WAGING PEACE

THE MACMILLAN COMPANY
NEW YORK · CHICAGO
DALLAS · ATLANTA · SAN FRANCISCO
LONDON · MANILA

BRETT-MACMILLAN LTD.
TORONTO

WAGING PEACE

by
C. Maxwell Stanley

A BUSINESSMAN LOOKS AT
UNITED STATES FOREIGN POLICY

The Macmillan Company   New York   1956

Library of Congress catalog card number: 56-12220

PREFACE

Survival is now the number one problem facing the United States. The expanding science of destruction offers us only two real choices: peace or devastation. Our search for the path to peace is now utterly urgent. The accelerated development of intercontinental missiles, space satellites, and more powerful thermonuclear weapons drives home this urgency.

Yet, much as we desire a peaceful world, we insist on peace with freedom. If the price of peace is slavery, that price is too high. We demand a secure peace — peace which will secure and protect our individual liberties, our traditions, our culture and our way of life.

This book is an attempt to analyze today's greatest world problem and to point out paths from among which we must choose. With this analysis as background, a recommended program for this country is suggested.

It is with great hesitancy that I undertake a book in a field normally reserved to the experts. I am motivated by personal conviction that the problem of achieving international peace and security overshadows all other national or international questions. I attempt this book as a means of exchanging my thoughts with others who are equally concerned.

Moreover, I sense the need for expression of thoughts and opinions by those who hold no governmental position. Such discussion and expressions are the means by which citizens of a democracy create an informed public opinion. This is needed to support the courageous and imaginative steps required to obtain a secure peace in the

v

Nuclear Age. Only thus will the United States assume its full responsibility as the leading nation of the free world.

Accordingly, this document is not the profound treatise of a historian, a diplomat, a scientist, or an expert. Rather, it is the attempt of a businessman—an engineer—to appraise the international facts of life. Its purpose is to reach some conclusions regarding the program which this nation should select and follow.

This analysis and appraisal draws heavily upon the vast sources of material, available to all who will read, developed by specialists and experts after exhaustive study.

It is directed not to the experts but to those many citizens who, though concerned with the international situation, have not made a detailed study of the requirements for a secure peace.

My appreciation and thanks are extended to those who have helped in the preparation and review of this book. I especially mention Dr. Arthur Rosenfeld for his review of Chapter 4; the Reverend Ned Gillum for his helpful suggestions; Mr. Edward McVitty for his research; the Reverend Edward A. Conway, S.J., for his keen criticism; and my son David for his contributions to Part III and for his assistance in editing the final manuscript. But most of all, I express my appreciation to my wife Elizabeth, not only for her long hours of reviewing and editing but also for her patience with the author during the hectic process of converting convictions into manuscript.

C. M. S.

Muscatine, Iowa
September 1, 1956

CONTENTS

PART I

An Estimate of the Situation

"It is our solemn obligation, I think, to lift our eyes above the lesser problems that seem to monopolize our time and to discuss and act upon what, by any standard, is the supreme problem before our country and the world."

—SENATOR BRIEN MCMAHON

"Mankind can extinguish itself, mixing science with arrogance and ignorance."

—DAVID BRADLEY, M.D.

"War is no longer an evil. In this age it seems intolerable."

—GENERAL GEORGE MARSHALL

"If freedom is lost, if the dignity of man is destroyed, advances on the material plane will not be 'progress' but a foundation for a new savagery. . . . Our supreme commitment . . . must be to win the peace—not a peace of totalitarian dominion but a genuine peace rooted in liberty."

—DAVID SARNOFF

"We are in the era of the thermonuclear bomb that can obliterate cities and can be delivered across continents. With such weapons, war has become not just tragic but preposterous. With such weapons, there can be no victory for anyone. Plainly, the objective now must be to see that such a war does not occur at all."

—DWIGHT D. EISENHOWER

Chapter 1

THE CHALLENGE

> Every top business executive must anticipate and recognize the problems facing his organization. He also must accurately appraise their magnitude. Unless he capably performs these functions his enterprise may be put out of business by unexpected factors.

HUMAN SURVIVAL and freedom are at stake. The threat of mass nuclear destruction hangs over us. The threat of communism generates fear and suspicion which undermine hard-won freedoms. Concentration on the arms race and the "cold" war impede progress toward a better world.

At no time in history has the challenge to man's creative ability been greater than now—the second decade of the Nuclear Age. The hydrogen bomb fuses together the problems of peace, security, freedom, and survival. The crisis is multiplied by the forthcoming intercontinental ballistic missile (ICBM) and space satellites.

What course of practical action can men pursue to save themselves and protect their freedoms?

THE CHALLENGE. The primary question of the twentieth century is whether we are capable of using the tremendous scientific, technical, and industrial developments of the last few decades for our welfare and benefit. Have we the wisdom and the unselfishness to use them wisely, or will they become a Frankenstein's monster, defy human control and destroy us?

Stated in another way, the question is whether we are capable of accelerating our development in the spiritual, moral, political, social, and educational fields. Can we here equal the great forward strides of the scientific and technical fields?

Unless we can, and unless we do, we shall be enslaved and perhaps exterminated by the very tools and implements we have created. If we can, and if we do, break through the log jam in these fields of human relations, the tools and implements we have created will usher in a new era of plenty. The possibilities of such an era are beyond the imagination of even our science-fiction writers.

PEACE OR WAR.   There are several aspects of this challenge. One is the question of peace and war. For centuries war has been an accepted means of settling differences between nations. War and the threat of war have been customary tools of foreign policy. War has been tolerated in spite of its accompanying death and destruction, although its use has been decried as inhuman and immoral.

But with the accelerated development of weapons of destruction, dramatized by the dropping of the first A-bomb on Hiroshima in 1945, a new era has begun. War is now obsolete. War has outlived its usefulness. War can no longer be relied upon to solve international problems. If this fact was not apparent at the close of World War II, it is now evident to anyone aware of the destructive power of the hydrogen bomb.

Complete war, waged with nuclear weapons, cannot be won. Both victor and vanquished will be battered and defeated, if not exterminated. General Omar Bradley said in 1948, "The way to win an atomic war is to make certain that it never starts." Man must find an acceptable way to eliminate war as an instrument of international diplomacy.

COMMUNISM OR FREEDOM.   Another part of the challenge today is the conflict between communism and freedom. Communism consists of a ruthless totalitarianism, based on a false ideology. It promises much, but in practice it makes man a slave of the state. Set against communism are the principles of freedom upheld by the democratic nations of the world. These endeavor to enhance the dignity and freedom of the individual and to make the state a servant of the people.

Communism seizes power by military force, subversion, treachery, and false promises. It is a dangerous foe because the Communists are willing to use any means to achieve their goal of world domination. However, the threat of communism is directly related to the problems of war and poverty. Is it not significant that the expansion of communist influence outside the Soviet Union has occurred during and following the chaos and conflict of World War II? Is it not also significant that communism's greatest appeal has been to those peoples who have received little or no material benefit from the industrial development of the recent century?

Communism has expanded its influence by capitalizing upon the sufferings of the impoverished and the hopes and dreams of those who want freedom and a better way of life. Communism cannot win in competition with freedom if the battle is fought in a world of peace and plenty.

The paradox of today is that the controversy between communism and freedom comes at a time when civilized man has developed the means and the methods which can bring a higher standard of living to the world. The great developments in the fields of health, industry, agriculture, and power now provide the tools with which a better material life can be obtained. But too great a portion of our natural resources, our scientific research, our thought and labor, and our taxes is required for armaments.

UPWARD STRUGGLE. Fundamental to the challenge is man's continuing struggle for independence, dignity, and economic improvement. This struggle is revealed in heroic efforts of colonies to obtain independence; in attempts to develop governments which protect human rights; and in the relentless drive for the things making a better material life.

The struggle is motivated by deep desires which have sparked man's forward progress through the centuries. Because they are ageless, their importance is sometimes overlooked in the face of the pressing problems of peace and war and the conflict between communism and freedom. But these basic urges for freedom, dignity, and a better life cannot be contained or suppressed; they permeate every problem and issue on the world scene.

Recognized and guided, these basic desires can exert a powerful influence in mobilizing world opinion to meet the challenge of today. Neglected or misguided, they will create explosive forces, shatter governments and institutions, and impede the world's ability to meet the challenge.

WHAT OF THE U.S.A.? At a time when the challenge to mankind is so acute, the United States of America has risen to a position of world leadership. We did not seek the position. In many respects we are not ready for its responsibilities; but, whether we like it or not, we are there. Our long championship of the ideas and ideals of freedom and human dignity, our development of a form of government which allows the inhabitants of a great continent to live and work in peace, our vast resources, our great enterprise, our increasing prosperity and our technical, scientific, and industrial development have all played a part in placing us in a position of leadership.

As the leader of the free world, we carry the responsibility of providing the vision, the courage, and the wisdom required to meet the challenge.

Bernard M. Baruch, a businessman-adviser to Presidents, puts it this way, "We must muster the strength of America—physical and spiritual—and use it wisely, generously, firmly in the cause of peace and freedom."

I am convinced that this great country of ours is falling short of this responsibility. Our policies toward the other nations and international activities fail to set the standards which may reasonably be expected of us.

Dazzled by our own strength, we rely too much upon military power to solve our problems. We forget the fact that no arms race has yet ended in anything but war. We overlook our great moral and spiritual heritage, and fail to utilize the universal appeal of such values. Consequently, we do an inadequate job of interpreting the objectives and goals of this nation to a watching world. Even our deep-seated desire for peace is not understood.

President Eisenhower has done more than any other American to assure the world of America's peaceful intentions. Yet the world remains suspicious, disorganized, and divided. Eisenhower's magnificent statements are undercut by the weakness of American foreign policy since World War I. We lack a definite program in our search for peace. We have no plan which gives promise of eliminating war without encroaching on legitimate national affairs. We tend to rely on the usual diplomacy when bolder steps are required.

The United States of America, strong and powerful as she is, cannot alone solve the problems of peaceful survival in the Nuclear Age. This can be done only by the concerted action of the nations of the world. But the task cannot be accomplished without our aid and leadership. The challenge rests squarely upon us.

But before we can lead, our citizens must face the problems and understand the facts. We must first throw off our lethargy and pessimism. Then we must determine the necessary objectives and plan a course of action which will take us toward those objectives. It will be neither an easy task nor a short one. It will require sound wisdom and great patience.

Arnold Toynbee dramatized the situation when he commented that man has lived a thousand years since the first A-bomb was dropped on Hiroshima. But most of that progress has been in the scientific, technical, and military fields. Now we must provide the political and moral leadership to accomplish comparable changes in other fields. We must match the thousand years of scientific advance to provide a world in which man will survive and peace and freedom will become a reality.

This is the challenge of the Nuclear Age. Have we the vision and wisdom, the courage and faith to resolve this dilemma of life and death?

Chapter 2

COMPETITIVE COEXISTENCE

> When an engineer is faced with a problem he starts by getting
> facts. His logical first step is to make a survey of the situation,
> gathering all available data and information. This process
> provides a background for intelligent study of the problem.

THIS CHAPTER, and the three which follow, attempt to
review the events which have led to the present international situation.

Today's situation may be described as a highly competitive coexist-
ence. It is peaceful to the extent that, as this is written, there are no
armed conflicts between the major blocs of the world. However, there
is a "cold" war with all of its conflict, its political and diplomatic maneuvering, its race for military supremacy, and its battle of propaganda.

THE DIVIDED WORLD.   The nations of the world today are divided into
three groups; namely:

1. The United States and those nations, usually designated as
allies, which are actively associated in resisting communism through
various regional programs of containment and mutual defense.

2. The Soviet Union, Red China, and their satellites, which are
usually designated as the communist world.

3. The neutral nations which are not actively associated with
either of the first two blocs.

The first and third groups are frequently referred to as the free
world. The classification of nations as between the first and third
groups is not always definite. The position of certain "neutral" nations
varies on different occasions and subjects.

The first group includes all of the nations linked with the United States by regional treaties of mutual defense and by other commitments for security. These nations, in addition to the United States, are:

NATO Members: Belgium, Canada, Denmark, France, Great Britain, Greece, Iceland, Italy, Luxembourg, Netherlands, Norway, Portugal, Turkey, and West Germany.

SEATO Signers: Australia, France, Great Britain, New Zealand, Pakistan, Philippines, and Thailand.

ORGANIZATION OF AMERICAN STATES: Argentina, Bolivia, Brazil, Chile, Colombia, Costa Rica, Cuba, Dominican Republic, Ecuador, El Salvador, Guatemala, Haiti, Honduras, Mexico, Nicaragua, Panama, Paraguay, Peru, Uruguay, and Venezuela.

Nations with which we have other military commitments: South Korea, Nationalist China, Japan, South Viet Nam, and Spain.

In addition, we have the unique situation of a military understanding with Yugoslavia, the only communist nation in Europe which is not controlled by Moscow. Yugoslavia, however, is hardly a part of the free world.

The nations of the communist group are: U.S.S.R., Albania, Bulgaria, Czechoslovakia, East Germany, Hungary, Poland and Rumania in Europe; and China, North Korea, Outer Mongolia, and North Viet Nam in Asia. The former nations of Lithuania, Latvia, and Estonia have been absorbed by force into the U.S.S.R.

Most of the other nations of the world fall in the third classification of neutral nations.

CONFLICT.   Deep controversies exist between the allies and the communist nations. The communist world, a group of closely linked dictatorships advocating the principles of Marxism, seeks to extend its reign and philosophy to include the entire world. Its vehicles for such extension include propaganda, economic pressure, intrigue, infiltration, subversion, and military power. Its goals are both ideological and territorial, aimed at the creation of a communist government of the world.

The United States and its allies, having fundamental principles quite opposed to those of the Communists, are banded together in spirit by common interests and on paper by treaties. They resist the spread of communism and seek to contain it within its present boundaries. Their principal methods include economic assistance, propaganda, diplomacy, and the development of military strength through collective security. Military force, with particular emphasis on strategic air power, has served as a deterring influence upon the Communists, both passively and actively—as in Korea.

Most of the neutral nations are sympathetic to the ideals of the free world rather than to the ideology of the Communists. They have usually supported the position of the free world in controversies within the United Nations. Otherwise, they have kept out of the power struggle between the allies and the Communists. Most of them have little or no military strength, and many have backward or undeveloped economies.

EUROPEAN DEVELOPMENTS.   When World War II ended in 1945, most Americans assumed that peace was assured and that there would be no more war. They believed the newly established United Nations would maintain international peace and security. There were great relief at the ending of World War II, and strong desire to return to peaceful pursuits.

Little heed was given to the voices which spoke of future trouble with the Soviet Union. In all honesty, it must be said that these voices were not easily heard. The spirit of cooperation between the Soviet Union, Great Britain, and the United States of America was high. Summit talks by Presidents Roosevelt and Truman, Prime Ministers Churchill and Atlee, and Premier Stalin, accompanied by propaganda favorable toward the Soviet Union, overcame most doubts about the intent of the Communists. So, heeding the clamor of "Bring the boys home," the United States and Great Britain pulled their military forces out of Europe, leaving only small contingents in Germany and Austria. The United States rapidly dismantled its military machine.

These events created a great vacuum in Europe which the U.S.S.R. was ready, willing, and able to exploit. It had already occupied Lithuania, Latvia, Estonia, Poland, Rumania, Bulgaria, Albania, and Hungary. By intrigue and infiltration the Communists forced the surrender of Czechoslovakia in 1948. They solidified their hold on East Germany and the occupied portion of Austria. The Communists accelerated their program of subversion and infiltration in Italy, Greece, France, and other European nations. While we were busy returning to peaceful pursuits, the Soviet Union came close to achieving control of continental Europe.

We awoke in 1947 to the realization that all was not peace and harmony with the Soviet Union. To check communist expansion in Europe, President Truman announced a program of containment. The first step was military and economic assistance to Greece and Turkey. This was followed quickly in 1947 by the Marshall Plan, which provided great assistance in rehabilitating and rebuilding Italy, France, West Germany, and other European countries. The resulting improved economic conditions helped to stem the tide of communist influence in these areas.

The high-water mark of communist expansion in Europe was the attempt to pinch off Berlin on June 18, 1948. This was successfully resisted by the Berlin Air Lift which gave a great moral victory to the cause of freedom. Shortly thereafter, the North Atlantic Treaty was signed and the organization of the NATO defense system begun. More recently, independence was granted to West Germany and plans have been made to rearm it.

With the growing military and economic strength in western Europe, including the presence of troops of the United States and Britain, the situation in Europe has become fairly stable. Communist influence in France, Italy, and other nations has been checked or is on the decline. The immediate Soviet military threat is less formidable.

DEVELOPMENTS IN ASIA.   On the other side of the world, communist influence has been rapidly expanding in Asia. By its late entry into the war against Japan, the Soviet Union seized much territory at little cost, occupying North Korea and large parts of China recaptured from Japan. Utilizing a well developed organization within China, the Communists capitalized upon the weakness of the Chiang Kai-shek government and the deep desire of the Chinese people for food and land reform. They scored a major victory in 1949 by completing their conquest of China, except Formosa.

This step set the stage for further expansionist pressure in Asia. After a period of consolidation came the invasion of South Korea in 1950 by North Korean forces supplied and directed by the U.S.S.R. Here, for the first time, aggression was resisted by military action of the United Nations. Such action, however, was made possible only by the accident of Soviet absence from the Security Council and by the presence of substantial United States military forces in nearby Japan. The United States carried the brunt of the requirements for money and machines for this war, and the United States and South Korea contributed most of the manpower. However, some sixteen members of the United Nations contributed fighting forces in the first attempt at collective security. Late in 1950, after the North Korean communist forces were defeated, Red China entered the war.

The bloody struggle continued until 1953 when an armistice was reached. This unsatisfactory agreement left Korea divided, with the Communists still in possession of the northern half of that unhappy country. The Communists promptly shifted pressure to southeast Asia. They gave assistance to the rebels in the "civil" war in Indo-China, where the French had been attempting unsuccessfully to stamp out revolutionary activities. The added pressure brought a quick collapse of the French at Dienbienphu, culminating in the partition of Indo-China at the unpopular Geneva settlement of 1954. Communist pressure continues in southeast Asia, all along the boundaries of Red China as well as in Viet Nam.

Efforts toward combating communism in Asia have been slow, but several recent moves have been helpful. The SEATO Pact of 1954 provides a defense treaty linking seven nations which have common interests in resisting communist expansion. The firm decision of the United States in early 1955 to use force to halt further communist movement toward Formosa has slowed activity there.

Of great improtance was the Bandung Conference of May, 1955. With a hopeful display of unity, this conference, involving some thirty Asian and African nations, boosted the morale of the world. Most of the participating nations were "neutrals." However, the conference indicated that most of them were aware of the communist threat and that they strongly supported the principles of freedom.

Nevertheless, the Asian situation is still fluid, and has not reached the stability achieved in Europe.

India is a question mark—refusing to align herself with either side in the controversy. The neutrals and the West irritate each other on such issues as colonialism even though both claim to support the principles of freedom.

THE RACE FOR POWER.   Since 1949 there has been a continuing race for military power, both nuclear and conventional. This race has fostered the greatest competition of arms the world has ever known. The United States has rearmed and has given assistance to its allies in strengthening their military establishments. We have accelerated the development of nuclear weapons and have created a Strategic Air Command with enormous striking power. This program has been successfully aimed at deterring the Soviet Union from precipitating a World War III. It has also served as a deterrent against major communist expansion.

In cooperation with our allies we have endeavored also to build conventional military power to deter the "little" wars and "minor" expansions and aggressions. Such efforts have included military and economic assistance, regional defense agreements, and arrangements for collective security. These activities have been only partially successful.

Throughout this period there has been constant competition for world opinion. Both the U.S.S.R. and the U.S.A. have sought support for their programs. In the early phases the Communists were highly successful. They impugned our motives, smeared us as warmongers and imperialists, and weakened our prestige in many parts of the world. Our own attempts in this propaganda battle were frequently inept and inadequate. Moreover, they were weakened by the hysterical fear of subversion and war which swept over this country from 1951 through mid-1954.

More recently, the successful creation of NATO and SEATO, the more reasoned approach of our government, and the sincere statements and actions of President Eisenhower have brought an increased understanding that the United States is dedicated to peace.

Military power, particularly that of nuclear weapons, appeared by 1955 to be sufficiently equalized to produce something of a stalemate. This fact, together with a growing unity and an improving economy in the free world, set the stage for a change.

Throughout this race for power the United Nations has managed to survive. It has served as a place to debate problems and to launch propaganda. This organization, its accomplishments and its failures, are further discussed in Chapter 5.

SPIRIT OF GENEVA.   The spring, summer, and fall of 1955 marked the rise, the summit, and the collapse of the so-called "Geneva spirit." This cycle marked a significant turning point in the conflict between communism and freedom.

Beginning in May, 1955, the Soviet Union's attitude toward the West became less belligerent. The Soviets accepted the Austrian peace treaty and withdrew their armies from Austria. They unexpectedly supported disarmament proposals advanced by Great Britain and France. They dispatched a mission of good will to Yugoslavia, exchanged visiting agriculturalists with the United States, and in other ways slightly raised the Iron Curtain.

The summit was reached at the Geneva talks in July between President Eisenhower, Prime Minister Eden, Premier Faure, and Premier Bulganin. The freer exchange of ideas and the lessened tensions at this conference raised hopes and expectations. President Eisenhower, emphasizing the need for acceptable disarmament, made his bold proposal for mutual aerial inspection. This proposal, reported to have been favorably received, was referred to the subsequent meeting of the foreign ministers of the Big Four.

To many, the Geneva Conference signaled a change of U.S.S.R. tactics—a greater willingness to talk and negotiate. But none of the problems of the world was solved at Geneva, and no basic change in communist objectives was announced. The arms race was not ended or slowed. World law was not established. Communist pressure in Korea, Viet Nam, Formosa, and other strategic points was not lessened.

The collapse of the Geneva spirit occurred in the few days of the Big Four foreign ministers' conference in October, 1955. They dealt with disarmament (including President Eisenhower's proposals for aerial inspection), reunification of Germany, and greater exchange of information and ideas between the East and the West. The foreign ministers, reporting no progress, adjourned after two weeks of futile discussion.

It is significant, however, that there was a continuation of the Soviet actions and attitudes which preceded the Geneva Conference. Messrs. Bulganin and Khruschev promptly departed on a sales trip to Asia, drumming communist virtues and promising economic aid. The Soviet Union became more interested in affairs around the Mediterranean. The Soviets sold arms to Egypt, and Communists increased their efforts to take over the anti-British uprisings in Cyprus and the opposition to French colonialism in North Africa. Everywhere there was more Soviet talk about economic aid, trade, and assistance to the underdeveloped nations.

TURNING POINT.   In spite of disappointments, the rise and fall of the Geneva spirit marked a significant turning point. The events associated with it were not accidental, but resulted from specific causes. Unless this fact is appreciated, and the causes are understood, the West will surely lose the next few rounds of its battle with communism.

The turning point, which has resulted in the complete revamping of Soviet foreign policy, is the result of at least three major factors.

The first factor is the current balance of power in the nuclear race. With the nuclear weapons and delivery equipment now possessed by the Communists and the free world, neither side dares launch the initial blow for fear of massive retaliation. Neither side can win an all-out nuclear war. This point was made clear by General Curtis E. LeMay of the United States Strategic Air Command, who said in December, 1955: "I believe it is too risky to begin a war under any conditions. No one can win a modern war. Even the victor loses."[1]

While the present precarious balance exists, nuclear war is not likely as the result of deliberate action. Although the hazard of World War III by accident or miscalculation remains, the mutual ability of massive retaliation deters acts which would provoke war.

The recent shifts in Soviet foreign policy indicate communist recognition of this fact. This common knowledge reduces the deterring value of the U.S. Strategic Air Command. Although it continues an effective deterrent against an all-out nuclear war, it now deters the U.S.S.R. only from an action which it may not wish to undertake. The Soviets can be reasonably sure we shall not resort to massive retaliation because of a minor incident or Korea-type aggression.

Hence, our threat of massive retaliation loses its power to deter other communist actions.

The second factor is the probability that armament developments in the near future will favor the Communists rather than the United States and its allies. The present balance in nuclear weapons delivered by jet bombers will be substantially altered if the Soviet Union develops intermediate-range ballistic missiles before we do. The IRBM is a missile having a range of up to 1,500 miles. This weapon will bring within communist range all of western Europe, northern Africa, Pakistan, the Philippines, Japan, Okinawa, and other Asian bases.

Such missiles can reach the capitals and major cities of all European countries in NATO and can reach our important overseas bases used by the B-47 bombers of the Strategic Air Command. When this occurs, the Communists can exert substantial pressure on our allies in the

[1] Curtis E. LeMay, "We Must Avoid the First Blow," *U.S. News and World Report,* Dec. 9, 1955, p. 38.

form of "ballistic blackmail" and can seriously reduce our ability of massive retaliation. If they achieve the IRBM before we do, they will have a gain in relative military position.

An objective reading of recent comments of United States scientists, military officials, and congressmen indicates the probability that the Soviets may be ahead of us in the development of missiles.

The third factor which results in a turning point is the ever shifting world opinion. The Soviet interpretation seems to be that there is currently a great opportunity to split our allies and the neutral nations from the United States and to win support and friends in Asia and Africa.

THE NEW LOOK.   A shift in emphasis of Soviet foreign policy was formally declared in a most important meeting of the U.S.S.R. Communist Party Congress in February, 1956. Elements of the new look include:

1. Repudiation of Stalin and dismissal of his works and ways as "twenty years of dictatorship and lies."

2. Substitution of the principle of "collective leadership," at least in theory.

3. Emphasis that the "world transforming, complete triumph of communism" is certain, and need not be achieved by war. The Communists now assert that war with capitalism is no longer inevitable.

4. A call for popular fronts with socialists to control parliaments and achieve communist triumph "by parliamentary means."

5. Expressions of sympathy and concern for the social and economic problems of the so-called "underdeveloped nations" and colonies.

It is significant, however, that the "new look" continues to call for maximum efforts to develop armaments and heavy industry, and for greater collectivization of agriculture. It is further significant that the U.S.S.R. has not in any way ended tyranny nor relinquished control over subjugated peoples.

But the "new look" is a real shift in emphasis.

The Communists will accelerate their wooing of nations in Asia, Africa, and South America by offerings of trade and economic assistance. Moreover, their "softer" line will seek to alienate these nations from the United States and to bring them closer to communist influence.

The "new look" also indicates efforts to strengthen the communist position in the "fringe" areas of the Middle East and Asia. These are the very points where we have the weakest conventional military deterrents and where the political situation is most volatile. It also indicates continued action on the part of the Soviet Union to keep the colonial issue boiling by extending support and encouragement to colonial peoples whose progress toward freedom has been delayed. Communists will try harder to take over legitimate anticolonial movements.

All of these are efforts aimed to drive wedges between the Western powers and the neutrals. The new Soviet policy will shift emphasis on the controversy between communism and freedom from Europe to the middle world—the area from Japan to South Africa. The new race for power in this area will seek the support and allegiance of neutral nations and nations which are now our allies. Its weapons will be ideas and opinions aimed at the hearts and minds of the peoples of these nations.

RACE FOR SPACE.   While the social, economic, and political battle rages in the middle world, the drive for military supremacy continues unabated. With new emphasis on the IRBM, the ICBM, and space satellites it, in effect, becomes a race for space.

As these means of delivery are perfected, they will be paralleled by developments in nuclear warheads. As one scientist has expressed it, the "boom grows bigger as the bomb grows smaller." The mating of more powerful nuclear warheads with ballistic missiles promises to provide the "ultimate weapon," the most frightful weapon conceived by man.

Hanson W. Baldwin, the military editor of the *New York Times* has recently written:

Dubbed ICBM in our research laboratories and Pentagon offices, the intercontinental ballistic missile has been called the "ultimate weapon." This giant ocean-spanning, mountain-leaping rocket—mated to a hydrogen warhead with a destructive capability of megatons (millions of tons of TNT)—is the supreme instrument of offense. It arches so high (600 to 800 miles above the earth) and moves so fast (12,000 to 16,000 miles per hour) that, once it has been launched, defense against it will be nearly, if not entirely impossible. . . . The ICBM will—when developed— threaten every city on earth not merely with damage but with destruction.

The implications are frightening—and sobering. In the early period of the coming ICBM era, before radar missile detection and possible antimissile defenses are developed, an enemy could probably devastate the United States with a surprise missile bombardment before we could even detect the attack—much less before we could launch a retaliatory attack. One or two missiles for each of our fifty biggest cities might cause 10,-000,000 to 50,000,000 casualties, knock out perhaps a third of our industrial capacity and turn parts of America into radioactive deserts.[2]

Such is the race for space now going on in Washington and Moscow. How soon? Scientists say it will not be long; certainly ten years—maybe five years—and perhaps only two or three.

Man will soon have the weapons to destroy himself.

[2] Hanson W. Baldwin, "I.C.B.M.," *Collier's,* March 16, 1956, p. 24.

Chapter 3

WORLD FACTS

A management decision based upon current operating statements and balance sheets may overlook basic trends. Therefore, a businessman reviews earlier records and reports to determine the prevailing trends. He seeks factors which enter into present conditions and which will affect future operations.

A SNAPSHOT of today's world provides only a partial view of the factors shaping world affairs. Fully to understand the problems which face our world, it is necessary to examine the elemental, long-range forces which influence man and his institutions.

Although any brief statement of these forces may be criticized as inadequate or oversimplified, we must start with some knowledge of them.

KEY FACTS.   The following ten facts cover the field in a general way:
1. The similarity of human desires.
2. The diversity of human institutions.
3. The continuing struggle for life.
4. The recent development of the tools of plenty.
5. The growing interdependence of nations.
6. The virtual collapse of colonialism.
7. The tremendous upsurge of nationalism.
8. The recent shifts of world leadership.
9. The continued existence of international anarchy.
10. The rapid development of nuclear power.

SIMILARITY OF HUMAN DESIRES.   Human beings the world over have similar basic characteristics. Their apparently great differences stem from the environments and the opportunities that have nurtured them. Given the opportunity, the most backward peoples can rise from degradation and achieve physical, mental, and social development comparable to that of more favored peoples.

An example is the rapid industrialization of Japan. Another is the accelerated development of native workers on some of the oil projects in such countries as Iraq and Venezuela. This is true because all peoples are born with similar physical, mental, and emotional equipment.

Moreover, all peoples are impelled by the same basic desires for self-preservation, protection of loved ones, comfort, recognition, and success. All peoples have deep spiritual and social longings. Again, the apparent differences are the result, not of the original characteristics, but of differing environments and opportunities.

It is important that we recognize these similarities. Unless we accept them, we shall raise artificial barriers between the peoples of the world, classifying some as first-class citizens, others as second-class.

If we accept the fact of similar basic characteristics, we can recognize that all peoples aspire to the same freedom, the same dignity, the same security, and the same peace. Such an approach lets us think in terms of equality of rights for all men and allows us to adopt policies encouraging less developed nations to move forward.

We Americans need to remember those unique words from our Declaration of Independence:

. . . that all men are created equal, that they are endowed by their Creator with certain Unalienable Rights, that among these are Life, Liberty and the pursuit of Happiness.

These words are as valid and appealing today when applied to the human race as they were in 1776 when addressed to the pioneers of our thirteen colonies.

Any approach to world problems which does not recognize and accept this fundamental fact is likely to promote disunity and racism and to enlarge differences between the developed and undeveloped nations.

DIVERSITY OF INSTITUTIONS. A second fact is that diversity, rather than similarity, exists in the institutions and patterns of life established by various peoples. The institutions, the patterns of life, and the cultures of peoples have been passed down from generation to generation, with the result that we now find great diversity among them.

Even though education and social development have a great leveling effect, people still retain many aspects of their inherited cultures, traditions, and religions.

In addition, there is diversity in the forms of government which nations have developed. Each form of government is influenced by the institutions which have been inherited. A prime example is the government of Great Britain, which, although based on democratic principles, retains aspects of a monarchy and of institutions which have been inherited from past centuries.

Moreover, the patterns of economic development are diverse. Not all nations have had equal opportunities and resources to develop their economic systems. Even as industrial progress comes to less developed nations, they do not all find it possible or desirable to select a system exactly like ours.

It is particularly important for citizens of the United States to recognize the existence of diversity. Our pride in our way of life and institutions is natural; but we must accept the fact that not all other nations have the conditions or the desire to duplicate them.

Because diversity is a fundamental factor, any program which seeks to protect the traditions and institutions of one nation must allow other nations to protect theirs. All nations must be free to exercise their judgment in the establishment and maintenance of their cultures, religions, traditions, governments, and economies. Recognition of this fact calls for international arrangements which protect diversity.

THE STRUGGLE FOR LIFE.   In many parts of the world the struggle for existence is the overpowering day-to-day concern of the great majority of the people. In such countries as China and India, a high percentage of the inhabitants do not have even the minimum requirements of food. Afflicted with disease, suffering from malnutrition, lacking proper shelter, they have little concern for anything beyond their struggle for life itself.

This continuing struggle for existence is not new. It has gone on for centuries, and it will continue until medical, agricultural, and industrial development in these underprivileged areas is adequate to meet minimum requirements. The impact of this fact upon world affairs is twofold:

In the first place, it causes certain nations and certain peoples to be so preoccupied with the struggle for existence that they have little time or energy to concern themselves with problems of world peace and world security.

In the second place, it explains why such people are so susceptible to the propaganda of the Communists or, in fact, of anyone who will hold out to them the promise of a loaf of bread.

It is important for us to recognize this. It explains the lack of enthusiasm of such people for our talk of democracy and free enterprise. A sick and hungry man cannot think clearly about freedom.

THE TOOLS OF PLENTY.   Mankind now possesses the tools which are capable of bringing a decent living to all the peoples of the world. This is a staggering and important fact of today. While it is a new fact, it is well known to scientists, engineers, and industrialists.

Though the struggle for life has gone on for centuries, it is only now that scientific and technical developments provide the tools of plenty. If their use can be extended to all nations of the world, revolutionary gains in the standards of living will result. Let us look at four of these tools:

Developments in medicine and health.
Improvements in agriculture.
Expansion of electric power.
Development of mass industrial production.

Modern developments in sanitation, medicines and medical care have made it possible for people to feel better and live longer. This has been fully demonstrated in many of the more highly developed nations. Moreover, test application in areas of underdeveloped nations has proved that the same results can be achieved there. The World Health Organization, a United Nations agency, has wiped out malaria over wide areas in several countries at a nominal cost.

Agricultural developments too have been at a rapid rate. The use of improved methods of cultivation, fertilizers, insecticides, and hybrid plants has greatly multiplied production per acre. Land reclamation, including drainage and irrigation, can provide somewhat greater acreage. These facts have been proved on a wholesale basis in many nations and on a test basis in nations of lesser development. The substitution of modern agricultural methods for the primitive practices still used in many parts of the world can bring amazing results.

My extensive professional work in the field of electrical power has convinced me of the close relationship of electrical power to improved standards of living and industrial production. Availability of electrical power is both a prerequisite to, and an index of, economic development.

Electricity is needed in underdeveloped countries not so much to provide lights and run appliances in homes but more as power for industry. Generation, transmission, and distribution of electrical power by conventional equipment is highly developed in many parts of the world. But in many areas the lack of adequate or economical fuel causes real power shortages. The new and rapidly developing atomic power gives promise of solving the problems of power supply in all parts of the world.

Another tool is that of industrial production, as demonstrated by the mass methods used in the United States. The benefits of industrialization, accompanied by the development of mass markets, are well known to every American businessman and industrialist. My personal experience with industry convinces me that application of these methods throughout the world will create great potential for industrial growth. These are the processes which need to be used in the "underdeveloped" nations, not only to provide the bare necessities of life but greatly to raise living standards.

Truly, it is a fact that scientific and technical developments have produced the tools of plenty. If properly applied, they can lessen the tight grasp of poverty now strangling many backward areas. Obviously, such developments will be gradual and must be accompanied by educational, social, and political growth. Nevertheless, it is significant that the tools of plenty are at hand. The need is to put them to work to cope with the problems of overpopulation and hunger.

INTERDEPENDENCE.   Increasingly, the nations of the world become more dependent upon one another. One of the factors bringing this about is the increased speed of travel, which has the effect of shrinking the size of the world. Air travel, which puts Paris only ten hours from New York and Manila under two days from San Francisco by commercial airlines, truly makes us all neighbors. The jet airliner will shrink the world still further. The science of rocketry promises further shrink-age: thirty minutes from Moscow to New York.

The speed of travel is paralleled by vast improvement in the means of communication. Using cable, radio, telegraph, telephone, and TV, we can communicate instantly with overseas points and even observe events as they occur.

The nations of the world are becoming more and more dependent upon one another for raw materials and for trade. With the increasing demands of modern industry, few nations are self-sufficient in their resources. They must look abroad for important raw materials. More-over, the trend toward specialization in industry often makes it desir-able to disregard national boundaries and to locate manufacturing plants with regard to resources, labor supply, and markets.

And perhaps most important of all, nations are finding that they are interdependent in the political sphere. In forty years of almost constant war and conflict since the outbreak of World War I, nations have been compelled, more and more, to associate themselves with one another in their efforts to obtain security. Even a powerful nation such as the United States publicly acknowledges its dependence upon its allies in its struggle for security.

Interdependence for security is heightened by scientific progress. No nation alone can handle the problems created by space satellites, intercontinental missiles, and nuclear weapons. Even peaceful uses of satellites and atomic power cannot be properly controlled by individ-ual nations.

In this shrinking world, no nation can be an island unto itself.

THE COLLAPSE OF COLONIALISM.   The period since the close of World War II has witnessed the collapse of colonialism as a going in-stitution. In 1946 the United States granted complete independence to the Philippines as the end result of a great experiment. After half a century of preparation, that nation became self-governing. Shortly thereafter India (1947), Pakistan (1947), Burma (1948), and Cey-lon (1948) were granted their independence by Britain and became independent members of the British Commonwealth. In addition, in-dependence has been achieved by Israel (1948), South Korea (1948), Indonesia (1949), Libya (1951), South Viet Nam (1954), Laos (1954), Cambodia (1954), Sudan (1955), Tunisia (1956).

Currently, a number of colonies are under trusteeships supervised by the United Nations. The objective of the trusteeship is, of course, the preparation of these people for their independence and self-government. Some of the trustee nations have neglected this duty, but several colonial areas are nearing independence.

The conference of Asian and African nations at Bandung in May, 1955, produced a unity of opposition to all forms of outside interference, including Western colonialism and the new colonialism practiced by the Communists.

Colonialism as a form of Western imperialism has passed its heyday. Self-determination and independence will rapidly be demanded by all peoples of the world.

Truly, colonialism is approaching its end in the free world.

RISE OF NATIONALISM.   The rise of nationalism has become one of the major factors shaping the destinies of the world in the middle of the twentieth century. The growth of nationalism goes back to the seventeenth and eighteenth centuries when feudal states and other political divisions were united to form nations.

The establishment of these nation-states, with cessation of warfare and easing of controversies within their boundaries, was accompanied by increasing security and prosperity. Political leaders were quick to take credit for such economic gains and to label them as national accomplishments. Much of the intense spirit of nationalism which prevails in the world today has sprung from such a valid source.

Nationalism is beneficial until it becomes so intense and short-sighted that emotion is substituted for judgment in international relations. When nationalism reaches such a stage it becomes chauvinism, and often gets completely out of control. An example is the extreme nationalism of Germany under Hitler. The doctrine of Aryan superiority and the warped concern over national interests fanned the hatreds and prejudices which led to World War II.

Nationalism, when it becomes extreme, blinds nations to their dependence upon one another. It encourages them to attempt a degree of self-sufficiency which cannot be achieved in today's complex world. Extreme nationalism, extending beyond the bounds of reason, also causes nations to depend upon military power to an unwarranted degree and to rely on a false sense of security that comes from armaments.

Today the world has an overdose of nationalism. This is true not only of the Communists but also of all of the larger nations of the free world, including the United States. The achievement of independence by former colonies often creates a national spirit patterned after the extreme nationalism of stronger nations.

It is most important that we recognize today's nationalism as extreme and beyond reasonable bounds. It increases the difficulty of finding the path to peace and freedom, which must be founded upon the interdependence of nations.

However, we need not blindly condemn all nationalism. Nationalism should mean sincere love of one's nation, and a deep desire to protect that nation and its people. Such nationalism will help us find the answer we are seeking. Americans always will be proud of, and loyal to, our country—and we should be. However, we need to remember the difference between enlightened love of country and fanatical nationalism.

SHIFT OF LEADERSHIP.   Since the beginning of World War II there has been a complete shift in world leadership. Prior to the beginning of that war, Great Britain, France, and Germany were the leading nations of Europe, and Japan was the leading power of Asia. These four nations, together with the United States, were nominally considered the Big Five in the world.

At the end of World War II, Germany and Japan were crushed in defeat and stripped of their independence. Both were occupied by the victors, and Germany was soon divided into East and West. Neither nation has fully regained its former power.

France, through her poor showing in World War II and her subsequent defeat, fell from her place of leadership. Liberation did not restore her to the top echelon. Her subsequent domestic crises, her inept failure in Indo-China, and her troubles in Africa prevent a return to her previous stature.

Britain, battered but victorious, remains a leader in the world, although she has lost her place as the major creditor nation. Furthermore, she has less influence as a part of the British Commonwealth than she formerly had as the head of the British Empire.

World War II and the events of the years immediately following catapulted the Soviet Union and the United States into positions of world leadership. This situation continues, with the Soviet Union as the leader of the communist world and with the United States as the leader and the most powerful member of the free world. This is a striking shift in leadership from that which prevailed before World War II.

A WORLD OF ANARCHY.   We live in a world of anarchy; that is, a situation in which there is no rule of law with respect to affairs between nations. In a condition of anarchy, each nation attempts to exert complete control over its affairs and claims the right to make final decisions in all matters respecting its contacts with other nations.

Anarchy has long since been eliminated in cities, states, and nations —in short, in every community except the world community. Within nations, individuals and states no longer are allowed to settle their disputes by force. Without exception, all nations have established a legal framework for enacting, interpreting, and enforcing laws which are binding on their citizens. Even the most backward and tyrannical nations have some machinery for maintaining law and order within their borders.

We readily accept this rule of law on a local basis. What would be our reaction if asked to sign a petition to abolish city laws, police force, and courts on the theory that men could maintain order by voluntary cooperation?

Nevertheless, we have world anarchy, for a rule of law has not been created on an international basis. In the absence of law, war and the threat of war are the ultimate means of settling disputes between nations when cooperation fails. The only restraints upon independent action by any nation are those imposed by treaties and agreements and by the pressure of world opinion. When these fail and violence occurs there is no "cop on the corner" to restore order and apprehend violators. There is no machinery which requires nations to resolve their disputes by peaceful means.

The United Nations, established by treaty, serves today to encourage peaceful settlement of differences, to encourage cooperation between nations, and to mobilize and focus world opinion. However, it has no authority to establish or administer world law in any phase of international life. (See Chapter 5.)

Hence, we continue to live in a world of anarchy with respect to relationships between nations.

NUCLEAR AGE.   The most dynamic new fact is that we are in the Nuclear Age. Since the dropping of the bombs on Hiroshima and

Nagasaki, the world is gradually realizing the magnitude of the revolution started by the splitting of the atom.

It is a revolution that has two aspects. On the positive side, the development of atomic power, with its useful by-products for industrial and medical purposes, can be of great value to mankind. Within a few decades nuclear power may become a major source of fuel for generation of electrical power, particularly in areas short of other fuels.

Many other peaceful uses are being found for the atom as research continues. Isotopes point the way toward unprecedented gains in the fields of medicine, health, agriculture, and industry.

Other scientific and technical developments are being accelerated by the Nuclear Age. These include the progress in rockets, which are the means of propulsion for missiles and space satellites. These promise benefits in transportation and communication, and also offer the engrossing possibility of space flight.

All of these developments of the Nuclear Age, if used for the benefit of mankind, will be of incalculable value.

The other side of the coin is the unprecedented destructive potential of nuclear weapons, particularly when mated with ballistic missiles. The two primitive atomic bombs dropped on Japan, followed by post-war research leading to the explosion of the first hydrogen bomb on Eniwetok in 1953, have added a new dimension to war.

Nuclear weapons are producing a revolution in military thinking. More importantly, they require a revolution in man's thinking concerning the prerequisites for secure peace and freedom.

An understanding of the potency of nuclear weapons is so important that it is dealt with more fully in the following chapter.

USE OF THE FACTORS.   The factors which have just been outlined should guide our thinking regarding primary forces and trends at work in the world today. They are more powerful than any nation or any people. They dominate the decisions and actions of all nations and peoples. If these forces are understood and dealt with intelligently and unselfishly, they can help to implement the great steps which must be taken to obtain a secure peace with freedom.

These forces, if misunderstood, overlooked, or evaded, will surely make the search for secure peace more difficult.

Chapter 4

DEATH UNLIMITED

Many successful enterprises have failed because they did not keep up with scientific and engineering progress. Industry carefully follows and evaluates technical development. It alters programs and products to take advantage of technical changes and improvements.

THE DESTRUCTIVENESS of war in the Nuclear Age as compared to that of World War II is so great as to elude the comprehension of our finite minds. It is as if the flood waters of the Mississippi River were compared to the flow of a fire hose. Nuclear weapons are so powerful that responsible political and scientific leaders candidly admit wholesale use of them would destroy much of the civilized world. Recently Thomas K. Finletter, Secretary of the United States Air Force from 1950 to 1953, said:

There seems to be almost no doubt but that the known weapons of today and the future may well, unless controlled, destroy the United States. Applied science for destruction is wholly out of hand; it is like a wild tiger running about the city streets.[1]

A full knowledge of the technical and scientific aspects of nuclear weapons is not necessary. We must, however, understand the potency of these devices.

NEW YARDSTICKS. The power of thermonuclear weapons is so great that new yardsticks are needed to measure their destruction. Until

[1] Thomas K. Finletter, *Power and Policy* (New York, Harcourt, Brace and Company, 1954), p. 392.

29

the first atomic bomb was dropped upon Hiroshima, the conventional measuring device was one ton of TNT, the standard explosive. The great destruction of World War II was caused largely by bombs having warheads containing up to four tons of TNT. This size was known as a "blockbuster," and it was an effective, powerful weapon. Toward the end of World War II the development of the B-29 bomber allowed an increase in size of blockbusters up to about eight tons of TNT. Doubling the size of the blockbuster was considered a significant advance.

But the first atomic bomb dropped upon Hiroshima from a B-29 bomber had a power equivalent to 15,000 tons of TNT. Thus, the first atomic bomb released nearly two thousand times the destructive force of World War II's largest blockbuster. Subsequent progress in the design and manufacture of atomic bombs and hydrogen bombs has dwarfed the Hiroshima and Nagasaki bombs. Consequently, it has been necessary to adopt new yardsticks which express the power of nuclear weapons in kilotons and megatons. One kiloton means one thousand tons of TNT; one megaton means one million tons of TNT. Using these new yardsticks, the power of various bombs may be expressed as follows:

	KILOTONS	MEGATONS
Blockbuster used in Europe in World War II	0.004	0.000004
Blockbusters available at end of World War II	0.008	0.000008
Atomic bomb dropped on Hiroshima	15.0	0.015
Atomic bomb dropped on Nagasaki	20.0	0.020
Latest atomic bombs developed*	500.0	0.5
First hydrogen bomb exploded in 1954	20,000.0	20.0
Potential hydrogen bomb*	100,000.0	100.0

* Largest size considered convenient.

The total TNT load in bombs dropped on Germany during World War II has been estimated at 2,200,000 tons. This is 2,200 kilotons or 2.2 megatons. Five of the latest atomic bombs would exceed this power, and a single hydrogen bomb—1954 variety—would have nearly ten times this total power. We do need new yardsticks!

AREAS OF DESTRUCTION.   These increases in explosive force are so immense they defy comprehension. It is easier to grasp the powers of these nuclear weapons by comparing the range and area over which their blasts can deal death and destruction.[2] The following table shows the comparative destructive effects of an 8-ton World War II blockbuster, a 20.0 kiloton A-bomb, and a 20.0 megaton hydrogen bomb. These destructive effects are expressed in distances from point of explosion for complete, severe, moderate, and partial destruction of normal buildings and structures:

EXTENT OF DESTRUCTION	8-TON BLOCK-BUSTER	20.0 KILOTON ATOMIC BOMB	20.0 MEGATON HYDROGEN BOMB
Complete destruction	0.037 mile	0.5 mile	5.0 miles
Severe damage	0.073 mile	1.0 mile	10.0 miles
Moderate damage	0.120 mile	1.6 miles	16.0 miles
Partial damage	0.150 mile	2.0 miles	20.0 miles

The following table is similar except that it shows the area of damage in square miles centered about the point of explosion.

EXTENT OF DESTRUCTION	8-TON BLOCK-BUSTER	20.0 KILOTON ATOMIC BOMB	20.0 MEGATON HYDROGEN BOMB
Complete destruction	0.004 sq. mi.	0.8 sq. mi.	79 sq. mi.
Severe damage	0.017 sq. mi.	3.2 sq. mi.	314 sq. mi.
Moderate damage	0.043 sq. mi.	8.0 sq. mi.	804 sq. mi.
Partial damage	0.068 sq. mi.	12.6 sq. mi.	1257 sq. mi.

The above figures for atomic and hydrogen bombs, prepared for structural engineers,[3] substantiate the statements that a single H-bomb is capable of paralyzing any American city.

Lewis L. Strauss, chairman of the Atomic Energy Commission, has confirmed this. In April, 1954 he reported on our first H-blast at a presidential press conference. The following exchange of questions and answers occurred:

A REPORTER: Many people in Congress, I think many elsewhere, have been reaching out and grasping for some information as to what happens when the H-bomb goes off. . . .

STRAUSS: Well, the nature of an H-bomb is that, in effect, it can be

[2] U.S. Dept. of Defense and Atomic Energy Commission, *The Effects of Atomic Weapons* (New York, McGraw-Hill Publishing Company, 1950).

[3] Philip W. Swain, "Bomb-blast table and charts," *Power*, August, 1954, p. 80.

made to be as large as you wish, as large as the military requirement demands, that is to say, an H-bomb can be as—large enough to take out a city.

CHORUS: What?

STRAUSS: To take out a city, to destroy a city.

A REPORTER: How big a city?

STRAUSS: Any city.

REPORTER: Any city? New York?

STRAUSS: The metropolitan area, yes (i.e., the heart of Manhattan, as he later elaborated).[4]

In addition, a hydrogen bomb of 20.0 megatons would make a huge crater. It is reported the Eniwetok bomb left a hole a mile in diameter and 175 feet deep—probably deeper than most existing bomb shelters.

Moreover, the intense heat would instantly ignite combustible materials up to a distance of five miles. This fire storm, fanned by its own heat and wind, would be fatal to people not sheltered. Within shelters, death would threaten because of intense heat and lack of oxygen.

RADIATION. Nuclear weapons add another dimension of death beyond the immediate effect of the explosion; namely, radiation. Both the atomic bomb and the hydrogen bomb release great amounts of radioactive material which gives off gamma and other rays. The radiation effects of this material are detrimental to the life and health of human beings if absorbed in appreciable quantities. The injury is similar to that caused by excessive radiation from X-ray equipment or radium.

Studies of the direct or prompt radiation effects from the Hiroshima bomb indicate that it was more than 90 per cent lethal for unprotected persons for a distance of 2,000 feet from the point of explosion, dropping to 10 per cent lethal at 6,700 feet.[5]

With a 20-megaton hydrogen bomb the lethal effect of direct or prompt radiation is not so important because of the great incendiary radius. Death by burning is quicker than death from radiation.

But damaging effects are not limited to direct or prompt radiation. They may be extended over vast areas as minute particles of material are carried off in the atomic cloud and show up as "fall-out" even at

---

[4] *Time*, April 12, 1954, p. 21.

[5] *The Effects of Atomic Weapons*, p. 376.

substantial distances. The most highly publicized case of this kind was the death and injuries which occurred among Japanese fishermen on the vessel *Fortunate Dragon,* which was some 80 miles from the first hydrogen bomb explosion at Eniwetok in 1954.

The Atomic Energy Commission in February, 1955, released a report on fall-out. It indicated that, under wind conditions frequently prevailing in the United States, death-dealing fall-out might be expected in a cigar-shaped area extending as far as 200 miles from the explosion. One analysis of this report showed that an explosion over Washington, D.C., could cause radioactive fall-out in a 20-mile-wide cigar-shaped zone extending 220 miles to New York City.[6] Radiation, decreasing with distance from the blast, was estimated as nearly 100 per cent lethal for unprotected persons as far as 140 miles, up to 50 per cent lethal at 160 miles, and dropping to between 10 per cent lethal and safe at 220 miles.

These facts have initiated lively discussion in the scientific and popular press. Geneticists are emphasizing radiation effects on human genes which influence reproduction and heredity.

A prominent authority, Professor H. J. Muller, considers ". . . no exposure is so tiny that it does not carry its corresponding mutational risk." [7]

Regardless of their conclusions, it is evident that radiation, either direct or fall-out, extends the death-dealing powers of nuclear weapons. It widens the area made immediately uninhabitable, lessens the need for accurate bombing, and increases the effectiveness of nuclear weapons in delivering knock-out blows.

THE COST OF DESTRUCTION. Popular opinion holds that nuclear weapons are extremely expensive. While it is true that vast amounts are being spent for atomic development, research, and production, it is also true that the cost of producing the explosive materials required in thermonuclear weapons is amazingly low.

One pound of fissionable material for an atomic bomb is reported to have a production cost of $10,000. But active explosive material for an H-bomb costs less than $50 per pound exploded. This is due to difference in nature of the material required.

If one pound of this active material is equivalent to 1,000 tons of

[6] "Facing the Fallout Problem," *Life,* Feb. 28, 1955, p. 24.
[7] H. J. Muller, "Genetic Damage Produced by Radiation," *Science,* June 17, 1955, p. 837.

TNT, the cost of explosive material equivalent to one ton of TNT is only ten cents. This may be compared to the World War II production cost of TNT: fifty cents per pound, or $1,000 per ton. This is a ten-thousandfold decrease in cost for a given amount of destructive power.[8]

MEANS OF DELIVERY.   The current means of delivery of nuclear weapons is the long-distance bomber, which has been vastly improved over the B-17, the B-24, and the B-29 of World War II.

Published information on our B-47 bombers, for instance, indicates a range capable of intercontinental flights (with refueling) and a speed of over 600 miles per hour at altitudes above 40,000 feet. Our B-52 bomber, just coming into production, is an even more potent aircraft. Its performance figures have not been published. However, it will replace B-36 bombers, which have a range of 10,000 miles, with a 5-ton load, and can fly at altitudes to 45,000 feet. Even these obsolescent planes are truly intercontinental bombers.[9]

DEFENSE.   Substantial efforts have been made to develop defense weapons and procedures to guard against strategic bombing. Progress has been made in radar warning devices, better jet interceptor planes, improved tactics, and in the development of guided missiles equipped with "homing" mechanisms.

In spite of these developments, there is little confidence in the ability of our defense forces to intercept and destroy any sizable portion of an armada of strategic bombers bearing nuclear weapons. A former Secretary of the United States Air Force has recently stated his belief that the defense efforts of the United States are grossly inadequate.[10] A news story about interceptor tests points out actual experiences under test conditions; they are not encouraging.

Probably no one knows the actual effectiveness of our defense program. The Air Force has tried hard to develop better defense methods, and undoubtedly our air defense is better than that available in World War II.

The trouble is that "better" is not enough. In World War II, if a defense force could consistently knock down 25 per cent of the enemy bombers, this was good enough. A 25 per cent rate of kill made

[8] Ralph E. Lapp, from address and notes.
[9] Jane, *All the World's Aircraft.*
[10] Finletter, *op. cit.,* Chap. II.

bombing unprofitable for the enemy. If a fourth of the bombers were lost on every mission, World War II bombers dropping TNT bombs could not do enough damage to justify the repeated losses.

But the hydrogen bomb has drastically changed this picture. Twenty to forty hydrogen bombs dropped on the vital industrial and communications centers of this nation would cause virtual paralysis. In order to drop forty bombs, only a few invading bombers would have to get through. Even a 90 per cent defense would not be good enough. An aggressor would gladly lose, for example, 900 out of 1,000 bombers when the other 100 could cripple the United States.

But no military leader has been optimistic enough to predict that the United States air defense could bring down 70 per cent or 80 per cent of invading bombers, let alone 90 per cent! It is little wonder that most informed observers contend that offense has outstripped defense. There is now simply no adequate protection against strategic bombing with nuclear weapons.

CHANGED PATTERN.   Any realistic appraisal of the kind of war which can be fought with present nuclear weapons is not at all comforting. Their power of destruction is unparalleled, unprecedented, and underappreciated. They drastically change the patterns both of offensive and of defensive military action.

Consider the comments made recently by M. Jules Moch, who for many years has represented France on the Disarmament Commission of the United Nations. Speaking in Paris in 1955, M. Moch observed that to destroy the whole population of France by strategic air attack would require 100,000,000 conventional one-ton bombs, 6,000 A-bombs like that dropped on Hiroshima, but only fifteen of the latest hydrogen bombs.

This staggering contrast is a realistic measure of the difference in war caused by nuclear weapons.

Unless an aggressor had such overwhelming power that he could eliminate with a single blow his opponent's ability to retaliate, he would surely be on the receiving end of nuclear weapons within a few hours. No one can predict the extent of destruction that would follow. A few days or hours might see all major cities obliterated, communication and transportation paralyzed, tens of millions of citizens exterminated, and great areas contaminated with radioactive materials. With such a beginning, both victor and vanquished would be losers. The blow to civilization could be staggering. It might be fatal if the war were carried to a bitter finish.

RACE FOR SUPERIORITY.   Our Manhattan Project during World War II devoted unprecedented scientific and industrial resources to atomic development. As a result, the United States took an early and definite lead. We were first with the atomic bomb, first with adequate plants to process atomic materials, and first with the hydrogen bomb.

However, the Soviet Union has shown an amazing ability to reach various stages of nuclear development earlier than anticipated by our officials. At the close of World War II, most experts predicted Soviet development of the atomic bomb by about 1952. These predictions were rudely shattered in 1949 when President Truman announced we had evidence of the first Soviet atomic explosion.

The exact status of Soviet production of nuclear weapons is a closely guarded secret. The general impression prevails that Soviet Russia has now produced a substantial stockpile. Moreover, there are indications the Soviets are not far behind us in the development of the hydrogen bomb. Many authorities believe the Soviets now possess an adequate number of nuclear weapons to deliver a paralyzing blow against the cities of western Europe, or indeed against this country.

The military planning of the United States has been based upon our possession of sufficient nuclear warheads and an adequate Strategic Air Command, dispersed in and beyond the U.S.A., to deter Soviet aggression.

As long as we possessed preponderant nuclear power, the fear of its use in massive retaliation was an effective deterrent. It may well have prevented Soviet invasion of Europe, though it did not prevent aggression by a communist satellite army in Korea.

Once both sides have an adequate stockpile of nuclear weapons and means of delivering them, there is no longer a monopoly of deterrent force. Because of the limited number of targets, a larger stockpile is of little value once a certain level has been reached.

Now it appears that both the Soviet Union and the United States possess the ability each to paralyze the other by striking the first blow. Such a situation, with the knowledge that this nation would not strike first, requires a further examination of deterrent power. Many observers contend that we need a greatly expanded Strategic Air Command in order to maintain an adequate deterring power capable of retaliating after the first blow has been struck against us.

Although this question is important, it fades into the background when one considers the onrush of ballistic missiles. Grave questions are being raised about our progress in their development. The furor in 1956 over our missile program seems to be more than just "politics as usual" in an election year.[11]

We are rushing to develop the intermediate-range ballistic missile (IRBM) and the intercontinental ballistic missile (ICBM) with ranges of up to 1,500 miles and 5,000 miles respectively. There are indications the Soviet Union may already have 800-mile missiles. Even with a crash program we may have difficulty catching up.

Neither the U.S.S.R. nor the U.S.A. dares relax a moment in the drive to maintain supremacy in these devices of destruction. A momentary advantage may quickly slip away if the other side gains a lead in scientific development.

A dictatorship like the U.S.S.R. has certain advantages in this race. The Soviets can concentrate upon it to a degree that is difficult in a democracy. They are training engineers and scientists at a rate which exceeds that of the United States. A free nation must inform its people and win public support before a new program can be adopted. The Communists are unfettered by such considerations, and can move more rapidly.

Against this we match our technical and scientific talent, and sincerely hope that our leaders give our armaments programs proper emphasis and urgency.

VANISHING MONOPOLY.   For a period of several years the United States enjoyed a complete monopoly of atomic weapons. The Soviet Union broke this monopoly in 1949, and is now believed to have a substantial stockpile of warheads, both atomic and hydrogen. Both Great Britain and Canada have had nuclear programs for some time.

However, at the present time, possession of nuclear warheads is believed confined to these four nations—the United States, the U.S.S.R., Great Britain, and Canada.

This monopoly will be further dissipated within a few years. We are now embarked upon an "atoms for peace" policy. This excellent

[11] John F. Loosbrock, "We Are Beating Ourselves," *Air Force,* March, 1956, pp. 43–46.

program has one unavoidable hazard: it will extend the opportunity for "atoms for war" to every nation which has a reactor and a supply of uranium. Power and research reactors can produce the materials required for bombs. Even though the rate of production is not comparable to that of the great United States plants, certain types of peaceful reactors can supply ingredients for bombs.

Moreover, the waste materials from reactors are radioactive and deadly. Disposal of these lethal wastes is one of the serious problems associated with the peaceful use of atomic power. Such radioactive dust can be used as a weapon.[12]

There are two means, then, by which nuclear reactors, presumably for peaceful purposes, can produce munitions. Materials developed in reactors can be stealthily accumulated to manufacture bombs, or the deadly wastes can be used as radioactive dust. Thus the monopoly will vanish, and many nations will have atomic weapons.

Unless adequately controlled, this situation will occur in a comparatively few years. Then the threat of nuclear attack or of nuclear "blackmail" will be rapidly widened. A nation need not accumulate a large stockpile of such devices to create difficult situations. An irresponsible ruler of a small nation with only a few warheads or a small amount of radioactive dust could blackmail a neighboring nation. Nuclear "trick or treat" would be a dangerous game. For example, what might happen if Egypt or Israel had nuclear weapons and threatened to use them if the other side did not make concessions?

ONRUSHING SCIENCE.   Nuclear warfare would be terrible with present weapons and means of delivery. Its destructive power, however, is puny and insignificant compared with the probabilities of tomorrow. Science is rushing pell-mell toward the ultimate weapons which will make pushbutton war a reality.

The promised delivery equipment is the intercontinental ballistic missile (ICBM). This device will be capable of carrying nuclear warheads from the Soviet Union to the United States. Propelled by rockets, an ICBM will rise almost vertically from its launching platform. Controlled by electronic devices, its power stages will detach as it is set on its course at speeds of perhaps 12,000 and 16,000 miles per hour. This means a flight time from Moscow to New York of 20 to 30 minutes.

[12] Hans Thirring, "The Noiseless Weapon," *Harper's Magazine,* Oct. 1955, pp. 44–46.

At maximum height the ICBM may rise some 600 to 800 miles above the earth. If the first ICBM has an accuracy error of 1 per cent, it will fall within fifty miles of its target. Scientists are seeking to perfect missiles which will strike within five or ten miles of the target, perhaps through use of automatic navigation or "homing" devices. Such accuracies are adequate. When the warhead is packed with megatons of thermonuclear explosive, a five-mile miss has nearly the same effect as a direct hit.

With accelerated development programs, these devices are promised in five to ten years—perhaps in only two or three. They will be preceded by the intermediate-range ballistic missile (IRBM). With a range of up to 1,500 miles, the IRBM will bring all of Europe, plus most of our African and Asian air bases, within range of the communist bloc.

Paralleling this development in delivery mechanisms, continued progress may be expected in thermonuclear warheads. Greater explosive power will be put in smaller bombs and missiles. The arsenal will contain not only atomic and hydrogen warheads, but the more potent 3F (fission-fusion-fission) weapon. The potential is so great that the term "biloton" is sometimes heard—meaning the equivalent of a billion tons of TNT. With its combined lethal powers of explosion, searing heat, and radiation, nuclear warhead development promises to keep pace with improvements of delivery systems. Indeed, we may already be able to make weapons more powerful than we need. When one bomb can now wipe out an entire metropolitan area, there is little advantage in making still bigger bombs.

The problems of defense against a rain of ICBM's or IRBM's are almost insurmountable. The 25-minute flight time from continent to continent offers no opportunity for mobilization or preparation. Missiles would be upon us almost before we knew they were coming.

The difficulty of intercepting a missile will be as great as that of attempting to shoot down a flying artillery shell. An eminent military writer, Mr. Hanson Baldwin, has said:

The ICBM—because it follows a ballistic trajectory outside the earth's atmosphere, because it flies so high and so fast—may become the world's first unstoppable weapon. Scientists envisage in theory a system of automatic tracking and intercepting missiles which might in time make possible a small "kill" rate. But the time between launching and impact is so short, the technical difficulties so immense, that any such defensive system is a long way off. Furthermore, even when it is developed, it can never be more than fractionally effective—and that just wouldn't be good enough. Only a few ICBM's would have to get through to knock out our own principal cities—a good part of our war making potiential. . . . The ICBM represents, for the immediate future at least, the ultimate triumph of the offensive in war.[13]

Along with missile development, science is making rapid strides toward space satellites. Both the U.S.S.R. and the U.S.A. are expected to launch one or more in 1957. When these are perfected, space platforms will be available for observation of foreign territory, communication, control of missiles, and possibly even for launching.

Once weapons now on the drawing boards and in the laboratories are perfected and produced in quantities, man will truly possess the ability to blast himself off the face of the earth. Military defense against them is an almost insurmountable problem, and civilian defense is an utterly fantastic concept. The only real defense against such weapons is to prevent their use. This calls for nothing less than elimination of war.

As long ago as May, 1951, in testimony before the Senate Armed Services and Foreign Relations Committees, General Douglas MacArthur said:

In war, as it is waged now, with the enormous losses on both sides, both sides will lose. It is a form of mutual suicide; and I believe that the entire effort of modern society should be concentrated on an endeavor to outlaw war as a method of the solution of problems between nations. . . .

[13] "I.C.B.M.," *Collier's,* March 16, 1956.

Chapter 5

THE UNITED NATIONS

A review of the present organization is a usual part of a management survey. What is the structure and effectiveness of the existing organization? How does it measure up to our needs and requirements? Are changes required to permit it to accomplish its purpose?

THE UNITED NATIONS was born in San Francisco in June, 1945—two months prior to the violent Hiroshima announcement of the birth of the Nuclear Age. It was hopefully organized to bring peace and security to a world tired of war. Its short life has witnessed success and failure, applause and condemnation, use and misuse. But it has survived in spite of conflict and now has gained public support. The U.N.'s survival and support are a tribute to growing recognition of the interdependence of nations and to a mounting demand for an effective international organization.

We must understand the structure of the United Nations, as well as its successes and failures, properly to appraise the role it can play in achieving a secure peace which will preserve and expand freedom.

HISTORY. The United Nations is the world's second attempt to form an international organization for the preservation of peace. Its predecessor, the League of Nations, collapsed when it was unable to prevent aggression. The League, created at the end of World War I at the urging of President Woodrow Wilson, was handicapped from the start by the absence of the United States as a member.

The inability of the League to preserve peace stemmed primarily from its lack of authority and power. It could not act by itself and was completely dependent on the cooperative action of its members. The steps which might have restrained Italy or Japan as they embarked on aggression were never taken. The member nations could not agree on the application of sanctions.

The United Nations Charter supposedly overcame the weaknesses of the League Covenant. A close comparison of these two documents reveals some improvement in the U.N. Charter and even some suggestions of greater delegation of authority. However, the fundamental principle of dependence on national cooperation rather than on delegation of authority to the world organization was carried over to the U.N. This repetition of the weakness of the League is clearly revealed by a review of the Charter.

PRINCIPLES.   The Charter of the United Nations was proposed and drafted by the coalition of nations which brought World War II to its victorious conclusion. Its broad outlines were developed at the Dumbarton Oaks Conference in 1944. The United States, Great Britain, and Russia laid the plans for its development. Many of the principles were agreed upon at Teheran and Yalta by Franklin D. Roosevelt, Winston Churchill, and Joseph Stalin.

These leaders were faced with the serious dilemma which confronted all nations. On the one hand, they recognized the utter necessity for a world organization to preserve peace. On the other, they were unwilling to give such an organization any real power or authority. It is completely dependent upon the voluntary cooperation of its members.

Moreover, the provisions of the Charter lodge the final control of all matters affecting security and aggression in the hands of the Big Five—the U.S.A., the U.S.S.R., Great Britain, France, and China. The effectiveness of the United Nations is thus predicated on continued cooperation between these powers.

The defeated nations of World War II were not included as members of the United Nations. Provision was made for their admission as they become "peace-loving states" and are "able and willing to carry out" the obligations of the U.N. Charter.

The United Nations is completely dependent upon voluntary cooperation of its members, and has no authority of itself. It cannot enact or enforce laws. It has no army and no police force. It can make recommendations but has utterly no power to enforce them. The U.N. Charter contains many fine promises; but if the member nations do not choose to keep these promises the U.N. is powerless.

The principal organs of the U.N. are: the General Assembly, the Security Council, the Economic and Social Council, the Trusteeship Council, the International Court of Justice, and the Secretariat.

THE GENERAL ASSEMBLY.   The General Assembly may consider any subject which is within the scope of the U.N. Charter, including maintenance of international peace and security, disarmament, and situations endangering peace and security. However, its functions, as established by the Charter, are limited to debate, study, and recommendation to U.N. members or to the Security Council.

Meeting annually, it receives agenda proposals on many important issues. In 1955 these included peaceful uses of atomic energy, disarmament, charter review, economic aid, the jurisdiction question involved in the Algerian and South African problems, and the colonial controversies in Morocco and Cyprus. In addition, it must deal with elections of new members, selection of members of the Security Council and other organs of the United Nations, and other affairs associated with the normal operation of the U.N.

Each member nation has one vote in the General Assembly. A two-thirds majority vote is required to place an item on the agenda of the General Assembly. Thus, one-third of the member nations (perhaps representing far less than one-third of the world's people) can keep any issue off the agenda and block discussion of its merits.

After being placed on the agenda, issues come to the floor of the Assembly to be debated and voted upon. Procedures are similar to those of legislative bodies—but with one vital difference: Resolutions proposed, amended, and adopted are only recommendations. Neither the member nations nor the Security Council is required to follow them. Regardless of their urgency and merit, the Assembly deliberations result only in recommendations which are followed or disregarded by each nation as it chooses.

This lack of legislative ability is often misunderstood, for the General Assembly has all the superficial trappings of a legislature. But it is only a "debating society," adopting suggestions and recommendations. Beneficial as such action may be in airing problems and forming world opinion, we must remember that the General Assembly cannot pass laws or regulations which are binding upon any nation or any individual.

Thus, every nation has a "built-in" veto: it can nullify any recommendation of the General Assembly by simply failing to obey it. The Assembly may propose, but the individual nations dispose. This is a far cry from a congress or parliament, for which the Assembly is often mistaken.

The Assembly is further prohibited from even making a recommendation on a matter of international peace and security while the Security Council is dealing with it.

In addition to its interests in the field of international peace and security, the Assembly can concern itself with studies and recommendations in other fields, such as, development of international law and promotion of international cooperation in the economic, social, cultural, educational, and health fields. In addition, the General Assembly has certain functions of study and recommendation regarding budgets, reports, the International Trusteeship system, and other organs of the United Nations.

THE SECURITY COUNCIL.   The Security Council too is a "recommending" body without authority to accomplish its objectives. The Charter confers upon it the primary responsibility for maintenance of international peace and security. It is also supposed to formulate plans for a system to regulate armaments.

The Council consists of eleven members with one vote each. Five are permanent members: the Republic of China, France, the Union of Soviet Socialist Republics, the United Kingdom and the United States. The other six are elected by the General Assembly. Decisions, except on procedural matters, require the affirmative vote of seven members, including the five permanent ones.

From this provision has come the "veto," whereby a permanent member can paralyze action of the Council. The more than sixty uses of the veto by the Soviet Union have made it a symbol of big-power disunity and of U.N. weakness. Its use clearly demonstrates the ineffectiveness of an organization whose structure requires unanimous agreement of a group of nations, be they large or small.

Criticism of the veto, albeit appropriate, overshadows other vital defects of the Security Council. Were the veto eliminated, the Council would still lack authority and ability to act. It could only make recommendations which might or might not be carried out by member nations. Its proposals are subject to the same "built-in" veto which confronts the General Assembly—the power of any nation (not just the Big Five) to refuse to follow the U.N.'s recommendation.

The Security Council's powers to deal with threats to peace and acts of aggression are limited to investigation and recommendation. The Security Council may seek solution by negotiation, mediation, conciliation, arbitration, and such peaceful means, calling upon nations to settle disputes. But it cannot compel settlement nor can it even restore or preserve order while it seeks a solution.

If such peaceful means are unsuccessful, and a dispute endangering security and peace continues, the Council can call on member nations to apply sanctions. Such sanctions, applied against the erring nation, might be in the economic or communications fields together with severance of diplomatic relations. But here again the Council only recommends. It cannot enforce nor apply sanctions itself. Such a call for sanctions may be respected or ignored by the member nations. When tried against Italy by the League of Nations after the Ethiopian invasion of 1935, the call was generally ignored.

If the attempted use of sanctions is not effective, the Council has the theoretical authority to "take action by air, sea or land forces . . . necessary to maintain and restore international peace and security." Action with what? With such military forces as individual nations are willing to send. The U.N. has no armed forces of its own. So again the Council's power is one of request and recommendation, leaving the decision to be made independently and separately by each nation.

The only such call to date by the Security Council followed the Korean invasion in 1950. It was successful only because the U.S.A. was willing to provide a disproportionate share of men and munitions. Only fifteen other nations responded with token forces, miserably inadequate without the large United States contribution. Most of the members of the U.N. either ignored the call, provided resources of minor value, or helped the aggressor. This test run clearly demonstrated the failure of action "by call." Such collective action is doomed before it starts by the uncertainty of participation of those invited.

Article 43 calls for agreements between the Security Council and member nations designating national military forces to be always available for collective action, coordinated by a U.N. military staff. However, years of discussion have not so labeled a single plane or a lone infantryman. Nor has the U.N. a sergeant, let alone a general, on its military staff.

Designation of troops and establishment of a U.N. staff would not assure prompt and effective action by the Security Council, because the forces to resist aggression would still be national contingents. Their availability would always be contingent on whether national governments would actually supply the forces when the Security Council called for them.

Nothing in the Charter gives the Security Council the authority to establish United Nations forces, with U.N. soldiers, U.N. weapons and U.N. commanders standing ready to resist aggression or to maintain order.

ECONOMIC AND SOCIAL COUNCIL.   This Council, consisting of eighteen members, may study, report, and recommend with respect to international economic, social, cultural, educational, health, and related matters with a view to creating conditions of stability and well-being among nations. It may also make recommendations for the purpose of promoting human rights and fundamental freedoms for all. The execution of any recommendations of this Council depends upon the voluntary action of the nations involved.

Many activities in this field are carried out by the specialized agencies which include:

Food and Agricultural Organization (FAO)
International Bank for Reconstruction and Development (BANK)
International Civil Aviation Organization (ICAO)
International Labor Organization (ILO)
International Monetary Fund (FUND)
International Telecommunication Union (ITU)
United Nations Economic, Social and Cultural Organization
    (UNESCO)
Universal Postal Union (UPU)
World Health Organization (WHO)
World Meteorological Organization

The following are in the process of being organized:

Intergovernmental Maritime Consultative Organizations (IMCO)
International Trade Organization (ITO)

The Economic and Social Council has the responsibility of coordinating the activities of these specialized agencies, all of which are established by intergovernmental agreements.

THE TRUSTEESHIP COUNCIL. This Council consists of the permanent members of the Security Council, members administering trust territories, and members elected by the General Assembly. Acting for the General Assembly, it concerns itself with the administration of the international trusteeship system. The purpose of this system is the administration of territories not yet ready for self-government. Examples include the area between Israel and Trans-Jordan, Somaliland, and many old League of Nations mandates.

THE INTERNATIONAL COURT OF JUSTICE. This court is established under the provisions of the Charter and the Statute of the International Court of Justice, which is annexed to the Charter. It may decide legal matters voluntarily submitted to it by nations, and may decide matters especially provided for in the Charter of the U.N. or in certain treaties. It may also give advisory opinions on legal questions at the request of an authorized body of the U.N.

No nation is required to submit its disputes to the International Court of Justice. The Court can decide a case only if both parties want it to do so.

Even if two nations refer a dispute to the International Court, its decision cannot be enforced unless both nations voluntarily obey the decision. Of course, the Charter states that members of the U.N. promise to comply with the decisions of the International Court. But the Court has no "sheriff" to enforce this promise. Again, the fact that the U.N. has no police or military forces is a serious weakness. Cases of failure to comply with the Court's decisions may be referred to the Security Council, which has no more powers in this field than in any of the others mentioned above. No other method of enforcement is provided.

The Statute of the International Court of Justice does not even attempt to provide machinery for enforcing the U.N. members' promise to refrain from "the threat or use of force." If another Hitler or Stalin starts a war or threatens one, the International Court cannot try him for violating the U.N. Charter. The International Court is not a criminal court, and it cannot hear any case which involves an individual rather than entire nations.

THE SECRETARIAT. The Secretariat, under the administration of a Secretary-General, provides staff for the operation of the United Nations. The Secretary-General may bring to the attention of the Security Council matters which, in his opinion, threaten maintenance of international peace and security.

ACCOMPLISHMENTS OF THE U.N. The United Nations has many fine accomplishments to its credit.[1] One important accomplishment is that it has survived its first ten years of existence. It is alive today in spite of the strains of a tense and unsettled world and in spite of those who have desired and predicted its failure.

The United Nations, by negotiation and conciliation, has prevented or ended aggression in several cases. It helped to save the independence of Iran and Greece. It brought the India-Pakistan war to an armistice in 1948. It also brought the Arab-Israel war to an armistice (1948) and has assisted in maintaining an uneasy truce. It contributed to the settlement of the Netherlands-Indonesian conflict and ushered the Indonesian Republic into the United Nations. In all of these instances the results have been accomplished by peaceful means, though often the U.N. was able only to end a war rather than to prevent it.

The United Nations called for collective military action to resist aggression in Korea. Here, for the first time in the history of the world, an international organization, acting through its members, opposed and resisted aggression with military measures. This step was possible only because of the absence of the U.S.S.R. from the Security Council at the time the vote was taken.

Recognizing this situation, the General Assembly took another forward step in 1950 when it passed the "Uniting for Peace Resolution." This resolution allows the General Assembly to recommend action in case of a veto in the Security Council on matters of aggression.

The United Nations has also achieved much through its specialized agencies. These organizations, working in the economic, social, health, and human areas, have made substantial beginnings in the great task

[1] Clark M. Eichelberger, *U.N.: The First Ten Years* (New York, Harper & Brothers, 1955).

of helping the peoples of the world overcome hunger and poverty and improve health. This work can help create a greater sense of community and understanding among the peoples of the world.

FAILURES OF THE U.N.   In spite of the worth-while accomplishments of the United Nations it has not been successful in maintaining international peace and security and in removing threats to peace. Its inabilities to deal with such problems have been evidenced by the following:

1. It has not prevented war. In addition to the Korean War, there have been numerous cases of armed conflict: Israel-Arab, India-Pakistan, Indo-China (Viet Nam), and others.

2. It did not obtain general and equitable participation in its one effort to use collective security to resist aggression in Korea.

3. It has been unable to get the member nations to agree to furnish any armed forces to the U.N. in future cases of aggression. Neither has it provided even a limited international police or military force.

4. It has not been capable of halting the arms race or of making any substantial progress toward disarmament.

5. It has been unable to prevent the expansion of the communist empire by force, threat of force, and subversion.

6. It has frequently been by-passed by its members who have deemed it necessary or desirable to seek solutions outside the U.N.

7. It has repeatedly denied membership to many nations which have met the requirements for admission. (This situation was partially corrected by the admission of most of these nations in 1955.)

An analysis of the reasons for these failures points to the inability of the U.N. to act if the Big Five are not in agreement. It also emphasizes the inability of the U.N. to compel any action and to make or enforce any decision unless all affected nations agree. The U.N. can only suggest, recommend, negotiate, conciliate, and plead as it seeks to solve a problem. It lacks the power to enforce a just decision.

Speaking before the U.N. Assembly in September, 1954, General Carlos P. Romulo of the Philippines emphasized U.N. weakness when he said:

We are compelled to admit that under the present Charter the United Nations is incapable of performing the service that it should for the peoples of the world in this atomic age; and it is the most important and urgent single element of that service to save humanity from the menace of atomic destruction. The question remains whether the good sense and good conscience of humanity will be asserted effectively and in time to forestall a war of annihilation with atomic and hydrogen weapons.

THE FUTURE OF THE U.N. Peace-loving people throughout most of the world support and look hopefully toward the United Nations. Such support is stronger today than it has been at any time since the U.N.'s birth. The nations are recognizing the need of such a world organization and are growing in their understanding both of its complexities and of its dynamic potentialities. This sentiment was expressed in nearly every address at the ceremonies at San Francisco in June, 1955, commemorating the tenth anniversary of the founding of the United Nations.

Now the serious questions regarding the United Nations are related to making it more effective. There is no real question regarding the urgency of its mission among men. Its acceptance among the nations of the world is so great as to compel its continuance by the great powers, including even the Soviet Union. But if it is to justify this faith, ways must be found to make the United Nations effective in the areas where it is now least effective—peace, security, and disarmament.

WHERE WE STAND. Having "estimated" the situation in these five chapters, where do we stand? A brief summary defines our position as one which is far from ideal.

Since the close of World War II there have been almost continuous strife and conflict between the free world and the Communists. World War III has been avoided, but the world is armed to the teeth with nuclear and conventional weapons. Communist expansion has been checked in Europe, where a stabilized condition has been reached at least for the present. In Asia, however, stabilization has not been accomplished, and communism is still expanding. Trouble is brewing in the Middle East. The "new look" in Soviet foreign policy creates a greater threat to the entire free world.

Underlying the conflict between communism and freedom are many fundamental forces which influence the attitudes of men and nations. These strong forces are continuing evidences of man's struggle toward a better life and a saner world. Such forces as nationalism, diversity, and the struggle for life often create disruptive conditions. But such forces as the common desire for peace and freedom, growing interdependence of nations, and the availability of the tools of plenty promote unity. All these forces can be helpful if properly understood and channeled.

Overshadowing all of these forces, and indeed even the ideological conflict between freedom and communism, is the impact of the Nuclear Age, offering both hope and fear. Its weapons have added new dimension to warfare which compels that nuclear war be avoided.

Apparently this conclusion has now been tentatively recognized by the Soviet Union, by the United States, and by other nations. But the actions and words of these nations scarcely indicate recognition that there is no alternative to peace in the Nuclear Age. Hence, the world needs to get on with the task of finding and developing the mechanisms for assuring international peace and security.

This focuses attention upon the United Nations, "man's best hope for peace." It has survived the years of postwar conflict and has gained in acceptance. How can it be effective in eliminating war, guaranteeing peace, and expanding freedom?

This question blends with others relating to our foreign and military affairs to create a single main problem: What should be our national program? How should we proceed toward our desired goal of peace and security? What elements should be contained in our policy? We must answer these questions wisely if we are to serve well our enlightened self-interest and to fulfill capably our role of world leader in this time of challenge!

PART II

The Alternatives

"We are here to make a choice between the quick and the dead.

"That is our business.

"Behind the black portent of the new atomic age lies a hope which, seized upon with faith, can work our salvation. If we fail, then we have damned every man to be the slave of Fear. Let us not deceive ourselves: We must elect World Peace or World Destruction."   —BERNARD M. BARUCH

"To cope with the atomic revolution, we need a political revolution of at least equal imagination and magnitude. Necessity is still the mother of invention. Our need is for peace, no longer as a mere convenience but as the indispensable condition of human survival."   —GENERAL CARLOS P. ROMULO

"The dogmas of the quiet past are inadequate to the stormy present. The occasion is piled high with difficulty, and we must rise to the occasion. As our case is new, so we must think anew and act anew. We must disenthrall ourselves, and then we shall save our country."   —ABRAHAM LINCOLN

Chapter 6

THE COMMUNIST PLAN

> Competition, an accepted fact in free enterprise, compels alertness and initiative. A manufacturer offering a new product fully acquaints himself with his competition. He examines the other products on the market, determines their merit and salability, and searches for their shortcomings.

WE START our examination of the alternatives by reviewing the ambitious and often confusing plan of the Communists. Their plan for a world order is indicated by their history, their literature, and their political maneuvering. As their philosophy is so repugnant to anyone knowing the true meaning of freedom and democracy, we have difficulty in understanding its appeal to others. Nevertheless, this appeal is proved by the expansion of communist domination and influence, and by the presence of supporters in prosperous as well as underprivileged nations. To combat the communist plan successfully we must understand their objectives and the methods they use to achieve them.

WORLD ORDER. The plan for a communist world, and its supporting ideology, is presented in the writings of Marx, Engels, Lenin, Trotsky, Stalin, and others. It began with the philosophy developed by Karl Marx and Friedrich Engels a century ago, called Dialectical Materialism. This philosophy not only inspired the revolution in Russia but gives a dogma to the Soviet and other governments now controlling some 800,000,000 people.

The philosophy is based on the premise that the universe and all that is contained within it can be credited to materialistic causes. This theory denies a Creator of the world. It reduces everything to matter. Both Marx and Engels contended that their work and philosophy had a scientific basis. However, neither of them adduced any real scientific proof. Even though their philosophy is full of inconsistencies, it has thrived on this century's interest in science and its seeming conflict with religion.

The communist doctrine, as propounded by Marx, is not only opposed to religion but is against all aspects of the civilization he knew in Europe during the middle of the nineteenth century. This includes capitalism, government, rulers, and the bourgeoisie—all who had risen above the worker. The communist formula, as developed by Marx and his followers, calls for the overthrow of monarchical forms of government in the name of self-government. This, however, is to be followed by a revolution of the proletariat or workers who will seize power and establish a dictatorship.

Under this dictatorship, both civil and international war will be used to establish power. In this period the population is to be educated, changed, and fitted "to assume the political reins." This educational process is for the proletarians themselves, to rid them of traditions or habits of the bourgeoisie. This process completed, the new socialist society will replace the old capitalistic society. Thus the dictatorship of and for the proletariat, through economic, political, educational, and cultural measures, will take the required steps to the ultimate dream of the Communists—a classless and stateless being. This dream will become reality because men can be changed and fitted to live in such a classless and stateless world.

It is quite obvious that the communist revolution in Russia is in the middle phase of this pattern. It is a dictatorship. It uses war and conflict to expand itself. The attempts to develop a new man are evident, both by education for the susceptible, and purges for the obstinate or unqualified. The dictatorships operating now in the Soviet Union and in Red China are still a long time removed from the stateless and classless communist heaven.

Doubts prevail that the current rulers of the Soviet Union have much interest in a classless and stateless world order. Certainly the Soviet Union becomes more and more stratified during the dictatorship phase. Nevertheless, the leaders make effective use of their doctrine and dogma, and to some extent it must influence their decisions and activities.

One tenet of their philosophy is that, given enough time, the capitalistic society is bound to collapse. This belief, along with the conviction, expressed by their philosophers and leaders from Marx to Stalin, that the period of dictatorship of the proletariat will be a prolonged one, extends indefinitely the time limit for the accomplishment of their objectives.

Such is the philosophy and ideology upon which the communist revolution and experiment is based. In the present middle stage, however, the state is supreme and can do no wrong. This philosophy was pungently expressed by Nikolai Lenin in 1920 at Moscow when he said:

Why should freedom of speech and freedom of the press be allowed? Why should a government which is doing what it believes to be right allow itself to be criticized? It would not allow opposition by lethal weapons. Ideas are much more fatal than guns.

STRATEGY AND TACTICS.   This ultimate goal of a stateless and classless world proletariat living as brothers has no present use except as a propaganda device. Communist organization is now in the middle stage, the period of dictatorships and of education to develop the ideal proletariat. Wherever they have gained control of a nation they have immediately established a ruthless and total dictatorship and have begun the process of education and elimination. Their obvious strategy of recent years has been to overthrow existing governments and establish communistic dictatorships. Their tactics to accomplish this are evident from a review of their activities.

In the first place, they endeavor to obtain adherents to their ideology wherever they can. This operation is carried on by their agents, covertly and underground when necessary, but through communist political parties where possible. This is a program of subversion, infiltration, and conversion which has had varying degrees of success.

A second characteristic of their activity is their prompt seizure of every opportunity presented by indecision and division in the free world. The overrunning of eastern Europe and the advances into North Korea and Manchuria are examples. A more recent one is the invasion of South Korea a short six months after the United States announced that their Pacific defense perimeter did not include Korea.

Closely allied is their equally prompt seizure of opportunities to inject themselves into economic, social, and colonial problems. Their 1956 change of foreign policy is high-lighted by their attempts to woo the nations of Africa and Asia. It is cleverly timed to coincide with growing criticism of the Western powers.

Another tactic is their willingness to use military force, or the threat thereof, to achieve their purposes in local areas. In general, this has been done by providing military know-how and equipment to their satellites and associates, who ostensibly are the prime aggressors. Thus far the U.S.S.R. has not committed its own forces and has pulled back its satellites when further advance seemed likely to precipitate a major conflict.

Another device is delay in such situations as the German and Austrian peace treaties, the deliberations in the U.N. Disarmament Commission and its military committee. This practice is dictated both by their belief that the collapse of capitalism is inevitable and by their need to overtake the free world in nuclear weaponry.

A further tactic is the practice of shifting quickly from a tough rigid position to a soft conciliatory one, or vice versa. This is related to their ability to take advantage of opportunities, to bide their time, and to adapt their actions to the tides and shallows of world politics.

This practice was demonstrated clearly in early 1956 by communist policy changes, including: collective leadership, an anti-Stalin move, intrusion in Middle East affairs, and an economic and social campaign in Africa and Asia.

WHERE IS THE APPEAL?   It is most difficult for Westerners, and particularly Americans, to understand the appeal of the communist ideology. We are convinced of the fallacy of Marx. We know that our free-enterprise system of today bears only slight resemblance to the capitalistic system which he condemned. We also observe the wide contrast between the promises and performance of the Communists. We compare their economic and social accomplishments with those of the more advanced countries of the free world. We also compare the freedom and the respect paid the individual in communist lands with that prevailing in the democracies of the free world.

Having done these things, we shake our heads in frustration and doubt. We simply can't see why communism should appeal to anyone. But it does appeal, and we must seek to understand the reasons.

A real effort is made to play on human needs and wants. To people who live in poverty-stricken hunger, the Communists promise food. To people suffering from an antiquated land policy, the Communists promise land. Those so circumstanced are not concerned with political philosophies. They hear only the promises of a loaf of bread or a plot of ground.

Then communism capitalizes on the basic desire for freedom and liberty. If a nation has been held as a colony and kept from any advance toward self-government—particularly if it has been suppressed by imperialist colonial practices—communism offers liberty and freedom.

Communism also plays on hatred and prejudices. It attributes all economic and social problems to class oppression, and develops antagonism against existing government. Using aroused hatred and prejudice, it kindles the desire to overthrow governments and economies.

Communism has raised semantics to a devilishly successful art. It has perverted the very terms which are fundamental to our Western ideals—peace, freedom, brotherhood, and democracy. These are everyday words in their propaganda. They purloin the very symbols of Western development and hold these to be attainable by their program.

Communist ideology, with its ultimate goal of classless and stateless society, holds up a heaven-like objective. It can be used to whip up a fervor, not unlike that developed by some religions, impelling men to slave and sacrifice for the ultimate goal.

And finally, as communism recruits its local leaders within a nation, it appeals to their very human urge for power and position. Preying upon frustrations, dissatisfactions, and hatreds, it offers authority and promises even higher position and influence.

With such a versatile array of appeals, it is not surprising that communistic propaganda has appeal, particularly in competition with some very inept propaganda on the part of the free world.

OTHER FACTORS.   Within the U.S.S.R., as within every communist country, are factors unrelated to communist ideology which are bound to have influence on decision and action. This will be increasingly true if it becomes evident to Russian leaders that world opinion is rising against them and that further expansion, both subversive and open, is increasingly resisted.

The U.S.S.R. is more than a communist ideology. It is also a ruthless centralized totalitarianism controlled by a handful of leaders. They guide the privileged members of the communist party which embraces only a small percentage of the population. This group has many reasons for preserving itself in power. Control gives them privilege, prestige, position, and possession. Is their primary allegiance to their ideology or to the preservation of their positions of power? They may well prefer to hold leadership within the nation rather than to risk their all by embarking upon expansion which might wreck all they have gained.

In addition, the U.S.S.R. is a nation as well as an ideology. It has the problems of national development and security which are common to other nations. Dependent upon its own efforts, it takes many steps to safeguard its security. Such an interpretation can be placed upon its expansion in eastern Europe where it sought friendly buffer states. How much of this expansion has been due to ideology and how much has been a search for security?

The U.S.S.R. apparently believes that it must find its security in military power, treaties and alliances and other devices. It is faced with the same temptations of extreme nationalism and with the same fears, prejudices, and insecurity which confront every other nation living in a world of anarchy. To the extent that its expansion has been dictated by considerations of national security, this expansion may cease if a secure peace is established.

The backward glance reveals that Russia has long been an expansionist nation. The postwar conquests of territory are in the areas where Russia historically has sought to expand. Traditional imperialism must have had some influence on Soviet leaders. However, they may well be more concerned with ruling as much of the world as they can without losing power than with being party-line fanatics.

Finally, the U.S.S.R. is made up of persons. These persons have normal desires for freedom, for understanding, for more food and better clothing. Although suppressed and controlled by a dictatorship, the 200,000,000 people of Russia proper are bound to influence national decisions. Their desire for a better life and greater freedom can only partially be restrained by ideology and dogma. Public opinion cannot be permanently and completely disregarded by any ruling group without endangering their position of leadership.

Such potential or existing forces are in conflict with communist ideology. Any compulsion to depart from the communist plan of world order must come from these sources, pressed home by the strength and unity of the noncommunist world.

One of our primary tasks is to develop such strength and unity on the part of the free world.

Chapter 7

OUR PLANS

Having reviewed competitors' products, a businessman looks at his own merchandise. He carefully appraises its strengths and salability and also its weaknesses and shortcomings. He uses such information to improve his product and to sell it effectively.

THE COMMUNISTS have a definite blueprint for the kind of world order they want. This goal guides their programs, activities, and positions. Their leaders can follow an over-all plan of military, economic, and political warfare as they strive toward world domination.

In contrast, the United States has neither a clear plan of an acceptable type of world order nor a unified program for assuring world peace and freedom. This is true in spite of a sound ideology and many worth-while programs. Although we constantly debate our national policies, we have failed to set up clear goals which may be considered as national objectives.

The free nations have difficulty understanding our motives, while we cannot comprehend their doubts about us. How has this situation come about?

IDEOLOGY. The beliefs and philosophies upon which the United States was founded and has grown strong have great appeal to men everywhere. They are in sharp contrast to those of communism.

Religious faith has played a fundamental role from the day the Pilgrims stepped ashore at Plymouth Rock. The vast majority of Americans believe in God. Our churches have a strong influence in local and national life. Deeply imbedded within our religious beliefs is a great respect for every individual human being as a child of God. We believe he has certain inherent rights which come to him from his Creator. Our Constitution and our form of government endeavor to increase the dignity of man and to protect his rights and freedoms. These same principles are embodied in our respect for, and protection of, minorities and our genuine concern for civil rights.

From this respect for the individual evolves our belief that states and nations exist to be the servants of man, not his masters. This idea, firmly implanted in our Declaration of Independence, our Constitution, and our Bill of Rights, serves as the foundation for our democratic form of government. The phrase, "of the people, by the people, and for the people," is the political interpretation of our religious beliefs and our concern for man.

Our great economic development has been achieved using a capitalistic or free-enterprise system. Government regulation and control of business activities, while increasing with the growing size and complexity of our economic life, have been held to a minimum in comparison with other Western nations. We rely primarily upon competition to avoid abuse. Our free-enterprise system has brought about the high level of our material standard of living.

A sincere sense of social responsibility is present in every community and is reflected in widespread charitable and civic activity. Individual giving to worth-while causes and emergencies is usually generous. Business organizations are increasingly accepting greater social responsibility.

Basically free from imperialistic aims, we have always believed in the principles of independence and self-government. We normally encourage and help peoples to obtain their independence.

Throughout the years we have desired peace and have maintained a very modest military establishment. Only since World War II have our peacetime standing Army, Navy, and Air Force assumed gigantic proportions. Our entry into both World War I and World War II was motivated by a deep desire to achieve a better world as well as self-protection.

Such ideals and principles have guided this country in spite of our failure to live up to all of them all of the time. These ideals and principles represent the fundamental beliefs of the overwhelming majority of our people.

PEACE AND PLENTY.   We have no lack of general aspirations which are supported by an overwhelming portion of our citizens. We want peace and plenty. We do not want war or conflict. We value our freedom and democracy. We put great stock in our free-enterprise, competitive economic system. We are sufficiently enthusiastic about our political and economic systems to urge them upon other nations. We love to help other peoples, particularly in emergencies, but we urge the old axiom that everyone should "stand on his own feet."

As long as we speak in such vague and ambiguous terms we have understanding and agreement. But it is different when we concern ourselves with the specific objectives and programs which we should support in the international field.

We are not accustomed to thinking in international terms, having enjoyed many generations of isolation during which we avoided entangling alliances and concentrated on our national development. Now, suddenly faced with the responsibility of world leadership, we do not easily comprehend the relationship of global problems to our ideology and our dynamic civilization. We seem unable to apply on a world scale our successful experience with political and economic systems which have brought peace and plenty within the broad confines of the United States. When we try to develop effective international objectives we often hesitate and stumble.

We have the aspiration of peace and plenty for the world, as well as for ourselves, but we lack agreement on the specific steps which must be taken to reach the goal. Hence, our fine aspirations frequently seem unrealistic and unrelated to the current world problems. We frequently find ourselves following negative programs, perhaps necessary but certainly uninspiring.

Such has been our experience since the close of World War II. A glance at the programs, positions, and policies of the United States in the postwar period conveys the impression that they have been extremely varied and unrelated. However, a more careful examination indicates that, after an interlude of unrewarded faith and hope in big-power cooperation, the actions of the United States have centered around a single policy; namely, the containment of communism. Certainly this objective has governed our major decisions and actions.

To advance this objective, we have molded our military, economic, and political policies and programs in a partially successful effort to confront the Communists with a stronger and more stabilized free world capable of deterring further aggression.

But we have not matched this necessary, negative policy with an adequate positive policy to achieve secure peace, plenty, and freedom.

CONTAINMENT.   In the early postwar years our policies were governed by great confidence that the Big Five would cooperate to maintain peace. This brief period of hope and faith ended on the hard rock of Soviet intransigence. From that day of disillusionment until the present time the principal element of our foreign policy has been containment, primarily of a military nature.

The various steps of our program to contain the expansion of communism both in Europe and in Asia have been outlined in Chapter 2. All phases of our foreign policy have been shaped around containment: military, economic, political, and psychological.

From a military point of view, our armaments and our alliances are aimed at providing deterrents against communist expansion by aggression. The major deterrent has been our Strategic Air Command armed with nuclear weapons and provided with bases encircling Russia in Europe, Africa, and Asia.

In the economic field, our foreign aid is now closely linked with the military preparations of our allies. This is a shift away from the original principle of the Marshall Plan which provided economic aid to war-torn countries. This plan, conceived in generosity and humanitarianism, and offered to Soviet satellites as well as to free nations, was a real boon in rebuilding the economies of western European countries and reversing the trend toward communism. But in recent years this approach has given way to close coordination of economic aid with military preparations.

In international politics our major activity is that of inspiring and helping our allies and the neutrals to oppose communism and Soviet expansion. Our activities in the United Nations are generally directed toward the same objectives.

In the psychological field our programs are aimed at achieving unity with our allies and wooing neutrals to join in resisting communism. We seek to counter communist propaganda and to place the responsibility on the Communists for failure to achieve international peace and security.

The program of containment has been bipartisan. Initiated by

President Truman, carried forward by President Eisenhower, it has had the support of Congress controlled both by the Democrats and by the Republicans. Moreover, it has been supported by an overwhelming majority of United States citizens.

Containment has had reasonable success in Europe, where the situation has been stabilized, but less success in Asia where communist influence is still expanding. To date, it has been of little value in coping with explosive situations compounded of colonial unrest, and local hatreds, such as those found around the Mediterranean and in southeastern Asia. Nor has the containment policy prevented the Communists from wooing nations such as Egypt and Afghanistan with economic aid.

EMOTIONAL REACTION.   In a very typical American manner, our disillusioned shift from a policy of hope and faith to a more realistic one of military strength and containment was accompanied by a great change in public opinion. The pendulum swung too far. This became noticeable only after our involvement in the Korean War. The trend was antiforeign and anti-United Nations as well as anti-Communist. This swing in public opinion reached its climax in 1953 and early 1954. Riding on despair and doubt, and inflamed by impassioned demagoguery and propaganda, it became a wave of hysteria and fear. It resulted in excesses of which the United States may long be ashamed.

Unfortunately, this episode helped the Communists by clouding the issues and diverting attention from the very real menace of world communism.

At the root of this episode were sincere but unanswered questions in the minds of many American citizens. Some of these questions had to do with our extensive involvement in Korea and the lack of assistance given by other nations. Others had to do with the control of Communists within the United States and the serious security issue high-lighted by the Alger Hiss case. Still others were concerned with the basic issue of isolationism versus internationalism.

Whatever the source, the result was hysteria and fear. Suspicion was rampant and guilt by association was common. Fear of communist subversion too often led to indiscriminate accusations against non-Communists. Public-opinion polls showed increasing belief that

World War III was imminent. All of this resulted in extreme concern for security, even if it encroached upon time-honored freedoms.

The wave reached the high-water mark at the opening of hearings before a subcommittee of the United States Senate when Senator Joseph McCarthy presented "McCarthyism," with all its fanfare and fantastic charges to a vast TV audience. But the frantic era collapsed only a few short weeks later as Senator Albert Watkins and his associates calmly heard testimony and voted to censure the same Senator McCarthy.

But though of comparatively short duration, this emotional reaction of public opinion in its revulsion to communism had a marked effect upon our foreign policy and upon its interpretation throughout the world. Fortunately, Americans now realize that we can fight communism more effectively if we avoid losing our heads.

OTHER PROGRAMS. Although "containment" has dominated our foreign policy since 1947, there have been other elements, such as the following:

1. Technical Assistance. This has been implemented both through the United Nations and through the "Point Four" program proposed by President Truman. Our talk on this subject has been supported by token financial contributions. (Recent appropriations for the U.N. Technical Assistance Program are at the rate of $12,000,-000 per year, while those for the United States program, exclusive of military assistance, are comparatively small.)

2. In addition to the direct grants of foreign aid under the Marshall Plan and now under Foreign Overseas Aid Program (FOA), which are closely linked to our policy of containment, we have other programs aimed at economic development. These include participation in international lending organizations such as the World Bank and the encouragement of American investment in foreign countries. These programs are all quite small as compared to our military spending.

3. Atoms for Peace. President Eisenhower's stimulating "Atoms for Peace" proposal in 1953 was enthusiastically received. It gave impetus to the search for constructive uses of the atom. The conference at Geneva in August, 1955, on the peaceful uses of atomic energy, the discussions and actions in the U.N. General Assembly

in the fall of 1955, and the subsequent twelve-nation negotiations indicate genuine interest and progress.

4. United Nations. We have given consistent support to the United Nations. At times we have utilized it in the manner intended. We displayed leadership in sponsoring the "Uniting for Peace" resolution, allowing the General Assembly to make recommendations dealing with aggression if the Security Council failed to do so. But at other times we have by-passed the United Nations and have developed most of our treaties and regional defense arrangements outside it. Since 1953 we have supported the calling of a review conference to consider amendments to the United Nations Charter.[1]

5. Independence. Culminating a long period of preparation, we dramatized the decline of colonialism by giving complete independence to the Philippines in 1946. In addition, we have consistently espoused the idea of self-determination. However, in the execution of our policy of containment we have frequently placed ourselves in positions seemingly supporting the colonial programs of our allies. Our attitude toward the peoples of the Soviet-dominated satellites has varied from resigned acceptance of their fate to a call for liberation.

6. Disarmament. As early as 1947, when the United States had a monopoly of atomic weapons, we recognized the need for international control of this awful power and proposed the Baruch Plan. It urged the creation of an international authority with power to control atomic materials and production.

But after the Baruch Plan was blocked by Soviet opposition we have, until recently, virtually abandoned any real effort to advance disarmament. In meetings of the United Nations Commission for Disarmament (and its subcommittee) and in our statements on the subject, we have often tended to emphasize propaganda rather than to seek a truly effective disarmament plan.

7. Publicity. We have constantly endeavored to tell our story to the rest of the world, utilizing the "Voice of America" as a primary instrument. This program, however, has been a bone of contention in the United States Senate, and charges have frequently been made that it is ineffective.

[1] Lawrence Weiler and James Hyde, *The United States and the United Nations: Political and Social Questions* (Carnegie Endowment for International Peace, New York, 1957).

CHANGE OF PACE.   Since early 1955, there has been a shift of emphasis in our foreign policy, apparently spearheaded by President Eisenhower's sincere desire to achieve peace. His leadership in these matters was evident even before the "summit" talks in Geneva in July, 1955.

The increasing emphasis on disarmament was high-lighted by the May, 1955, appointment of Governor Harold E. Stassen as a Special Assistant to the President on disarmament matters. It has been dramatized by President Eisenhower's bold proposals at the Geneva Conference for mutual aerial reconnaissance and exchange of information on military establishments.

Such proposals, and others which have been discussed in the U.N. Disarmament subcommittee, are concerned with an "early warning" system aimed at lessening the likelihood and the fear of a surprise nuclear attack. This approach as a "step" to disarmament currently dominates the administration's thinking. No over-all plan for disarmament with effective controls has been proposed; in fact, there is indication of continued reliance upon a balance of power to achieve peace.

As recently as September, 1955, Secretary of the Air Force Donald A. Quarles firmly stated that the United States had no intention of disarming and that it sought "peace through effective deterrents." This approach is the same as that which Winston Churchill called "a peace of mutual terror." Nevertheless, the proposals for alarm systems are held by many to be a preliminary step or gateway which may not only lessen the likelihood of major aggression but create a mood leading to a "limitation of armament agreement."

With respect to the United Nations, we sponsored and actively supported a resolution in the 1955 General Assembly favoring, in principle, the calling of a review conference to consider amending the U.N. Charter. It calls for a "committee of the whole" to study the time, place, and procedure of such a conference and to make a report in 1957. In his address before the General Assembly of the U.N. in September, 1955, Secretary of State Dulles mentioned the veto, universal membership, and provisions for disarmament as possible subjects for Charter revision.

During and since the "summit" talks at Geneva in July, 1955, we have restated our willingness to negotiate with the Soviet Union to seek a path to international peace and security. At the present writing, there have been no concrete results of major significance, and neither side has been willing to compromise on any of the major issues.

The success of our policy of containment in Europe, and the apparent recognition by leaders of both sides that nuclear war must be prevented, have created a situation of lessened tension. The shift of the cold war to economic and political battlegrounds in the Middle World, extending from northwest Africa to southeast Asia, has not yet been met by an adequate program on the part of the United States. Proposals for limited increases in foreign aid are meeting resistance in Congress.

INTERPRETATIONS.   There have been varying interpretations of the actions of the United States in the ten years since the end of World War II.

The Communists have interpreted our actions to be those of a "warmonger" who seeks by every device to start World War III to gain domination of the world. Through skillful propaganda they have thus portrayed us to the watching world. The Communists have taken advantage of the free world's lack of unity to drive a wedge between us and our allies and to discourage the neutrals from following our leadership.

This propaganda has had its effect. It has hammered at real doubts which the inconsistencies and uncertainties of our actions have raised. It has been easy for the Communists to interpret our emphasis on military strength as a preparation for war. It has been easy to question our sincerity when we have seemed to support colonialism. At times it has been difficult to determine whether we shared the sincere belief of most of the world that the United Nations is the one great hope for peace.

Among our friends who know and understand the United States there has been little doubt as to our desire for peace. However, there has been concern as to our maturity and ability to fill a position of leadership. We have risen to the heights to propose fine plans, only to swing back to shortsighted actions. At times we have indicated an understanding of the necessity for controlling armaments and aggression on the world level, and at other times we have appeared satisfied to depend upon the shopworn practice of power politics.

There is lack of unity in the United States, as indicated by well-publicized expressions of difference, even within the political party of the administration. It causes other nations to doubt whether we have stable objectives in the international field.

In the spring of 1955 there seemed to be improvement in our position. The sincerity of our desire for peace was more adequately demonstrated. This fact, together with the increased stability of the free world, created a backdrop for the favorable reception of the leadership demonstrated by President Eisenhower at Geneva in July, 1955.

However, these gains have not been sustained. President Eisenhower's illness removed him from active leadership for several months. The foreign ministers' conference in October, 1955, brought no tangible results. The shift in announced Soviet policy creates new problems. The race for supremacy in ICBMs accelerates, and our progress in it becomes controversial.

Add the political charges and countercharges of a presidential election year, and the interpretation of our foreign policy becomes utterly confused. We may, in fact, ask the question: Have we any generally accepted foreign policy beyond containment of communism?

THE GREAT VOID.   An honest appraisal of our purposes, our program, and its interpretation by the rest of the world indicates a definite void.

The void is in the lack of a long-range national policy to guide our efforts as we seek to achieve secure peace. Such a program or policy must not only state the laudable objectives of peace, plenty, good will, freedom, and security; it must also contain specific steps toward these goals. It must chart the programs by which we hope to attain these objectives.

There is great need for such a policy determination, both at home and abroad. At home it would overcome confusion and give understanding and unity to our citizens. Within the free world the effectiveness of the communist program would be greatly reduced if our allies and the neutral nations could be sure of our objectives and how we propose to achieve them.

To the Soviets it would make clear the conditions under which we would be willing to agree to disarmament, and the basis we propose for a secure peace.

This void can only be filled by the development of a better-informed public opinion and by discussion and debate of the issues involved in our national policy, including a realistic appraisal of nuclear warfare. Such a policy should be bipartisan, placing national interests above party politics.

Unless and until such a national policy is evolved, we shall be seriously handicapped in our efforts to achieve the secure peace and safeguard the freedom which we all desire.

Chapter 8

HIGHWAYS AND BYWAYS

Most decisions in the fields of engineering and management involve a choice from among various alternatives. Even if one alternative seems unmistakably desirable, all possibilities warrant examination. An alert executive will frequently list the alternatives, jotting down the advantages and disadvantages of each.

WHAT PATH should the national policy of our country follow? A poorly marked byway wandering through the woods of international anarchy—or a highway running open, straight, and true toward the goal of secure peace with freedom?

There is no lack of ideas concerning roads to peace. Nearly everyone has a plan for reaching the desired destination. Many of these have merit, but others are impractical to the point of being "crackpot."

Some of the plans are simple ones, involving a single program or objective, claimed to be the sole key to peace. Others are complex, involving a number of programs and objectives. Their supporters allege that the battle for peace must be waged on many fronts.

A little study shows that the simple, single programs fall into a few groups, as do the parts of the more complex multi-purpose plans. This permits the following classification of alternate suggestions, with a brief description and a statement of the merits claimed for each.

POWER

One group of plans is based on power, meaning, of course, military power. Many advocates of such plans maintain that power is the only force understood by the ruthless dictators of the world. They further

73

contend that the free world cannot be secure unless it possesses military power to hold the Communists in check. There are several variations on the same theme, all with definite overtones of military emphasis.

POSTURE OF STRENGTH.   This is the program pursued by the United States since 1950, labeled by the term often used by President Dwight D. Eisenhower. It seeks, with the aid of our allies, to maintain military strength so great that the Soviet Union will not risk war. It is based upon providing deterrents against aggression, the principal one now being our Strategic Air Command armed with nuclear weapons. Its supporters state that the purpose of this military power is defense only, and it is to be used only if an attack is made against us. The United States and her allies are to be held together by treaties and other "collective security" agreements.

Currently, the "posture of strength" program includes the following:

1. Maintenance by the United States of a strong military organization with a current annual budget of nearly 40 billion dollars.

2. Occupation, with assistance from our allies, of forward bases which encircle the Soviet Union and increase the deterrent power of our Strategic Air Command.

3. Full-scale participation in the North Atlantic Treaty Organization (NATO), a military defense system designed to deter or resist any Soviet move toward western or southern Europe.

4. Military aid and guarantees to nations in other parts of the world, including Yugoslavia (which is not a member of NATO), the members of the Organization of American States, the members of the Southeast Asia Treaty Organization, and other nations in the Near East and Far East.

5. Continued development of weapons, including ICBMs, space satellites, and more powerful thermonuclear warheads.

6. Development of a continental defense against foreign air attack.

The maintenance of this "posture of strength" has required the location of United States troops and bases in many parts of the world, unprecedented commitments for mutual defense, and huge expenditures for our peacetime military establishment.

FORTRESS AMERICA. This plan is based upon the premise that the United States should not be involved in military and defense commitments with the rest of the world. Rather, we are urged to limit our efforts to North America, or at most to the Western Hemisphere, and make these areas impregnable. Such a proposal implies that we do not need allies and are capable of going it alone. Its advocates maintain that we should concentrate upon defense of the Western Hemisphere or the North American continent, keeping some military outposts in the Pacific and in the Atlantic. Such a defense system would be supplemented by a strong Air Force capable of massive retaliation if we are molested.

Through this armed isolation, we would supposedly free ourselves from involvement in world affairs. We could allow the communist controversy to run its course, concentrating our attention on domestic affairs.

BALANCE OF POWER.   Some recommend a return to the classic device of balance of power which has allegedly been effective during certain periods of history. It is the device which was used in an attempt to maintain peace in Europe prior to World War I and to World War II.

The balance-of-power approach has usually involved two opposing groups of nations linked to their associates by treaties and alliances. A third nation or group of nations, free of long-term alliances with either of the two opposing groups, seeks to prevent aggression by supporting the weaker group, thus maintaining a balance. The theory is that as long as both opposing blocs have approximately equal strength, neither will start a war.

Britain has, in the past, provided the balance which has sometimes stabilized conditions in Europe. This has been possible because of her detached geographical position, her great naval strength, her generally peaceful intent, and her highly developed sense of responsibility.

Balance of power is, of course, based upon the theory that military power is the prerequisite of peace. Its supporters see in this historical device the means of stabilizing world conditions, lessening the threat of war, and reducing the load of armaments.

Today there is no third nation or group of nations powerful enough to wield the balance. Most of the world's military power is held by two opposing groups: the alliance led by the United States and that which is led by the communist empire. Britain is now closely allied with the United States and can no longer play her former role. India and other neutral nations have little military power.

Some balance-of-power advocates believe that as Germany and Japan rearm, these nations will exert a balancing force. However, at present there are only two sizable military blocs in the world. Therefore, balance-of-power advocates hope that United States and Soviet strength will remain approximately equal.

Thus, from an American point of view, balance of power calls for most of the military measures which are part of the "posture of strength" policy. One difference is that "posture of strength" advocates would have more nations become allies of the United States, while many believers in a balance of power want to keep a belt of neutral nations between the United States and Russia.

PREVENTIVE WAR.   The extreme position of power policy is advocated by those who favor a preventive war. They call for war upon the Soviet Union by the free world at a time and place selected by the free world. They contend war should be waged before Soviet military strength is great enough to allow the U.S.S.R. to strike the first blow. Supporters of this program rest their complete faith in power and war. They believe that World War III is inevitable and, since that is so, we had better beat the Communists to the punch.

RELIGION AND GOOD WILL

Another group of suggestions is based on faith in the principles of religion, good will, and brotherhood. These suggestions are diametrically opposed to those based upon military power. Their supporters believe spiritual and moral force is the most effective means of obtaining peace.

RELIGIOUS FAITH.   All dedicated followers of Christianity and other principal religions believe that wider acceptance and practice of religious faith would change the world. They point out that if all men would submit to the will of God and live according to His directions there would be no need for war. Therefore, all churches are working to bring about a great growth of religious belief and practice. Most religious leaders agree that this great change will not occur overnight, and that it will require many decades or centuries of hard, patient work and prayer. Therefore, many of them also urge their followers to support immediate political and economic measures which they believe will reduce the danger of war. Responsible leaders of Protestant, Catholic, and Jewish faiths strongly support the United Nations and seek to strengthen it. Moreover, most of them recognize the need to end war and substitute law and order on an international scale.

WORLD BROTHERHOOD. Many people believe that brotherhood among men is the best road to peace. They contend that if men could know and understand one another, they would not fight. They urge that we devote more time and money to study of other nations, world travel, international exchange of students, and so on. Those who emphasize brotherhood usually support some of the approaches to world community which are mentioned later in this chapter.

PACIFISM. Between World War I and World War II strong waves of pacifism swept over this country. This attitude was engendered by a belief in the futility of war, by disillusionment with other methods of eliminating war, and (in some cases) by a desire to withdraw in isolation behind the bulwarks of the Atlantic and the Pacific. These same factors still give birth to suggestions of a program of pacifism. Those who support these views believe no good can come of war. They allege that avoidance of military preparations on our part will be met by a softening of attitude on the part of the aggressors. Others devoutly believe the sin of war is not justified under any circumstances. Such advocates, sincere in their beliefs, are frequently followed by individuals who embrace pacifism as an escape from the pressing realities of today.

CONCILIATION TOWARD U.S.S.R. Another school of thought suggests we can obtain tranquillity in the world by adopting a policy of "live and let live" toward the Communists. Its supporters believe that such an attitude would assure brotherhood and understanding, and that this good will would solve many of the problems of the world, or perhaps make their solution unnecessary.

This emphasis on conciliation sometimes approaches a policy of appeasement, or removing United States barriers to communist expansion. The advocates of a "soft" policy toward the U.S.S.R. claim that the Soviets are afraid of the United States, and that our military program provoked the present Soviet intransigence.

INTERNATIONAL COOPERATION

Another series of ideas centers upon the theme that the only difficulty on the international scene is the lack of cooperation between nation-states. It is claimed that the United Nations and diplomatic negotiation provide all of the tools required to prevent war. Hence, only cooperation is needed. Some of the variations of this approach are:

GREATER USE OF THE U.N.   One suggestion is for greater use of the U.N., particularly by the permanent members of the Security Council. It is urged that all problems and difficulties should be brought to the United Nations for discussion and settlement. These proponents contend that the powers of mediation, negotiation, and conciliation provided by the United Nations Charter are adequate to handle all situations. They see no necessity for strengthening of the United Nations or changing of its Charter. The U.N.'s sole deficiency, in their opinion, is absence of willingness to use the United Nations in the method intended.

DIPLOMACY.   Others suggest that the established processes of diplomacy provide the ways and means for solving the problems of the world. Supporters of this view put great faith in the diplomatic processes and their ability to compromise differences. Some would have the diplomats start with the little problems and gradually move on to the more complicated ones. Many advocates of diplomacy-as-usual propose that it be used as an adjunct to greater use of the United Nations.

SUMMIT TALKS.   Related to proposals for greater use of diplomatic processes is the suggestion of more meetings of the leaders of the great powers. Supporters of this idea put great stock in face-to-face meetings of national leaders as a key to greater cooperation. They point to the cooperation during World War II when President Roosevelt, Prime Minister Churchill, and Premier Stalin were in constant contact and met at Teheran and Yalta. Most advocates of this approach urge its use in conjunction with normal diplomatic processes and perhaps with greater use of the United Nations.

SETTLEMENT OF ISSUES.   The idea is also advanced that settlement of some or all of the issues between the Communists and the free world would relax tensions and promote understanding. The issues referred to include such controversial ones as: reuniting Germany, Korea, and Viet Nam; free elections in Soviet satellites; cessation of Soviet subversive activities in other nations; United States air bases near Russia's borders; and release of prisoners. We have challenged the Soviet Union to reach agreement with us on such problems as a token of good faith in their declared peaceful intent.

WORLD COMMUNITY

Another group of ideas embraces the premise that the first prerequisite of peace is the creation of a world community. Its advocates contend that peace cannot be achieved or maintained unless we first develop a greater community of interest and custom. They say that men and human institutions must become more similar before peace will be possible. The definition of a "world community" varies greatly with particular interests and viewpoints. Some define world community as adoption of uniform political and economic systems throughout the world. Others would settle for far less. Specific areas of development through which a world community might be sought include:

LANGUAGE.   One school of thought considers differences in language the primary barrier to understanding. This group wants a universal language, such as Esperanto, or more general use of some established language, perhaps English or French.

EDUCATION.   Many contend that a true world community cannot be created until all peoples achieve comparable educational levels; others, that only illiteracy need be overcome. They, therefore, urge concentration upon education and communications to provide a more informed and enlightened world population.

HEALTH.   Another point of emphasis is health. Certainly, health standards need to be improved in many parts of the world. This is believed to be possible through the application of public-health and medical practices which are well advanced in the United States, western Europe, and other nations.

ECONOMIC. Still others believe the basic requirement for world community is greater equalization of economic opportunity and standards. This, they claim, will let peoples rise above poverty and starvation and become concerned with world peace. Here again, modern techniques are recommended: improved agriculture, greater use of power and mass industrial production. Increased United States economic aid to underdeveloped nations is urged. Greater freedom of trade through relaxation of tariffs is also put forward as a method of improving the world economy.

Many insist that economic improvement must be based upon wider use of free enterprise as practiced in the United States.

SOCIAL STATUS. Some say the primary requirement for a better world community is improved social status of peoples throughout the world; including land reform, protection and fair treatment of minorities, respect for civil liberties, and similar items.

POLITICAL INSTITUTIONS. Another factor frequently cited as a prerequisite for world community is similarity of political structures. Its proponents believe there can be no world understanding with people living under political systems having divergent forms and beliefs. An extreme point of view is that all nations must have the same form of government. Americans subscribing to this point of view want all nations to have democracies with representative government. Others demand that all peoples have independence or be in the process of preparation for independence.

IDEOLOGY. Finally, there is the idea that world community cannot possibly develop until all peoples subscribe to similar ideologies. It is contended that so long as communism and freedom are in conflict, no progress can be made toward global peace. This view insists that the strife between these two ideologies must be resolved before peace can be achieved.

DISARMAMENT

Another group of suggestions centers upon the theme of disarmament. Some who advance such ideas believe the tools of war must be eliminated. However, there are vast differences in the meaning of the term "disarmament." It is a word which seems to mean different things to different people. Some of the current definitions and associated disarmament proposals follow:

OUTLAWING WEAPONS AND WAR.   One type of "disarmament" calls for outlawing weapons, or even war itself. Such proposals are usually concerned with nuclear weapons. All nations would solemnly promise by written treaty not to use atomic or hydrogen bombs or weapons. Some of the proposals include the outlawing of further tests or development of such weapons. Others are limited to their use in offensive warfare. Still others call for the U.S.S.R., Great Britain, and the U.S.A. to ban the use of nuclear weapons against major cities. And occasionally it is suggested that the simplest solution is to ban war itself.

ARMS LIMITATION.   Another current meaning of "disarmament" is arms limitation. Such limitations might apply either to nuclear or to conventional weapons, or both. They would also limit the size of armed forces, with established levels for the major nations. Each nation would promise not to maintain armaments or military forces in excess of the agreed level. Such a program might or might not have some means of inspection to indicate violations of the agreement.

ALARM SYSTEMS.   Recently attention has been focused on "disarmament" ideas providing systems of inspection capable of detecting concentrations of military power which could launch an offensive. The intent is to eliminate surprise attack by sounding an advance alarm. President Eisenhower's offer to the Soviet Union of exchange of military blueprints and inspection by aerial photography is the most striking proposal of this type. This proposal, augmented by ground inspection and other controls, has been submitted to the subcommittee of the Disarmament Commission of the United Nations. While not actually disarmament, such "alarm" systems are being considered in disarmament discussions as interim steps or "gateways" to disarmament.

UNIVERSAL ENFORCEABLE DISARMAMENT.   At the other end of the scale is universal enforceable disarmament. This would involve not only the elimination of all national arms—nuclear and conventional—but also the establishment of adequate enforcement procedures. Its proponents state that enforcement would require inspection forces in the hands of an international organization, together with world military forces to prevent aggression. It is claimed that such a step would take from nations the ability to wage war. Its supporters also urge safeguards to assure justice and to protect the rights both of individuals and of nations. Many contend that these safeguards can come only through a strengthened United Nations with the beginnings of world law.

WORLD LAW

A final set of suggestions for achieving secure peace centers upon the establishment of world law. Supporters of these suggestions believe that only law can end world anarchy, maintain justice, safeguard disarmament, and furnish the means for peaceably settling international differences. They contend that world law can only be created by an international organization with authority to enact, interpret, and enforce law. Six approaches to establishing world law are listed.

EVOLUTION OF UNITED NATIONS.   Some supporters of the United Nations contend that it has a sufficiently flexible Charter that through evolution it can assume the authority required to develop world law. They support this position by pointing to changes which have occurred in the U.N. since 1945, notably the "Uniting for Peace" resolution of 1950. They believe that the world will gradually permit the U.N. to assume the greater powers necessary to provide the minimum world law necessary for international peace and security.

LIMITED FEDERATION.   Specific proposals have been advanced for the transformation of the United Nations into a world federation, including all nations, with authority limited to the control of armaments and prevention of aggression.[1] Steps suggested for transforming the United Nations into such a federation by means of Charter revision include:

1. Delegation to the United Nations of authority to enact world law in the limited field of armaments, armaments control, and aggression; this authority to be exercised by a revised General Assembly with more equitable representation.

2. Creation of an executive or administrative agency within the

---

[1] *Policy* (New York, United World Federalists, 1956), and *How to Give the United Nations the Limited Power to Prevent War* (New York, United World Federalists, 1954).

U.N., with powers of inspection and policing in the limited fields of armaments control and aggression. This agency would have sufficient armed forces to assure peace and prevent aggression.

3. Enforcement of world law in the field of armaments control and aggression upon the individual as well as upon the nation. Under this proposal any individual, even a national official, could be arrested and brought to trial for violations of the laws in this field.

4. Revision of international courts and tribunals to allow them to settle peacefully certain types of differences which are bound fo arise between nations.

5. Erection of adequate safeguards to protect individual liberties against U.N. interference, and to prevent encroachment by the strengthened United Nations upon the internal economies, cultures, traditions, religions, and political institutions of member nations.

Those who support this program contend that it provides the basis for foolproof disarmament and peace, with full protection of the diversities among nations and their peoples.

ATLANTIC UNION.   Another of the proposals for an extension of the rule of law is Atlantic Union[2]. It is an outgrowth of Federal Union as originally propounded by Clarence Streit. He advanced the idea of a union consisting of those nations of the world which have had considerable experience in democratic government; for example, Australia, Belgium, Canada, Denmark, France, Great Britain, Netherlands, New Zealand, Norway, the Philippines, Sweden, Switzerland, the United States, and others.

Currently the Atlantic Union Committee proposes a similar federal union initially limited to the democratic nations of NATO. The name comes from location of these nations near the Atlantic Ocean.

The organization would be a union of the nations based upon the principles of federation. The government so created would handle foreign affairs, military preparations and defense, and other matters relating to international affairs. The Atlantic Union would become a major power in the world, with a great preponderance of industrial and economic strength. The Union would also control currency, tariffs, and trade. Common citizenship would be provided within the Union.

[2]*Atlantic Union: Why?* (Washington, D. C., Atlantic Union Committee).

Other nations would be admitted to the Atlantic Union when their standards, in terms of education, civil rights, economic development and form of government, reach levels comparable with those of the nations originally comprising the Union.

Those who support this program contend it would assure unity among the nations bearing the free world's burden of military defense. Thereby, it would create military and economic strength capable of halting the expansion of communism. They also claim it would provide great economic advantages to its members, thus encouraging other nations to advance, embrace democracy, and become members of the Atlantic Union.

FEDERATION OF FREE WORLD.   Another suggestion is a federation of the free or noncommunist nations having some of the features of both a "limited federation" and an "Atlantic Union."

Its supporters contend a federation of the noncommunist world is needed to maintain military and economic strength to deter communist aggression. Most advocates would first attempt the organization of a universal world federation with authority limited to the control of armaments and prevention of aggression as outlined above.

They believe communist expansion could best be prevented if all nations were members of a limited world federation. However, they fear the Soviet Union would not join a federation which would take away Soviet military power.

Failing to achieve a universal federation within a reasonable time, they would organize a similar federation of the noncommunist nations with these variations:

1. The federation might be organized under the provisions of Article 52 of the United Nations Charter.

2. The delegation of authority, structure, method of operation, and safeguards would be similar to those listed above under "Limited Federation," but would apply only to member nations.

3. Adequate power would be given to maintain a substantial military establishment. This would be necessary, as universal disarmament could not be undertaken so long as the communist nations remained outside the organization and maintained high levels of armaments. The required military power would have to be provided either by the free-world federation alone or in cooperation with national forces.

4. The door to membership would be held open to the communist nations. When they entered, the free-world federation would become a universal federation and universal, enforceable disarmament could be achieved.

Its advocates claim such a free-world federation, as a step toward a limited world federation, provides means for a strong military force if alliances prove unworkable. In this respect, it is similar to the Atlantic Union. However, its supporters would encourage membership of many nations in Asia, Africa, and South America which would be excluded from an Atlantic Union.

REGIONAL FEDERATION.   Still another approach to the ultimate goal of world law is that of regional federation, such as a United States of Europe, or a federation of noncommunist Asian nations. It is claimed that a number of regional federations, perhaps organized under provisions of Article 52 of the Charter, would provide benefits comparable to those provided by the United States of America. Nations, in effect, would become states, trade barriers would be eliminated and the benefits of a larger community provided.

Many supporters urge regional federations simply because of the benefits to the nations involved. Some supporters contend a group of regional federations would be a step toward world law, as it would reduce the number of governmental units, eliminate local frictions, and increase the use of supranational organizations.

SUPERSTATE.   The most extreme of the ideas for world organization calls for a world government of maximal powers, frequently referred to as a superstate.

A comprehensive proposal for this type of organization is found in a proposed world constitution drafted by a group of scholars at the University of Chicago in 1947. This proposed constitution provides for a world government having universal membership, and having broad powers. It would give the world government powers comparable to those now held by the federal government of the United States.

With such broad powers it would not only maintain peace in the world but would also be concerned with economic, health, social, and educational problems of all nations. Furthermore, supporters would have it guarantee freedom to all men everywhere and develop local and national governments based on democratic principles. One of its functions would be the elimination of want and poverty.

Such a proposed organization has objectives going far beyond international peace and security. It has often been labeled a superstate or supergovernment. Its proponents claim that in order to maintain peace, a world government is required with all these powers.

ROAD MAP.   With numerous possibilities suggested as routes to peace, a road map is needed to distinguish the byways from the highways. We must chart our course and select the best route to our destination. Such a task is a complex one, for most of the proposals discussed above have some merit. What basis shall we employ in making our selections?

Chapter 9

YARDSTICKS

Specifications are a well known engineering tool. They are written statements of conditions or requirements to be met. Specifications serve as yardsticks to measure the quality and performance of a product or a structure.

FROM THE MANY alternative programs listed in the previous chapter must come the ingredients of an adequate national policy for the United States.

Each of the suggestions needs to be examined from various points of view: moral, social, political, legal, and economic. In addition, the practicality and feasibility of each must be considered. Such an evaluation should indicate the elements of a policy for the United States which will not only serve our enlightened self-interest but will also meet our responsibility of world leadership.

OBJECTIVE. What should be the primary aim of United States foreign policy? Are our traditional statements of objectives adequate? Are the customary practices of diplomacy sufficient?

No thinking American can be satisfied with the shopworn approaches which have permitted the present chaotic world conditions. New targets and objectives are needed; fresh methods and approaches are demanded. As General Douglas MacArthur commented recently,

The old methods and solutions no longer suffice. We must have new thoughts, new ideas, new concepts, just as did our venerated forefathers when they faced a new world. We must break out of the straitjacket of the past.

87

Should not our primary objective be secure peace with freedom? Does not this simple phrase express our need? Peace—real peace— something more than the mere absence of war; secure peace—lasting and permanent—with the threat and scourge of war eliminated, that is our goal.

We need a peace which will secure all nations against outside interference, in which they can develop their own economies, cultures, and traditions.

Of course we insist on "peace with freedom." We do not want peace at any price—especially not at the price of tyranny. We do want the kind of peace under which our individual freedoms and liberties will be secure.

"Secure peace" or "peace with freedom" are used interchangeably in this book as a short label for the recommended objective of United States foreign policy.

Is not this a minimum prerequisite to achieving the inspiring objectives expressed in the preamble of the U.N. Charter?

WE, THE PEOPLES OF THE UNITED NATIONS DETERMINED
to save succeeding generations from the scourge of war, which twice in our lifetime has brought untold sorrow to mankind, and
to reaffirm faith in fundamental human rights, in the dignity and worth of the human person, in the equal rights of men and women and of nations large and small, and
to establish conditions under which justice and respect for the obligations arising from treaties and other sources of international law can be maintained, and
to promote social progress and better standards of life in larger freedom . . .

The simple idea, "secure peace with freedom," says this almost as well and in many fewer words.

FUNDAMENTAL GOALS.   Once we have chosen a secure peace with freedom as our basic objective, how shall we choose the programs to achieve this objective? The six goals listed below may be used as yardsticks to measure the desirability and acceptability of programs which are considered for incorporation in our national policy.

1. *Preservation of Our Freedom.* It almost goes without saying that we should never adopt a program or policy which impairs our

basic individual liberties. Freedom has enabled this country to prosper. Certainly the first objective of our foreign policy is the protection of these hard-earned rights and the maintenance of our traditions and practices which enhance the dignity of man.

2. *Maintenance of Our Security.* Likewise, we demand that our foreign policy (including military policy) protect us from attack or invasion. As long as nations are free to maintain and utilize military power, we must necessarily adopt the diplomatic and military steps which we consider necessary for our protection.

3. *Containment of Communism.* Our opposition to communist expansion is almost a corollary of the goals stated above. We believe that the communist ideology destroys the fundamental freedoms and dignity of man and corrodes religious and spiritual values. Hence, it is inevitable that we consider restraint of communist expansion as a necessary yardstick. We must go further and seek the ultimate decline of communism, hoping that the peoples under communist rule will eventually be free.

4. *Avoidance of World War.* The enlightened self-interest of the United States, and of every other nation, requires us to find ways to avoid World War III. As the destructive power of nuclear weapons becomes better understood, there is increasing realization of the futility of using war to settle international differences. Therefore, our policy must endeavor to avoid war but must do so in a manner which will not be contrary to the above three goals.

5. *Development of a World Community.* We have had a long-standing interest in programs which help to build a better world community. We have consistently supported activities aimed at improving educational, social, and economic levels throughout the world. The need for world development has never been greater than now. We must continue to encourage and support such programs and activities.

6. *Increase of World Unity.* In addition to those programs which develop a better world community we should, by attitude, word, and deed, foster greater political and ideological unity of the world. Such unity will help us cope with immediate problems and will provide a necessary base for a secure peace.

If we can adopt programs and policies which will simultaneously advance these six goals, we shall have an enlightened and effective national policy.

REALISTIC PROGRAM.   Another test which must be applied in examining the various programs is that of realism. By "realistic" is meant a program which is both obtainable and adequate. Thus, an idea may fail to be "realistic" either because it is impossible of achievement or because it is inadequate to meet the need. Our programs must be sufficiently bold and imaginative to provide adequate answers to the problems of today.

Furthermore, no program or policy can be realistic unless it squares with our basic moral, spiritual, and political principles. If it is contrary to these, it will not be accepted at home.

It is also quite apparent that any program or policy, to be realistic, must be in keeping with today's facts of international life. It cannot be geared to world conditions of fifty years or even ten years ago. It must be fitted to the political, social, economic, and scientific realities of the Nuclear Age and the new problems of tomorrow.

Still another test of realism is a program's ability to meet immediate problems at the same time it promotes progress toward the ultimate goal of secure peace with freedom. It must make sense in the divided, chaotic world of today and also advance us toward the more unified and peaceful world of tomorrow. It must also be capable of standing the test of time if progress toward a sound solution is slower than desired.

A final test of realism is economic feasibility. There is a definite limitation to the monetary commitment which we can and should bear. Any program which requires expenditures and taxation in excess of an acceptable level will not be supported by the American people.

COMPLEXITY.   A program which meets the yardsticks outlined above must consist of several elements. It cannot be a simple program with a single idea. Certain parts of national policy will, of necessity, be compromises between the ultimate that may be desired and the more immediate which is attainable.

The unique challenge of the Nuclear Age requires long-range objectives which may need to be pursued for a number of years. But there are also immediate problems which must be dealt with while we work toward the long-range objective.

And finally, an over-all program and policy which meets these goals will not be an easy one. Its achievement will certainly require great effort, great patience, and great dedication. There is no easy road to a secure peace. It is no simple task to reverse history, eliminate war, and substitute peaceful settlement. But discussion of the problems of achievement can better be deferred until the over-all program and policy are selected and understood. Therefore, we proceed with an examination of the merits of the many alternatives.

PART III

A Bold Approach

"The fact of international anarchy in a world of highly interdependent states is one of the primary causes of modern war. Hitler, Mussolini and Tojo were incidental to the basic cause of World War II."
—VICE ADMIRAL EMORY S. LAND, U.S.N. (Ret.)

"In this H-bomb era, we stand on the rim of hell, the potential destruction of our entire world civilization. The prime challenge to humanity is to find honorable peace so that mankind may live." —WALTER P. REUTHER

"International disarmament of both conventional and atomic weapons requires an international authority with power to inspect, control and impose punishment, swift, sure and condign, against any transgressor." —BERNARD M. BARUCH

"Peace is our objective; the advancement of the rule of law is the means. We have little time to waste . . ."
—HENRY R. LUCE

"The founders of our nation showed a political wisdom which has rarely if ever been matched. Surely, however, their effort did not exhaust the political genius of the American people. They invented and bequeathed to us an ordered society of spiritual and intellectual freedom. Such a society ought to be able to produce the new ideas needed to meet changing conditions. That is for us to demonstrate. Now, when new peril threatens, it behooves us to prove our worth. May we not, in our generation, emulate what our forebears did in their generation, and find the way to develop international order to shield national life? That is the challenge of our time. Let us dedicate ourselves to meet it."

—JOHN FOSTER DULLES, SECRETARY OF STATE

Chapter 10

POSTURE OF STRENGTH

A starting point for any new program is the present. Even though a manufacturer embarks on the construction of a new plant to produce a new product, he must still deal with his present situation. Enthusiasm for the ultimate goal must be tempered with attention to the immediate problem.

WE ARE NOW ready to select the elements of an adequate program and policy for the United States. Consisting of seven items, it will be labeled the Seven-Point Program.

As we evaluate alternate programs we must first consider present world conditions. Unless the program we select deals adequately with today's problems it cannot guide us to the better world of tomorrow.

ANARCHY. The first fact which must be faced is that anarchy prevails in today's world. Anarchy means there is no law but the law of the jungle: might makes right. Each nation is free to act as it wishes, unrestrained by any higher law or authority. No power exists which can compel a nation to honor treaties or commitments, to follow a path of justice, or to respect the rights and territory of any other nation.

Under such circumstances, nations are free to pursue selfish and even stupid objectives. A dictator, a group of national leaders, or a political party may seize control of a government and embark on a program of aggression.

Examples within the last few decades include: Japan under the leadership of its war lords, Italy led by Mussolini, Germany dominated by Adolf Hitler, and now the Soviet Union ruled by the Communists. Viewed against this background, the current Soviet threat is not a new phenomenon. It is different in time, place, strength, and strategy—but not in its basic nature. The Communists, like former imperialists, seek world conquest.

Faced with such situations, nations desiring peace and security historically have relied upon two devices: diplomacy and military force. By use of diplomacy they attempt to erect bulwarks of world opinion against potential aggressors, to placate them by concessions, or to develop mutual treaties of defense. Most diplomatic endeavors are backed by military force. The success of diplomacy is often directly related to the power of the armed forces which support it. When diplomacy fails the only recourse is war: the use of the military force which backs the diplomacy.

None of the events since World War II has changed this situation. Anarchy still rules in international affairs. The United Nations, as now constituted, is simply another tool of diplomacy. By negotiation, it may avoid or limit aggression. By collective security, it may provide a means for nations jointly to wage war against an aggressor, as was done in Korea; but it cannot protect even the small nations against war. Inasmuch as it can act only with the unanimous accord of the great powers, it is completely helpless to guarantee the security of one of the Big Five against another.

Because we cannot now depend upon the United Nations to provide security, we have no alternative to reliance upon military force to protect our interests. This we must do until other means are provided to enforce peace. This we must do even as we seek steps which will develop law and order and make dependence on force unnecessary. As long as we live in a lawless world we are compelled to keep ourselves militarily strong. Failure to do so would be national suicide.

Once we could depend upon the broad expanses of the Atlantic and the Pacific to isolate us from potential aggressors. Now, however, with modern aircraft and missiles, security by isolation is gone. We no longer have the protected position which we enjoyed from 1776 until 1914.

REJECTIONS.   We must cross off as presently inadequate any program based solely on good will, international cooperation, or world community. Important as these factors are, they are incapable of restraining a ruthless nation with evil intent. Moreover, though each of these factors can and must be a force in making a better world, no one of them is strong enough today to remove the need for a restraining force to control and deter the lawless.

So we must eliminate "pacifism" and "conciliation toward U.S.S.R."; these programs are completely inadequate in a world of jungle lawlessness.

Similarly, we cannot accept "international cooperation" by itself as an adequate solution. Such cooperation is most important, but it must be considered as a means to an end rather than as an end in itself.

Reliance on cooperation alone is utterly utopian. It assumes that all nations will always be "good," and will always be able to agree. But we are human beings, not angels. Even the people of a small town cannot govern their affairs by cooperation. They cooperate through the Chamber of Commerce, but they also establish a city council and police force.

Various forms of international cooperation—greater use of the United Nations, diplomacy, settlement of disputes and talks at the summit—are all desirable. However, these are only tools to use in our search for solutions to our problems; they are not answers in themselves.

We must not rely on world brotherhood and the improvement of the world community as adequate methods of meeting the immediate problem of security for the United States. We recognize the need of a better world community and resolve to intensify our efforts to achieve it. But these are slow-moving forces requiring decades and generations. As such, world brotherhood and world community cannot be relied upon alone to meet the pressures of today.

If we are wise, we shall not reject religious faith. Rather, we must acknowledge its tremendous importance in today's world. However, it would be unrealistic to abandon all other programs and rely solely on the power of religion to solve our dilemma. That power is very real and very great, but religious leaders agree that it works slowly. We still need immediate measures to keep the human race from slaughtering itself. However, we must beware of rejecting religion as impractical; it is not. The task of building secure peace with freedom is so great that only a genuine religious faith can inspire us to do the job. Man must change his world, but he needs help from a higher power.

THE PLACE OF FORCE.   For the present we must rely upon the maintenance of strong military forces to achieve three necessary objectives:

We use military power in an attempt to guarantee our national security at a time when there is no world law or world authority capable of doing so. We are compelled to rely upon it as the ultimate means of preventing and discouraging aggression against our nation.

Next, we rely upon military force to provide deterrents against communist expansion into adjoining territory. With our allies we endeavor to erect bulwarks along the communist borders in Europe and Asia to obtain stability and to prevent aggression.

Finally, we use military power to buy time in which to develop a better means for maintaining secure peace.

These three objectives are necessary to the enlightened self-interest of the United States. To achieve them we have no alternative to maintaining our military strength. We do so even though it is contrary to our basic distrust of the military. We do so sincerely believing it to be an indispensable aid to peace but hoping it will not be long required.

Our next questions relate to the kind of military force and preparations we need.

ALLIES.   In spite of the occasional suggestions that we "go it alone," there is general agreement that we must have allies and must work with other nations. Military experts have ably presented the case in favor of allies. They show how allies lessen the strain on our economy and resources and provide more powerful deterrents against a potential aggressor.

In spite of the frustration arising from the inherent impossibility of smooth cooperation among sovereign nations, allies are still the lesser evil.

Our adoption now of a completely unilateral program would be a backward step, greatly weakening our position.

A policy of continued cooperation with other nations eliminates two of the possibilities which were discussed under "Power Policy"; namely, "Fortress America" and "Preventive War."

The "Fortress America" approach is an extreme form of unilateral action by the United States: a return to nineteenth century isolationism. Abandonment of our allies would be completely out of step with the growing interdependence of nations. All of Europe, Asia, and

Africa would be easy prey for the Communists. Even with all our riches we haven't the raw material nor the industrial might to match the rest of the world. The adoption of such a policy would be a foolhardy risk of our freedom and a renunciation of our position as a world leader.

A "preventive" war against the U.S.S.R. would be an even more extreme return to isolationism. Any move in this direction would quickly disassociate us from our allies and leave us friendless and alone. A "preventive" war could not prevent, for it would surely unleash the retaliatory power of Soviet nuclear weapons upon us. Moreover, it would be completely repugnant from a moral point of view and would be a total reversal of our past policy in pursuit of peace and freedom. "Preventive" war is an idea that must be emphatically rejected.

We need allies and our allies need us. The quest for a secure peace is not the private property of any nation, not even of the United States. It warrants the concerted effort of all nations.

A CONTINUING PROGRAM.   Our present armaments program was begun under President Truman about 1948 when Soviet intransigence was fully recognized. It was rapidly accelerated during the Korean War. Under this program we have budgeted over $350,000,000,000 in the fiscal years 1950 through 1956 for our Army, Navy, and Air Force. We now have the most powerful military machine we have ever maintained in peacetime: it numbers about 3,000,000 men. The major elements of this program were outlined in Chapter 8.

This program must be continued to accomplish our desired objectives. Of necessity, comments on the United States armaments program are limited to general observations. Military strategy and tactics are fields for the experts. To render competent judgment, one needs adequate information regarding our own military establishments, those of our allies, and of the Communists. Though it is beyond the scope of this book to deal with military strategy and tactics, there are certain general observations which are pertinent.

Certainly the program must be adequate to fulfill its purpose. Its nature and size should not be governed primarily by its cost. It would be false economy to maintain a program which is too weak to buy the time we need in which to find other means of securing a lasting peace. Unfortunately, the general public has no measuring devices to determine the adequacy of the program. We are willing to support a proper program but must trust our military and governmental leaders to determine its content. Nevertheless, we must not hesitate to raise certain pertinent questions regarding its adequacy. Below are a few of these.

QUESTIONS

1. Both the U.S.A. and the U.S.S.R. now apparently have large stockpiles of nuclear weapons. Are we reaching a stalemate in nuclear weapons? If so, does our Strategic Air Command have the capacity to survive an initial attack and still deliver a massive retaliation? This is an important question, for it is most unlikely that circumstances would arise under which we would deliberately strike first. Hence, our retaliatory power must be ample to absorb an initial attack and still deliver a crippling blow. Otherwise, the Strategic Air Command will lose its value as a deterrent against World War III.

2. Have we also adequate deterrents against the "little wars" and "minor aggressions"? Does our military program provide a "posture of strength" against further chipping away by communist satellites such as we have witnessed in southeast Asia in the last few years? If we are committed to a program of containment of communism, it must be contained in Asia as well as in Europe, and we need deterrents against small expansions as well as against major aggressions.

3. What of our defense against an air attack? Is it adequate? What is its effectiveness? Can it detect and down a reasonable percentage of the planes in an invading air armada? If so, what do we do for defense against the new missiles which are being developed? Is there any defense against them? These are all questions which are unanswered so far as the public is concerned. As a result, there is great difference of opinion as to adequacy of military defense measures.

4. How about research and development in the military field? Is it adequate? Are we keeping ahead of the Soviet Union? These questions may be raised with particular emphasis on the ICBM and the space satellite. Many responsible authorities question whether we have an adequate lead over the Soviet Union. Are we making proper use of our scientists and engineers as we attempt to maintain a lead in technical development? Nuclear weapons of today and their means of delivery become obsolete so rapidly that an apparent lead can be lost overnight if our research and development are not well advanced.

5. What about the relative balance between our Army, Navy, and Air Force? Is the present division of strength and appropriations based upon our true needs, or is it a carry-over from previous practices? Is it determined by an appraisal of our military needs or as a compromise between competing branches of the armed services?

6. Is adequate progress being made toward the unification of our military services? Is the waste which tends to clog any military machine being eliminated? Most of us do not oppose spending for a military program but we want full value for each tax dollar.

7. What about civilian defense? To say the least, the program of civilian defense has received indifferent public acceptance and support. What is wrong with it? Are its procedures and methods inadequate? Can any program of civilian defense really be effective against nuclear weapons?

8. Is the public being adequately briefed on the potency and effectiveness of modern weapons? Is a cloak of secrecy labeled "military security" being unnecessarily used to withhold facts which are needed to maintain an informed public opinion? While there are obviously limits to the material which should be declassified and published, there are many who believe more adequate information could be and should be released to the public.

To maintain a proper "posture of strength," favorable answers are needed to at least the first six questions. To obtain intelligent public support, all eight questions must be answered with a "yes." There are grave doubts that such positive answers can be given to all eight questions.

Therefore, laymen may properly raise such questions and call for answers from our responsible political and military leaders in language we can understand. When such answers are negative we must demand changes in our policies to correct the deficiency.

U.N. SECURITY FORCE.   Although our security now depends upon national military strength, real advantages could result from the prompt establishment of a United Nations military force. This is true even though it would occupy a role secondary to national armaments.

A limited U.N. security group would have numerous advantages:

1. It would enable the United Nations to enforce the terms of armistice and to patrol borders in such troublesome spots as Korea, Kashmir, Viet Nam, and Israel.

2. It would provide a limited military organization to deter or deal with minor aggressions. If U.N. military forces were in existence, nations would be less reluctant to support action against aggressors. The Uniting for Peace resolution would be given more real meaning.

3. Potential aggressors would be less likely to attack a weak nation because the presence of a U.N. military force would make it more likely that aggression would be resisted. What if the United Nations had possessed military forces at the time of the Korean invasion and the Communists had realized the likelihood of resistance? Perhaps that aggression would never have occurred.

4. The availability of a United Nations security force, although small, would help divide the burden of resisting aggression more fairly among the nations of the world.

5. It would give practice and experience in solving the problems of operating a world military force. Larger U.N. armed forces surely will be required someday to maintain peace and order in the world.

The United Nations security organization proposed above should not consist of national contingents as provided in Article 43 of the Charter. Rather, it should be an organization recruited, paid, trained, and commanded by the United Nations and responsible directly to the United Nations. It could be used effectively in crises upon order of the U.N. General Assembly.

Even as we are busy maintaining our "posture of strength" with national forces, we should press for the establishment of a United Nations security force. We should press for its establishment by the United Nations General Assembly in order to by-pass the Security Council where it would certainly be vetoed. The cost of maintaining such a force, even though we contributed a substantial portion, would be minor compared to our national expenditures, and would be a wise investment.

Such a force would become the nucleus of the modern world military organization which will be required to maintain a secure peace.

WE CANNOT DEPEND ON POWER ALONE.   While we must at this time depend upon national military strength to provide a reasonable degree of security, we must avoid making this dependence permanent. There is no certainty that military power will guarantee peace, even though we determine to use it for that purpose.

Even a casual review of the history of the last few hundred years reveals that armament races in the past have usually ended in war. Such was the case with the competition for power prior to World War I and World War II. Even though a balance of power may be achieved for a while and may delay the outbreak of hostilities for years or decades, the end result of national competition in armaments has been war. This sobering fact should check overenthusiasm about the security given by military power.

As long as major military establishments exist, there is the chance that war may be precipitated even though no nation desires it. This may occur by accident, by misinterpretation of the actions or movements of an opponent, or by the maniacal decision of an individual or a nation. Wars have occurred in the past by accident and are perhaps even more likely to occur accidentally in the "pushbutton" era when time is the key factor in launching a retaliatory blow.

While military force continues to be used in the "fringe" areas, for example, Indo-China, the Israel-Arab conflict, there is always the possibility of a "little" war widening into a major one. A group of allies, each a sovereign nation, will have great difficulty in maintaining a concerted policy in the "fringe" areas where the little controversies arise. Moreover, each such dispute is seen through glasses tinted by the viewing nation's interests and prejudices. It is from such "little" wars in the "fringe" areas that accidents or misinterpretations are most likely to arise which would precipitate world war.

The probable deterioration of NATO is another reason for avoiding dependence upon military power alone. Already NATO has difficulties in getting full compliance from all of its members. Once the Soviet Union has ballistic missiles of intermediate range capable of blasting western Europe and reaching United States advance bases, it will be increasingly difficult to maintain NATO strength. Ballistic blackmail by the U.S.S.R. can well impair the effectiveness of NATO.[1]

As long as huge military establishments exist there is the further chance that the leaders of some nation may be tempted to risk war to satisfy selfish goals. Wars have been started in the past because national leaders have thought it would be to their advantage to strike while they had temporary superiority. With mechanized warfare, the

[1] "The Prospect for Disarmament," *New Republic*, Oct. 24, 1955.

advantage can shift quickly to a nation scoring a technical advance in weapons over its competitors. There is no escaping the fact that the mere existence of military power presents a continuous temptation to use it.

Once the ICBM is developed, reliance on military power becomes reliance on mutual terror. When both sides have the "ultimate" weapon, a great premium will be placed on surprise attack. The restraining force will be terror, mutual terror, which will make for mutual fear. The motive of fear is not a responsible one on which to build our hopes for security and peace. Minds motivated by fear do not act with responsibility and sanity.

Moreover, mutual terror is basically an evil concept. It is evil because it depends upon force to shape a man's destiny. Such a belief is completely contrary to the ideas and ideals by which man has advanced.

We must ever be aware of the fallacy of the argument that military strength can be counted upon to avoid war. The fallacy arises from the fact that the ultimate reason for military power is its use in warfare. In a showdown, armaments must be used to compel, and their very use is war. Nothing could be more dangerous than for us to accept this fallacy. We are now tempted to place undue reliance on military power after many generations of strong opposition to militarism.

Rather, we should recognize that military force, while essential today, should have and must have the primary function of buying time to find solutions in our search for a secure peace. These solutions must certainly include the establishment of law and order by peaceful means, the ultimate elimination of national armaments, and an end to the institution of war. It is important, however, that we not only accept the time bought by military strength but use that time in a determined pursuit of peace with freedom.

We cannot repeat too often the urgent necessity of *waging peace*.

ITEM ONE—MAINTAIN MILITARY STRENGTH. Continue our present program which has been identified as a "posture of strength." It involves the maintenance of adequate military strength, in cooperation with our allies, to deter communist expansion and aggression. It is an interim step, necessary as long as nations are dependent upon their own national strength to maintain security in a world of anarchy. It cannot be abandoned until we have achieved a rule of law in the world and have provided other methods for preventing aggression.

Chapter 11

A HELPING HAND

Progressive business leaders are concerned with the community in which they must operate. Programs aimed at creating a better community are supported even if no direct benefits are expected.

IT IS NOT enough to maintain a posture of strength. There is another task which we need to pursue with equal diligence. We need to extend a helping hand to all those nations which are endeavoring to alleviate misery, poverty, and unrest among their people. Such help is needed not only to develop a more wholesome world community, but also to erect bulwarks against the spread of communism.

The recent shift in Soviet policy emphasizes trade and economic aid, and stresses concern for the underdeveloped nations. We have a great stake in the future of these countries. If India and other Asian countries slide into communist domination, Moscow will control—and claim to speak for—a majority of the world's population. There is real danger that this may happen unless we awake to the need and the opportunity.

The neutral nations of Asia and Africa, proud of their newly won independence, are desperately trying to accelerate their economic and industrial development. Such gains are necessary if they are to remain free and resist the lure of communism.

Businessmen should be the first to recognize the magnitude of the task these nations are undertaking. They seek to accomplish in years what usually has taken decades. Businessmen can also understand the need for economic and industrial progress to support higher standards of living, better education, and individual freedom.

We should quickly appreciate the important role of free enterprise in many phases of economic and industrial development. We should urge its use to minimize the need for governmental programs. At the same time, we know that some phases of economic development cannot be accomplished by private enterprise. In such instances, we should be the first to urge the United States or the United Nations to undertake suitable programs.

President Eisenhower recently spoke in support of expanding economic assistance to the nations of Asia and Africa which are confronted by the Communists. He said:

> Inevitably these nations must look abroad for assistance, as ours did for so many years. They want help, first of all, in real and enduring friendship. They want help in training skilled people and in securing investment capital to supplement their own resources.
>
> For such help they will look to us as the most prosperous and advanced economy of the world.
>
> Foresight will compel an understanding response from us. In our own enlightened interest we can and must do much to help others in pursuit of their legitimate aspirations.

NOW IS THE TIME.   Never has there been a greater need around the world for a helping hand.

Colonialism is dead—a dozen nations have recently achieved independence and others are near the goal. The peoples of Asia and Africa, long exploited and dominated by colonialism, are throwing off the yoke and demanding independence, dignity, and a better life.

The teeming populations of the world will no longer be satisfied with the lot of their forefathers. They are determined to break the shackles which restrain them and to struggle upward.

A great revolution, largely peaceful, is surging through the underdeveloped nations of Asia and Africa and, to a lesser extent, South America. This fact is emphasized by many competent observers who know these areas, have visited their leaders and studied their problems.[1]

A young friend just returned to the United States of America from

[1] Norman Cousins, *Who Speaks for Man?* (New York, The Macmillan Company, 1953); and John Cowles, *Des Moines Register,* Feb. 5, 1956.

three years' missionary service in South Korea and a six months' tour through Asia provides firsthand verification. From his visits with young people in these areas, he tells of their strong determination for independence, dignity, security, and economic progress.

The conflict between communism and freedom will be waged in these areas in the next few years. Neutral India, Burma, Indonesia, Egypt, and others will be wooed by the Communists. If this courting is successful, the Communists will accomplish their dream of dominating Eurasia, except for the small area of western Europe.

This would be a serious setback to the cause of freedom. It would bring within the communist orbit a majority of the peoples of the world, unlimited resources, and great industrial potential.

The Soviet Union recognizes the opportunity. The Soviet shift in emphasis from Europe to Asia and from military to social and economic warfare confirms this. The visit of Bulganin and Khrushchev to Burma, India, and Afghanistan put their program in high gear, using propaganda interlaced with offers of financial and industrial help.

Unless the free world—and particularly the United States—meets this challenge, we are apt to stand by idly while Moscow and Peiping plant, cultivate, and harvest a bumper crop. Their probable immediate aim is to make these countries neutral toward communism and wean them from the Western world. Success in their efforts would be a staggering blow to Western morale. We must critically examine the attitudes and methods we have used, and bring them in line with reality.

THE EXAMPLE OF INDIA.   India is a good illustration. Many an American considers India to be ungrateful for the United States' aid, unsympathetic to the free world, and leaning a bit toward communism.

He doesn't understand why India insists on neutrality. He thinks India should associate with the Western military powers. He believes India should view the United States as a champion of freedom, democracy, and free enterprise, the very things India needs. As a result, public opinion is unfavorable toward India, and this is reflected in the debate and action of our Congress.

It will be a tragedy if we allow false impressions to create a rift between the great subcontinent of India and the great democracy of the United States.

India is simply following many of the practices we adopted as a young nation.

India has only recently achieved independence with a bloodless revolution. In 1947 Britain granted independence, allowing India to become a member of the British Commonwealth.

India has her hands full with internal problems. Her 400,000,000 people have living standards so low they are scarcely comprehensible to one who has not seen them. Under the leadership of Prime Minister Nehru, India is trying to accomplish centuries of progress in a few years. Land reform, improved methods of agriculture, health programs, expansion of industry, broadening of education are but a few of her needs. Competent observers indicate that India is making real progress.[2]

This program is being carried out by a democracy. India has not resorted to a dictatorship, benevolent or despotic, as have many countries undertaking rapid modernization.

The success of India in resisting communism has been remarkable considering the illiteracy and poverty of its citizens.

In order to concentrate on its domestic problems, India has tried to maintain strict neutrality. This is just what the United States did after the Revolutionary War. Indeed, we followed a policy of neutrality, with very few lapses, from 1786 until World War I. Even after World War I we reverted to neutrality until engulfed in World War II. India believes she needs neutrality while she concentrates upon internal development problems.

In pursuit of this policy, India has sometimes appeared overly friendly to Red China and unfriendly toward us. A good explanation of this was once given by General Carlos P. Romulo of the Philippines. He asked: "What would you do if you had on your border a nation whom you did not trust and whom you feared might invade you, whereas across the seas there was another nation whom you did not fear and whom you did trust? Would you not," he continued, "be friendly to the border nation even at the risk of being misunderstood by the nation across the sea?"

There is little evidence that India is actually unfriendly toward the United States. Recently, Prime Minister Nehru said:

[2] Chester Bowles, *The New Dimensions of Peace* (New York, Harper & Brothers, 1955).

America is a great and powerful country, but for my part, if I may say so with all modesty, I do not attach much importance to America's bombs. I do attach importance to a great vitality and great integrity which sometimes, if I may say so, point in the wrong direction—gets excited—but essentially gives it strength.

Mr. Nehru said the United States' real strength was deeper than its financial, industrial, or technological strength, and "the more that comes into play the happier it will be for the world!"[3]

India needs the help of the West and the West needs India. If India can succeed in her great peaceful revolution, she will become a tower of strength for the principles of freedom and democracy. If India fails and is pulled toward the communist sphere, it will be a great loss to the free world.

India merits every bit of assistance we can extend to her. But India, a proud country, has recently spoken against direct national contributions from the U.S.S.R. or the U.S.A. and has urged all assistance be channeled through the United Nations. Basically India wants know-how and credit, not gifts.

The problems of other nations with newly won independence are similar to those in India, with some variations. Most of these nations are at a stage of political development similar to that of the United States of 1790. Their economic and social condition is even more backward than that.

A Midwestern businessman, recently returned from an extensive Asian trip, calls for the United States to extend the helping hand. He classes such aid and understanding as one of our most important opportunities. Unless we assist needy nations to strengthen their economies, he says, they will, out of necessity, turn to the Communists for help.

If these needs and opportunities are met, the United States can be of inestimable assistance in advancing and protecting freedom. We dare not pass by the opportunity to strengthen world unity by building a stronger world community.

THE TASKS.   The building of a better world community has many aspects. The political phase is outlined in later chapters. Here we are concerned with the social, educational, and economic phases:

[3] *New York Times,* Jan. 30, 1956.

Living Standard. No genuine world community can develop when a billion or more people are underfed and plagued with illness. People with empty stomachs have little interest in world politics. Nor do their leaders have much time for international problems. Improved living standards are a prerequisite for united action in many areas. There is a great need for technical assistance to help underdeveloped nations help themselves. Technical assistance can show untrained peoples how to obtain adequate food, better health, sanitation, and other necessities. There is an ever growing need for development of industry, transportation, communication, irrigation and power facilities to raise standards above the subsistence level. Community, in the best sense of the word, will not come to a world half prosperous and half starving.

Knowledge. But a better world community is also dependent upon knowledge and education. Better education is required to provide the professional men and technicians needed for the development of agriculture and industry. It is also needed as a basis for self-government and self-improvement. Moreover, it is basic to understanding and exchange of ideas. Community, in which individuals actually communicate with one another, will not come to a world half educated and half illiterate.

Understanding. Scattered individuals or groups become a community as they get to know one another and work together. Understanding depends to a considerable extent upon the mingling of people and the exchange of ideas. This calls for better communications, not only in writing but by direct personal contact—such as mutual tours of inspection and exchange of students. As we become acquainted we not only gain in understanding but we also find it easier to cooperate.

APPROACH. Economic development of the world's underdeveloped areas is essential. It is the basic prerequisite which will enable these peoples to help themselves. What should be our answer to the economic competition of the Communists? Certainly we should not merely imitate their program. Neither should we abandon the worthwhile parts of our current economic assistance programs. However, we should set our own pace and develop a sound over-all program. Our program should meet the real needs and desires of the nations we propose to help. It should also square with fundamental American principles. A few suggestions follow:

1. Promote sound economic growth. Our activities must be fitted to the state of development of the nation we are assisting. If its real need is elemental improvements in agriculture and health, we should not attempt to introduce advanced mechanical equipment.

2. Help others to help themselves. Outside help, essential though it is, cannot by itself raise any nation's standard of living. Hard work by the people being helped is also essential. Hence, our efforts should be cooperative and aimed at assisting underdeveloped nations to grow in their knowledge and ability to help themselves.

3. Use private business and nongovernmental organizations to the fullest extent practicable. As a businessman, I believe that private enterprise should undertake all phases which it can handle properly. No program should be carried forward by the United Nations or the United States if private business is willing and able to do the job.

4. Use United Nations agencies whenever possible. In general, no project should be handled unilaterally by the United States if it can be done adequately by a United Nations agency. U.N. projects involve greater participation of nations and greater sharing of costs.

5. Separate military and economic aid. Programs aimed at improving economies and living standards should be undertaken because they are sound in their own right. We should not use economic aid to buy military alliances. We should not label military aid as economic assistance. We have sometimes made these mistakes and they have made other nations suspicious that we are trying to bribe them.

6. Maintain a continuing program. A concentrated program covering a few years, like the Marshall Plan, will not be effective in Asia and Africa. There the need is for assistance over a longer period of time but at a lower rate. Just as we have a continuing military budget aimed at security, we need a continuing budget for economic aid. In the long run, it can be equally beneficial to our country.

7. Consider foreign aid as an investment. It should not be regarded as a "give-away" or a charity. Rather, it is a necessary investment from which we can reap benefits. If it helps the under-

developed nations to help themselves, we will gain lasting benefits. In addition, it will help build a sounder world economy and a greater world market. Beyond this, it can help raise morale and self-confidence and do much to stem the tide of communism in the neutral nations of Asia and Africa.

HOW MUCH INVESTMENT?   Few people are familiar with the amount of our current expenditures for economic assistance. Most think we are spending far more than is really the case.

The proposed 1957 budget for "foreign aid" submitted to the Congress by President Eisenhower totaled about $4,900,000,000. The Congress compromised on an appropriation of $3,766,570,000. How much of this is allocated to real economic aid and technical assistance? An analysis of the appropriation request is revealing. The breakdown follows:

Foreign Military Assistance and Direct Forces Support		$2,017,000,000
Foreign Defense Support (includes economic support of Turkey, Formosa, and Pakistan)		1,162,000,000
Subtotal		$3,179,000,000
Nonmilitary Foreign Aid		
Technical Assistance	$152,000,000	
Development Assistance	350,000,000	
Miscellaneous	85,570,000	587,570,000
Total		$3,766,570,000

Thus, 2 billion dollars is earmarked for direct military purposes. If these funds were not given to our allies, we would need to spend an equal or greater amount to assure our present posture of military strength. Such expenditures could just as well have been added to the budget of our Defense Department.

Another 1.1 billion dollars is closely tied to military defense. If it were not provided to our allies we would no doubt need an equal or greater expenditure to achieve comparable military position. By supporting the economies of such nations as Turkey, Nationalist China, and Pakistan we permit them to maintain needed military forces.

This leaves only $587,570,000, or 16 per cent of the requested appropriation, as "nonmilitary." This is a more accurate indication of our bill for economic aid to offset the communist threat. This is equivalent to about $3.50 for every person in the United States.

This amount is only one-sixth of one per cent of the gross national product of the United States, which in the third quarter of 1955 was at the annual rate of $392,000,000,000, or an average of $2,376 for every man, woman, and child.

Compared to this, our direct expenditures for the armed services are around $38,000,000,000 per year, or about $230 for each person in the United States.

Is this amount for foreign aid adequate or would we benefit by a greater investment? The answer is a matter of judgment based upon the comparison of benefits and costs.

We cannot plead financial inability to maintain and expand such programs. We should expand them, and do so promptly and cheerfully—not as inefficient "give-away" projects but as well planned technical assistance.

PRIVATE ENTERPRISE.   There is a tendency to overlook the part private enterprise can play in building a better world community. This tendency often leads to proposals for grandiose governmental activities.

Believing as we do in the benefits of free enterprise, we should encourage participation of business on a world-wide basis wherever it is practicable. There are four areas in which private enterprise can contribute substantially; namely:

Finance. Capital is required to develop a nation. It is necessary for communications and transportation systems, irrigation and land development projects, industry, and for many other purposes. Economic development can be accelerated if outside capital is available. Just as European capital was invested in the United States in the nineteenth century to advance our expansion, so can foreign capital accelerate development in many nations. As we are the major creditor nation in the world today, underdeveloped nations must look to us for loans to finance improvements. Private financing should be encouraged in the form of loans to governments, to business firms, and to industrial corporations.

Management. Many American industrial concerns have established profitable plants and businesses in foreign countries which have contributed to the economic growth of these countries. Oil-producing companies in Arabia and Venezuela, manufacturing companies in Europe, Mexico, and South America are examples. Such enterprises have served not only to develop natural resources but also to provide merchandise, income, and employment for the local people. Where management has been foresighted, it has made maximum use of local personnel with a resulting increase in local income, leading to improvement in education and standards of living. These benefits of private ownership and operation in other countries have been obtained not only in the underdeveloped areas but also in some of the more advanced nations.

Substantial benefits flow from such programs. The National Planning Association has analyzed several of them.[4] One is the Creole Petroleum Corporation in Venezuela, where a valuable resource has been developed. The economy of the country has been improved. The company has been conscious of the "trusteeship" nature of its operation. As a good citizen, it has employed local people for over 90 per cent of its staff. It has increased pay levels, raised standards of housing and sanitation, built and supported schools, and generally made for better living. It has consistently increased local purchases of material and supported economic development beyond its own operations. Its community sets standards for the surrounding area.

Enlightened business leadership in many fields—manufacturing, mining, oil, or retail merchandising—has brought similar benefits to many parts of the world.

Know-How. Private enterprise can furnish knowledge and skills which are necessary to develop resources, expand industry, and create adequate communications and transportation facilities. Services of this type are being rendered by many engineering and consulting organizations retained by foreign governments or foreign business enterprises. In addition to such activities, business and industry can provide information and key personnel for the actual construction and operation of projects in other countries.

Licensing foreign manufacturers to make various American products is another way to provide "know-how." Many American

[4] National Planning Association, *United States Business Performance Abroad:* No. 1, Sears, Roebuck De Mexico, S.A.; No. 2, Casa Grace in Peru; No. 3, The Philippine American Life Insurance Company; No. 4, The Creole Petroleum Corporation in Venezuela.

concerns find opportunities in this way to expand their own business and aid other nations' economies. This licensing method can be used when conditions do not warrant investment or actual operation by American firms.

Trade. Private enterprise is the key to wider world trade and to the reduction and removal of trade barriers. A breaking down of these barriers is a necessary step toward greater world community. Underdeveloped nations must have access to items produced in the more highly developed areas. In turn, many industrialized countries, including the United States, need access to raw materials.

Two-way trade is needed to let underdeveloped nations pay for their purchases and avoid subsidization. Freer trade will not only speed economic development, but will improve morale and understanding. Trade, not aid, is the chief steppingstone to economic progress. World trade is a field in which American enterprise has particular opportunities. As we are the world's creditor nation, we must either increase trade or raise our foreign aid far beyond what will otherwise be needed.

In spite of the popularity of the slogan "trade, not aid," some spokesmen for private enterprise are the principal opponents of lower tariff barriers. The necessary steps to free world trade should be taken in the broad interests of the United States. We know this will cause temporary hardships and readjustments in certain limited segments of our economy.[5] But the national interest requires us to proceed toward freer trade, giving attention to these special problems.

Where necessary, our government should give financial help to industries which cannot compete with foreign imports, while these industries convert to other products.

THE TEST. Private enterprise has a great opportunity in connection with the economic phases of developing a better world community and meeting the communist threat in this field. If business leaders will rise to this challenge, the principles of free enterprise can be extended.

Many of my fellow businessmen lack the courage of their convictions. Frequently they condemn government aid to underdeveloped nations; at the same time they oppose freer trade. Others criticize the

---

[5] Committee for Economic Development, *United States Tariff Policy* (November, 1954).

U.N. technical assistance program but refuse to support private exchange of "know-how."

Private enterprise is being tested. Has it the will and the desire to help expand the world economy? Everyone who classifies himself as a business leader should seek the answer to this question. To the extent that private enterprise fails to meet this challenge, we will be compelled to initiate broader programs through the United Nations or through our government. This is true because we cannot permit the Communists to take over the underdeveloped nations.

Reasonable changes in our laws are necessary to encourage greater world trade and more private American investments overseas. These changes might include:

1. Lower tax rates for foreign earnings of U.S. corporations.

2. A government insurance program to protect American investors against the danger that foreign governments will seize or nationalize their overseas investments.

3. Gradual elimination of tariffs and import quotas.

4. Long-term loans to aid conversion of our few industries which cannot survive in a free market; these should accompany the gradual elimination of trade barriers.

5. President Eisenhower's proposed bill to simplify customs regulations and eliminate some of the red tape which now clogs world trade.

The great success of American private enterprise is due largely to the ability of business leaders to see and follow their own long-range self-interest. The self-interest of both American business and our nation now demands that we businessmen help build a better world community.

PRIVATE ORGANIZATIONS.   Fortunately, economic aid is not limited to the United Nations, the United States, and business firms. A great deal of effective work has been done for years by religious and philanthropic organizations.

The missionary work of the churches has long been a helpful factor. The underlying motives of missions have been spiritual and religious, aimed at man's soul. But they have been concerned with technical assistance, education, and health as well as with spiritual activities. They have established and maintained schools from primary to university levels. They have sent medical missionaries with their preachers and teachers, and have built hospitals and improved sanitation. They have sent farm experts to demonstrate ways of improving primitive agricultural methods.

These activities of the churches, undertaken with real concern for the individual, have clearly demonstrated the desire and ability of man everywhere to improve his lot when given the opportunity. Such programs have been technical assistance at its best. The cost has been nominal. The churches have trained local people to carry on and expand the programs.

In recent years other private organizations have established programs of technical assistance. These have included the privately endowed foundations and, to a limited extent, educational institutions and groups of individuals. All of these activities are worthy of continuation and expansion. They are supported by private contributions and avoid the red tape and complications of governmental operations.

Many private organizations also help to arrange exchange students, information, and culture. Such activities need encouragement because of their real value in increasing knowledge and understanding.

U.N. AND U.S. PROGRAMS.   There are other needs which cannot be handled by private enterprise or private institutions.

Private enterprise cannot invest unless it can make a profit in the long run. Church and philanthropic organizations are limited to the funds which their supporters are willing to give.

There remain other activities which must be undertaken either by the United Nations or by the United States if they are to be accomplished. Needs which cannot be met by private enterprise or private organizations fall into two broad categories.

First, there is "technical assistance"—showing people the basic principles of public health, agriculture, and other technical skills. Such projects have been included in our "Point Four" program and the U.N. technical assistance program. Much of this work consists of sending teams of experts in agriculture, sanitation, public health, and so on, into underdeveloped countries. There they show the people how to achieve greater agricultural production, eliminate diseases such as malaria, and make similar improvements. The cost of these programs has been remarkably low in comparison with their accomplishments.

Another type of project which cannot be handled by private enterprise is illustrated by a United States Marshall Plan mission carried out in Greece under the supervision of Walter Eugene Packard.[6] One part of that project changed Greece from a rice-importing to a rice-exporting country. Starting with a 100-acre test plot, Packard showed the farmers of the Anthele community how to reclaim land on the edge of a vast salt plain. A $10,000,000 annual gain to the national economy was accomplished with an original investment by the United States of $43,000.

There are still other types of projects which cannot be entirely self-liquidating. These include roads, large dams, water-supply systems, and similar items. Even in this country, such projects are usually handled by governmental agencies. The need in this field is principally financial. Either grants or long-term, low-interest loans to national governments are needed.

Our recent commitment (later cancelled) to Egypt for the first $100,000,000 for the great Aswan Dam on the Nile River is an example. A loan by the Export-Import Bank to Liberia for roads into an undeveloped area is another example.

Such are the tasks which free enterprise cannot handle and which must be undertaken by the United States or the United Nations if they are to be accomplished. To make our program more effective in these areas, the following policies are suggested:

1. Increase appropriations to the United Nations technical assistance program. Continue our own Point Four program but coordinate it closely with that of the United Nations.

2. Provide special United States economic assistance from time to time where there is a clearly demonstrated need. Examples are assistance in Korea and Viet Nam; these nations are striving to ward off communism and to recover from the ravages of war.

3. Participate in the Special United Nations Fund for Economic Development (SUNFED) which is badly needed to handle major projects, outside the technical assistance program, which cannot be financed by loans.

4. Expand our participation in international lending agencies which finance self-liquidating projects. These include our Export-Import Bank and the World Bank (International Bank for Reconstruction and Development).

5. Use our surplus farm products, when practicable, to alleviate

[6] Charles Ianine, "American Miracle Worker," *Christian Science Monitor* Jan. 14, 1955.

hunger. President Eisenhower's January, 1956 offer of food to flood-stricken parts of Europe is a good example. The August, 1956 sale of wheat and other commodities to India is another.

Such programs will require increased appropriations beyond those currently earmarked for economic aid. The amount of increase needs to be carefully examined to assure that the funds are being effectively used for economic development which will result in greater world unity, higher standards of living, and increased resistance to communism.

An increased investment by the United States is warranted from two points of view. First, it can help erect bulwarks against the spread of communism. Second, by raising standards of living, it will make a definite contribution to a sounder world economy which will be directly beneficial to us.

DISARMAMENT SAVINGS.   Several years ago the late Senator Brien McMahon introduced a resolution in the United States Senate. It called for the United States to commit to an economic development fund a substantial portion of the savings which would result from disarmament. This proposal has been repeated by many others, both here and abroad, and there is strong support for it. The amounts which could be made available and the benefits which could come from them are amazing. Contrast the nearly $40,000,000,000 now being spent annually by the United States for its military establishment with the $12,000,000 we are currently contributing to the U.N. technical assistance program.

If we were relieved of the current military burden and diverted only 30 per cent of it (about $12,000,000,000) to economic and technical assistance, this would provide an annual amount more than ten times our total current expenditures for all forms of economic aid. Add to this a portion of the funds of other nations released by disarmament, and the funds available for worth-while and lasting projects will be tremendous.

Many have suggested the formation of a World Development Fund into which the armed nations would agree to put a portion of the proposed armament savings for a period of years. Such a fund should be administered by the United Nations and be used for the economic development of the world. The United States should seriously consider a commitment to use a portion of its disarmament savings for building a better world.

Such a pledge to use part of our disarmament savings for economic development should help to crystallize world opinion in favor of world law. However, progress toward a better world cannot wait for the achievement of disarmament. It should continue and be expanded along the lines which have been discussed in this chapter.

ITEM TWO—LEND A HELPING HAND.   Continue and expand our support of programs aimed at building a better world and creating a stronger world community. Broaden our efforts to include activities of private enterprise, nongovernmental organizations, our government, and the United Nations. Commit a portion of our potential savings from disarmament to an expanded program of technical assistance and economic development.

Chapter 12

RESPONSIBILITY FOR PEACE

A cardinal principle of management calls for the selection and use of a proper organization to accomplish a desired objective. Frequently, a choice must be made between different organizational patterns. Failure can result if the wrong organization is selected. Failure can also occur if the proper organization is by-passed or misused.

AS WE TURN to a consideration of the possibility of substituting world law for world anarchy, one of the first questions concerns the assignment of the responsibility for peace. Should the individual nations of the world keep this responsibility or must it be lodged with a world organization or institution?

CAN NATIONS DO THE JOB?   Throughout recent centuries the responsibility of trying to maintain world peace has rested with the various sovereign nations. There have been brief exceptions from 1921 until about 1933 and in the decade since World War II. During these periods a portion of the responsibility (but little or no authority) has been given to the League of Nations and to the United Nations.

During these centuries many wars have occurred and the security of nations has frequently been violated. The conflict of national interests has often been too great to permit effective cooperation to avoid war.

Even when national interests have been similar, simple shortsightedness and inertia have prevented "collective security" from becoming effective. The evidence is overwhelming that separate nations are incapable of maintaining international peace and security.

Nevertheless, it is necessary to examine this evidence carefully before concluding that the nations cannot by themselves maintain a secure peace. The far-reaching impact of the answer demands such an examination. If nations cannot perform the task, there is no alternative to delegating the responsibility for maintaining peace to a world organization. This is a major decision because such a delegation must involve authority as well as responsibility. The answer to the question must be found, therefore, not in our preferences or prejudices but in an objective analysis of the abilities of nations to do the job.

HISTORY OF WAR.   During the entire history of modern nation-states, war has left a bloody trail with ever increasing violence and destruction. The customary devices of treaties, alliances, mutual security pacts, balances of power, armaments, and defense mechanisms have been used by nations in their efforts to avoid war. Such devices, used down to the beginnings of World War I and World War II, have been ineffective even when neither side wanted war and when their leaders actually tried to avoid it.

Most wars have been started by an aggressor nation in an effort to increase its territory or to capture a highly desirable prize. Examples include the Franco-Prussian War of 1870, Japan's occupation of Manchuria in 1931, the Italian conquest of Ethiopia in 1936, the German invasion of Poland in 1939 which triggered World War II, and the North Korean Communists' invasion of South Korea in 1950. In such instances, the conflict was deliberately started by a nation seeking to achieve an objective it believed attainable through war. The attacked nation, in most instances, has been unable to protect itself, as it has usually been outmanned and outgunned.

In other instances, war has occurred with little or no desire on the part of either side. Many historians now place World War I in this category. In these instances, conflict was started, not by desire, but as the result of a chain of circumstances which made war seem inevitable. Such wars have occurred in spite of treaties, alliances, and balances of power. They have occurred when both sides have been strongly armed to defend themselves. They have occurred even after desperate eleventh-hour negotiations.

An objective reading of history clearly shows that nations have not been able to maintain peace and security when acting either individually or through alliances.

This inability has been recognized by nations on several occasions. As far back as the Congress of Vienna (1815), after Napoleon's defeat, proposals were made to set up international machinery to keep the peace, including an international army and "positive guarantees."

More than a hundred years later, at the close of World War I, the necessity of an international organization to enforce peace was widely recognized when the peacemakers assembled in Paris in 1919. The creation of the League of Nations showed that the nations recognized this need. During World War II there was renewed recognition of this need. In spite of the previous failure of the League of Nations, steps were taken to create the United Nations.

History not only shows that nations have been incapable of maintaining peace; it also gives evidence that this weakness has been recognized in brief moments of introspection and self-examination at the close of great wars.

DEVELOPMENT OF LAW.   History presents other evidence that dependence upon nations for the maintenance of secure peace is bound to fail. This is found in the process by which law and order have been extended over greater areas and populations up to the level of nations.

Slowly but surely throughout recorded history, man has been in the process of expanding the rule of law to ever greater areas. This onward march has increased the unit of government from the family group to the tribe, from small tribes to larger ones, from tribes to cities, from cities to states, and finally from small states to nations. Each of these steps has followed a similar pattern, or at least one which has included common elements.

First, there has been a conflict of interest. Two tribes or cities or states have become more mobile or have developed greater desires. They have both wanted to use the same hunting ground, territory, or resource; to control the same river, road, or pass; or to dominate the same commercial outlet, market, or port. This conflict of interest has resulted in an open dispute.

Sometimes the controversy has been settled by peaceful means, through a deal or a compromise. More often, attempts at negotiation have failed to reach agreement. Then there has been an increasing demand for the use of force to settle the difference. Often, no peaceful settlement has been attempted, and force has been used from the beginning of the dispute. Use of force may be merely threatened at first, but sooner or later the force has been used and war has resulted. Often there has been a series of skirmishes or battles between periods of peace or truce.

But inevitably, if the conflict of interest has continued, one of two events has occurred. Either one of the groups has conquered and subjugated the other, or the leaders of the two groups have reached an agreement to unite their groups. By one or the other of these two processes, there has finally emerged a central power or authority capable of establishing a rule of law over the combined groups.

More often than not, the rule of law has been extended by conquest and has been harsh and dictatorial. But occasionally leaders have possessed the wisdom to recognize common interests and benefits and have created a rule of law by peaceful means, which in many instances has been more tolerant and has allowed the smaller groups to keep their own institutions.

However, whether by conquest or consent, the result has been the creation of a political authority extending over a greater territory and a greater number of people. Within that territory and among those people the extension of a rule of law has resulted in peace. The differences between the original groups have been settled by peaceful means, whether by arbitrary and dictatorial edict or by the democratic use of legislatures and courts.

In other words, whenever political units have clashed, use of war has been ended only by setting up a single government with enough power to end the fighting. This new authority must be strong enough to keep its members from starting wars even if they want to fight. Thus, they are forced to settle their disputes by peaceful means. The use of force and the threat of force as between the units is thus ended.

The most recent examples of this process are found in the formation of the nations of the world. Two examples illustrate the process: Germany and the United States.

Prior to 1870, the territory which became Germany was divided into a number of states, including Bavaria, Prussia, and others. Each of these states was a little nation. Each maintained a military force, patrolled its borders, imposed tariffs, and had its own currency. Conflicts of interest had long existed among these states, and they were frequently involved in wars with one another.

By 1865 Prussia emerged as the most powerful of the group and, under the leadership of Bismarck, embarked upon a forceful merger, using either the threat or the exercise of military power. Maneuvering war with Austria in 1866, Prussia defeated her rival and compelled a German reorganization without Austria. Bismarck then ruthlessly annexed several states which had supported Austria. Prussia's power then compelled the northern states to join a German Confederation. The defeat of France in the war of 1870 added Alsace-Lorraine and brought in the remaining South German states. In 1871 the new German Empire was proclaimed.

There emerged a Germany with a single monarchy and a single national military establishment. Law and order, generally tolerant and just, was extended over the nation, and the differences of the German states were no longer settled by the threat or exercise of force.

The United States, on the other hand, achieved its national government without the use of conquest or force. The thirteen colonies, having gained their individual independence in the Revolutionary War, were separate and sovereign states with democratic forms of government. However, between the close of the war and the adoption of the Constitution in 1787, there were increasing conflicts of interest. Disputes over tariffs and boundaries grew more bitter. As chaos increased, trade and commerce declined. War was avoided only by a narrow margin, for at one time the militias of Pennsylvania and Connecticut were drawn up in opposing array.[1]

The efforts of the thirteen colonies to work together through a treaty, the Articles of Confederation, were failing when the Constitutional Convention met in Philadelphia in 1787. Only after prolonged deliberations, often on the verge of breakdown, did the common sense and good will of our leaders prevail. The adoption of the Constitution created the United States, and a rule of law was extended over the entire area.

The lesson of history is clear: small states have been able to end war among themselves only by creating a higher government and by giving it enough power to keep them from fighting.

Doesn't this same rule apply to today's nations? Their efforts as

[1] Carl Van Doren, *The Great Rehearsal* (New York, The Viking Press, 1948).

separate nations to prevent war have failed. This should be no surprise. The states of Germany and the United States had more things in common than do the nations of the world today. Yet their similar traditions and beliefs did not keep them from fighting. Isn't it ridiculous to believe that the nations, whose present conflicts and differences are so much greater, could achieve peace by their own efforts alone?

Years ago Alexander Hamilton clearly stated this lesson: "To look for a continuation of harmony between a number of independent, unconnected sovereignties in the same neighborhood, would be to disregard the uniform course of human events, and to set at defiance the accumulated experience of ages."

COMMON SENSE. This conclusion from history that separate nations are incapable of maintaining a secure peace is supported by many thinkers and writers approaching the matter from various points of view.[2] There is no need to repeat the detailed reasoning of those who have concluded that the responsibility for peace must be given to a world organization. Rather, a few basic thoughts are presented:

The agency charged with the responsibility for maintaining a secure peace must be capable of acting promptly when a threat of aggression arises. Prompt action is impossible with a group of nations which must each make its own decision after aggression threatens and can take concerted action only if there is unanimous agreement, at least of the major powers. Prompt action can be expected only from a world organization which has authority to act immediately when action is necessary.

Similarly, the agency charged with the responsibility must act with dispatch whenever predetermined conditions arise. If potential aggressors know that aggression will be promptly detected and resisted, they will be faced with a major deterrent. Past experience shows that when the unanimous agreement of a group of nations is required there can be no certainty of action. Unanimity is lost if any one of them senses an opportunity for individual advantage by failing to act with the others. A football team with eleven quarterbacks would seldom score a touchdown; the game might be over before they could agree

[2] Emery Reves, *The Anatomy of Peace* (New York, Harper & Brothers, 1945); and Cord Meyer, *Peace or Anarchy* (Boston, Little, Brown and Company, 1947).

on the next play. It is equally difficult for a group of separate nations
to act promptly.

The organization responsible for peace must take a truly international point of view, rising above the selfish or petty interests of any
nation. This is essential because it will be required to enforce decisions and actions upon member nations. So long as the responsibility
rests with nations, there is no impartial judge or referee.

The organization charged with the responsibility must be safeguarded from sabotage by a nation with aggressive intent or evil desire. Human nature being what it is, we must expect that another
Hitler, Mussolini, or Stalin will arise in the future, take control of a
national government, and seek world domination. As long as the responsibility is left with nations, such a regime in a major power can
effectively sabotage collective action—witness the Soviet use of the
veto.

If we want fair and firm enforcement of a rule or law—be it in
sports, industry, or local government—we do not ask the participants
to work together jointly to enforce it. Rather, we designate a referee,
a manager, or a police force to enforce the rule with promptness and
consistency.

The same elemental principles apply to securing peace. Enforcement of predetermined rules is required, and such enforcement can
be effective only if exercised by an international or world authority.

THE INTERNATIONAL ORGANIZATION.   The case for lodging the responsibility for peace with a world organization is overpowering, whether
looked at from the viewpoint of history or of common sense. We have
no other choice. If we want a secure peace we shall have to pay the
price. Like many of the decisions we must make in business and domestic life, it is not always a matter of choosing what we like but of
accepting what must be.

We can no more avoid the use of a world organization to maintain
world peace than we can avoid a city government to maintain local
order. This need was well illustrated in the Boston police strike of
1919. Stripped of a city enforcing agency, law gave way to disorder,
looting, and riot.

It is inevitable that a rule of law will be extended over the world.
In no other way can peace be secured. Instead of resisting the inevitable, the peace-loving nations of the world need to accept it and estab-

lish by agreement—not by conquest—a rule of law which protects national interests and human rights.

Once this necessity is recognized, we can turn our attention from the "why" to the "how" and "what."

The first question which must be raised is what international organization shall be selected to carry the primary responsibility for securing world-wide peace. The answer is obvious: the United Nations. We should utilize the United Nations, not because it now possesses the authority and power to do the job, but because it is a going organization which can be improved.

The U.N. was created for the task we now propose; it has survived the first ten hard years, and it is supported by a great reservoir of favorable world opinion. Moreover, it has a staff and a secretariat which have gained in experience from both success and failure. What would we gain by throwing away this resource and investment and creating another world organization?

CRUTCH OR VEHICLE?   The next question to consider is the manner in which the United Nations is to be used. Can it be effective unless we use it as the foundation of our foreign policy? Why shouldn't we use the United Nations as a vehicle instead of as a crutch?

As a crutch, the United Nations is merely one more device to supplement other means of diplomacy and negotiation—employed if advisable, by-passed if other procedures seem more promising.[3] As long as we use it as a crutch, we shall appear to be half in and half out of the United Nations.

On the other hand, if we select the U.N. as a vehicle, it becomes the primary instrument of our foreign policy. We should utilize traditional methods of diplomacy and negotiation to support the United Nations. Of course, until the United Nations is strengthened and given greater authority and power, there will be problems which it cannot handle and objectives which it cannot achieve. In such instances, we should first attempt to use the U.N., even if we doubt its effectiveness. We should turn to other methods only when compelled to. Such a policy will point out the weaknesses in the United Nations which must be corrected, and will avoid any charge of by-passing it.

This decision between "crutch and vehicle" is not unlike a person's attitude toward religion. To some it is only a crutch, used on Sundays or when human resources fail. To others it is a moving force in their

[3] Weiler and Hyde, *The United States and the United Nations.*

lives—influencing their every attitude and action. As long as the U.N. is considered a Sunday or emergency institution, it will remain an ineffective "crutch."

The decision to make the United Nations our basic instrument of foreign policy must be followed by two courses of action. Until the United Nations can be strengthened we must use it in its present form in every practicable way. At the same time we must work for the necessary changes in the U.N. to permit it to achieve a secure peace.

Discussion of how to use and support the present United Nations follows, and the necessary changes are dealt with in later chapters.

SUPPORT.   Three elements are involved in supporting the United Nations as the keystone of our foreign policy.

One important element is financial support. In 1955 our total contribution to the United Nations and all of its specialized agencies was $65,669,977. This amounted to about forty cents for each citizen of the United States—less than two packs of cigarettes a year. This is only a small fraction of one per cent of the amount we are spending on our military establishment. No sound question can be raised about our ability to contribute many times $66,000,000 a year to the organization responsible for securing peace.

We have never failed to pay our share of the United Nations budget, but appropriations have sometimes been made in a grudging and uncertain manner. We should fully, promptly, and cheerfully meet our financial responsibilities to the United Nations. Moreover, we should not hesitate to increase our financial support, within reasonable limits, whenever it will make the organization more effective.

Support also involves our attitude and our comments about the U.N. It cannot be claimed that the United States has failed to place its influence behind the United Nations. Both President Truman and President Eisenhower have repeatedly spoken in its behalf and have called upon the American people to recognize it as man's best hope for peace.

Public support for the United Nations is indicated by a Roper Poll taken in 1953.[4] This survey showed overwhelming support for the United Nations and majority support for strengthening it. The following table from the survey report speaks for itself:

[4] Elmo Roper, "American Attitudes on World Organizations," *Public Opinion Quarterly,* Winter 1953-1954, p. 407.

Attitudes About World Organization

Per cent

1. We shouldn't get tied up in any *more* alliances or joint commitments with other countries and we should aim at getting out of as many as we can as soon as we can. (This is the isolationist view.)   9

2. We should continue to work along with the United Nations just about as we have been, gradually trying to make it better as time goes on. (This is the United Nations "as is" view.)   21

3. We should immediately get behind *strengthening* the United Nations and do everything necessary to give it more power and authority than it has—enough to actually keep even a strong nation from starting a war. (This is the stronger United Nations view.)   35

4. In addition to continuing with the United Nations, we should also unite with the friendly democratic countries into one government in which each member nation would in effect become a state, somewhat like the different states in this country. (This is the democratic-union view.)   6

5. We should start now working toward transforming the United Nations into a real world government of *all* nations of the world, in which every nation would in effect become a state, somewhat like the different states in this country. (This is the world-government view.)   11

6. Some of these ideas are good, but we won't get any of them working in time to prevent war, so we'd better not rely on them. (This is the hopeless view.)   7

No opinion   11

Total   100%

In spite of this wide following there has been much bitter and misinformed criticism of the U.N. One extreme is the call to "get the United States out of the United Nations and the United Nations out of the United States." Does such an invitation to return to isolationism make sense in the Nuclear Age? Or is it as irresponsible as a proposal to abolish the municipal government of Chicago because one does not like the way it is being run?

If the United Nations is to become the base of our foreign policy, it deserves constructive but informed criticism. To support such criticism, there is definite need for more adequate information on the United Nations, its accomplishments and its failures, and especially on the urgency of making it a success.

And above all, support of the United Nations implies its use whenever possible. Practice in the use of the United Nations will not remove its major defects, but it will help develop morale, spirit, and experience. Nothing succeeds like success, but success cannot come without use. And even when the present United Nations proves incapable of dealing with certain problems, attempts to use it will point out defects, increase the demand for changes, and build a greater unity in the free world.

The U.N. needs to be used if it is to survive. Failure to use the U.N. will weaken and undermine it. General Carlos P. Romulo, delegate of the Philippines to the U.N. from its organization in 1945 until the present, pointed to this danger in 1954, when he declared:

But the heart-sickening truth is that the U.N.'s demise is being brought on by the free world. We are steadily sapping the U.N.'s strength by bypassing it, by cutting away at its political prestige, and by deliberately failing to tap its mine of potential power. We talk lots of sweet talk about it, but refuse to give it the political vitamins it needs.

How can we make better use of the U.N.? These are a few suggestions:

PEACEFUL SETTLEMENT. The United Nations has often obtained peaceful settlement of disputes through commissions and other devices, even under its present inadequate powers. Its ability to contribute in these areas can be enlarged by a determination on our part to utilize the United Nations in every instance. We should not resort to other methods of settlement until the United Nations has demonstrated its inability to produce results. This means bringing all problems involving threats to peace to the Security Council, which is technically in continuous session, and demanding prompt action. If a veto results, the matter should be taken to the General Assembly under the Uniting for Peace resolution.

Unless there is a real emergency, only after such efforts have failed should action be taken outside the United Nations. Efforts to effect peaceful settlement through the United Nations will help mobilize world opinion and place stigma not only upon the offending nation but upon any nation which blocks action by veto. Timely presentation to the U.N. of such problems as Indo-China might have brought about far happier results than the tragedy of Dienbienphu and the unhappy armistice negotiated at Geneva.

The recent volatile conflict between the Arabs and Israel is the kind of issue which should be the concern of the United Nations. This situation clearly threatens the peace and security of the whole world. Hostilities between the two factions could easily expand into world war.

The U.N. helped achieve an armistice between the two factions in 1948. It has maintained truce observers in the area since then. However, as tensions mounted in 1955, the United States and Britain by-passed the U.N. Even as the U.N. General Assembly was in session from September to December, 1955, we sought action outside the U.N. We did not bring the issue to the Security Council until March, 1956, when many observers were predicting immediate outbreak of war. The subsequent mediations of Mr. Dag Hammarskjold, Secretary-General of the United Nations, averted war and have maintained a precarious truce up to the time this is written.

Wasn't this a proper matter for U.N. action all along?

Shouldn't the United Nations firmly demonstrate that world opinion is strongly against war in this area? If border patrols from outside are required, should they not be placed there by the United Nations? Britain and the United States talk of intervention if necessary to assure peace. This step is helpful, but a United Nations declaration, supported by a majority of U.N. members, would be far better.

Neither Britain nor the United States is a popular candidate for this task. Britain is unpopular because of her recent domination of Egypt, her current controversy in Cyprus, and her oil interests in the Middle East. The United States is unpopular with the Arab nations because of her long-standing support of Israel and because of the way we have sided with Britain and France in recent colonial issues before the United Nations General Assembly.

Early in 1955 the United States and Great Britain should have carried this issue to the Security Council and, if necessary, on to the General Assembly of the United Nations. Ordinarily, we should not act bilaterally until the United Nations has grappled with the problem and has proved itself incapable of handling the situation.

But again, in the current Suez Canal issue, Britain, France and the United States have initiated or supported multilateral action by a group of nations without utilizing the United Nations. So far there has been no serious effort to use the United Nations.

COLLECTIVE SECURITY.   As long as collective security remains the only available deterrent to aggression, continued efforts should be exerted to take advantage of the provisions of the United Nations Charter. Even though such action might be blocked by a Soviet veto, efforts should be renewed, in compliance with Article 43 of the Charter, to designate forces to be turned over to the Security Council if needed. Continued efforts should also be made to develop a United Nations general staff to direct collective action when required.

Let us not fool ourselves: these measures would not make the U.N. effective. Even if Article 43 were complied with, the U.N. would still have no military forces of its own. The agreements to designate forces for future U.N. use could still be broken by any nation. However, if even a few of the nations were willing to keep their promises, these steps would give the U.N. more prestige than it now has.

As suggested in the previous chapter, the formation of a genuine United Nations security force, consisting of men hired, paid, and commanded directly by the U.N., would have a beneficial effect.

Use of U.N. investigating commissions, like the one in South Korea at the time of the 1950 invasion, is desirable in all trouble spots. That commission was quickly able to pin the responsibility for aggression upon North Korea.

All such steps enlarge the U.N.'s ability to deter or resist aggression.

AGENCIES AND COMMISSIONS.   The United Nations can also be made more effective by greater use of its specialized agencies and commissions.

All of the specialized agencies operate without the veto restriction because they are responsible to the General Assembly. As participants in these agencies, we need to continue our financial support and in some instances to increase it. Certainly, we should develop a broader program of technical assistance under the U.N.

Not only do we need to continue our participation in these agencies; we should give them better publicity and public understanding in order to help crystallize public opinion behind the United Nations.

Worth-while studies are being carried out by some of the commissions established by the United Nations, including the Commission on

Code of International Offenses, the Disarmament Commission, and
others. The work and activity of these groups should be encouraged
and expanded.

ATOMS FOR PEACE.   President Eisenhower's famous "atoms for
peace" plan has enjoyed a fine reception. The President, in 1953,
called for immediate use of atomic science for peaceful purposes—
power, health, and research. He suggested this be done without await-
ing establishment of controls over nuclear weapons. The program was
urged as a step in international cooperation and a beginning in nuclear control.

This proposal has caught the interest and imagination of nations
everywhere. There is great interest in peaceful use of the atom. The
United States and Britain, as well as the U.S.S.R., have offered to
make uranium and other nuclear materials available. Scientific knowledge and "know-how" are being exchanged.

Proposals have been made that this program be administered by the
U.N. In 1955 the Tenth General Assembly went on record favoring
the development of the program under the United Nations. A commission was established to develop procedures.

World control is desirable for certain aspects of "atoms for peace."
"Peaceful" reactors can be used to develop "belligerent" fissionable
material which can become nuclear weapons. The need for inspection
and control was made clear recently by Admiral Strauss, Chairman
of our Atomic Energy Commission.

This statement, coming just after President Eisenhower had made
a specific offer of nuclear materials, points up the problem.

"Peaceful" reactors must be inspected to prevent diversion to military use. Furthermore, the disposal of atomic wastes will soon create
problems which are international in scope.

Constructive results can come from handling "atoms for peace"
through the U.N. Such a procedure can give the United Nations a
chance to cut its teeth on a problem of international signficance, and
can give valuable experience in inspection and control. More importantly, it can cut down the diversion of nuclear material to military use.

ITEM THREE—USE THE UNITED NATIONS.   Decide that the responsibility for maintaining a secure peace must be delegated to the United
Nations. Use and support the present United Nations to the maximum
even as we seek changes to improve it.

Chapter 13

RULE OF LAW

No business could long operate without law. Businessmen rely on law so constantly they take it for granted. Yet if law, government, and police were suddenly removed, no private property would be protected, no contract would be enforceable, not even life would be safe. Business has traditionally stood for "law and order."

BEFORE we consider what changes are necessary to strengthen the United Nations so it can maintain a secure peace, we must define the specific need. This may be done by stating responsibilities in precise terms rather than in vague ones like "establishment of just and durable peace," or "elimination of war."

There are two fundamental responsibilities which must be delegated to the United Nations: the establishment of world law and the achievement of enforceable disarmament. These two basic needs are entwined and are completely dependent upon each other.

The subject of law is dealt with in this chapter, while disarmament is discussed in the following one.

The terms "world law" and "rule of law" are used interchangeably, law being the opposite of anarchy. The current threats to peace result primarily from the anarchy in today's world. A rule of law is the world's most fundamental need. Without law, we cannot bring sense and order to world affairs.

RULE OF LAW. Law is generally held to be a fundamental prerequisite of both peace and freedom. This is just as true on the world level as on the local, state, or national level. Order, peace, security, individual rights, and abandonment of individual use of force come only when law is substituted for anarchy. The writings of many historians, political scientists, and experts in the fields of law and government stand as testimony to this truth.

Numerous contemporary leaders in this country have called for world law. These include President Eisenhower, past Presidents Hoover and Truman, the late Robert A. Taft, Adlai Stevenson, General Douglas MacArthur, Chief Justice Earl Warren, and such business and industrial leaders as Henry Luce, Bernard Baruch, and David Sarnoff.

Law may be defined as a rule of conduct prescribed by a supreme governing authority and enforced by its sanctions. In other words, the following basic elements are involved in law.

1. A supreme governing authority, with
2. power to make rules of conduct and having
3. the ability to enforce these rules.

However, if law is to be just—and we insist on that—certain judicial procedures are also required. Their purpose is to interpret the law, assure its equitable application, and protect the individual rights of all who are subject to the law.

A rule of law also normally provides means for peaceable settlement of disputes. Under the protection of law, force is no longer needed by individuals or groups to resolve their controversies.

We are here concerned with conduct related to peace and security; namely, control of armaments and prevention of aggression. Let us see how law deals with these matters within any state of the United States.

A legislative body—the lawmaking authority—defines and prohibits those acts which are harmful to the rights of others and prescribes the penalty for violation. For instance, in the field of "armament control and prevention of aggression" as applied to individuals, the State of Iowa prohibits possession of concealed weapons except by authorized permit. It also declares illegal such acts as murder, assault and battery, robbery, and so on. Penalties are prescribed for the violation of such statutes.

When individuals violate these laws they may expect to be apprehended by the police—the enforcement authority. If the police catch one man in the act of beating or robbing another, they stop the aggressor and restore order.

Violators may also expect to be charged with a criminal offense and to be tried by a court of law—the judicial authority—to determine guilt and fix the penalty.

As law-abiding citizens we do not carry weapons or organize ourselves in vigilante committees to obtain security. Rather, we look to the policeman on the corner to enforce a rule of law which guarantees our safety. The certainty of punishment by enforcement agencies provides the deterrent which limits use of physical violence.

Law protects everyone's freedoms by deterring or apprehending those who invade other people's rights. As law-abiding citizens we give up the "right" to beat up our neighbors or take potshots at someone we dislike. This is no sacrifice for the great majority of us. We are glad to give up our "right" to use force against others, because in return we receive the greater benefit of protection against violence. We look to the rule of law to maintain order and peace. We no longer attempt to defend ourselves by individual or cooperative measures.

Numerous safeguards are built into such a system to protect individual rights and freedoms. Others are established to review constitutionality of legislative enactments, to prevent or correct arbitrary actions of the enforcement arm, and to assure just decisions by the courts.

The simple example just described includes all the elements of a rule of law applied to the preservation of peace and security. Such a system of law does not work perfectly, nor does it prevent all crime. But law is the best thing man has yet devised to limit conflict and protect individual rights and freedoms.

In a similar pattern, law is applied within the states, cities, and towns comprising most of the nations of the world. This is true even within totalitarian nations, although their rules of conduct may be prescribed by command or edict rather than by legislative action.

A rule of law assumes that because *some* citizens will not cooperate to maintain order, the responsibility and the necessary authority must be delegated to a governing organization. It further assumes the presence of criminals and people of evil intent and arranges for the enforcement of approved rules of conduct upon them. It also recognizes the possibility of abuses in the administration of law and establishes safeguards and balances to correct and minimize them.

Only on the world level do we seek peace and security without law. Only there do we find no established and enforceable rules of conduct prohibiting arms, aggression, mass murder, and war. Only there do we hope that cooperation is adequate to provide peace and security.

Why have we overlooked the simple, elemental fact that law is essential for a secure peace? How long will we remain blind to the need for world law to end the costly and bloody use of war—the trademark of anarchy?

Only when we grasp and accept these fundamentals will we make progress toward the difficult task of reorganizing the United Nations.

LAW AND DISARMAMENT. Great emphasis has properly been placed upon disarmament. It is not necessary here to debate the question as to whether world law must precede disarmament, or disarmament must precede world law. Both are necessary, and neither can be fully achieved without the other.

If war is eliminated as a means of resolving international differences, not only must nations give up the use of armaments, but also means must be provided to enforce peace. World law provides a method which can be fair and just. It thus fills the void created by the elimination of military power as an instrument of foreign policy.

Moreover, world law offers the surest way of making disarmament enforceable. It provides the means for effective civilian control, and the safeguards which we must demand before we can safely accept universal disarmament.

RESPONSIBILITY OF U.N. Therefore, the primary responsibility which must be assigned to the United Nations is the establishment and maintenance of world law. Nothing less than this gigantic task is an adequate commission.

Such a rule of law must be established by a governing authority to which power has been delegated. It just cannot develop out of good will and world community. It must be created by an international institution receiving its delegated authority and power from the people of the world.

Such a strengthened U.N. must act as a supreme governing authority in its sphere of jurisdiction. For this reason great care must be exercised in defining its powers. It seems reasonable and conservative that the U.N.'s powers should be strictly limited to those which are needed to achieve a secure peace. No greater power or broader function should be delegated than is essential to achieve our objective.

Therefore, it seems logical to limit the functions of world law to three specific areas:

1. The control of armaments and armed forces
2. The prevention of aggression
3. The provision of means to aid peaceful settlement of disputes between nations.

These are the minimum functions required to prevent war. Because the nations of the world are not yet likely to accept a greater range of world law, proposals exceeding the minimum will only increase the difficulty of obtaining agreement. Furthermore, it is unwise to give any governing body more power than is absolutely necessary. The author dislikes "big government" on any level.

The establishment of world law, strictly limited to these areas, will not be a panacea. It will not solve all of the world's problems.

But by eliminating war and securing peace, we can break the shackles of fear and suspicion and lift the burden of armaments. Relieved of these, men everywhere can turn with greater singleness of purpose to the social, economic, and political problems which cry for solution. Progress in these areas will be limited as long as the overpowering concern of national leaders is with military security and strategy. Therefore, the U.N.'s top priority should be the achievement of secure peace through law.

However, at the same time the U.N. assumes the responsibility of maintaining peace through law, it must continue many existing activities and programs. These include the work of the specialized agencies, the Economic and Social Council and the Trusteeship Council and the International Court of Justice. In fact, these activities should be enlarged and expanded whenever they will create a better world community or greater unity.

Most of these agencies have been far more effective than the U.N.'s peace-keeping machinery. Voluntary cooperation seems to work better in the fields of health, education, and economics than in preventing war. It would be unwise to give the U.N. power to make and enforce laws in these many fields.

In summary, the primary responsibility we must delegate to the U.N. is the establishment of a rule of law strictly limited to the control of armaments, prevention of aggression, and peaceful settlement of controversies between nations.

"The only alternative to war or international anarchy is the estab-

lishment of the rule of law," said Sir Anthony Eden of Great Britain
to the House of Commons in July, 1950.

ENFORCEMENT ON INDIVIDUALS.   In order to be effective, law must
be enforced on the individual person. This is now the case at local,
state, and national levels.

If an auto driver in Jackson, Michigan, violates a traffic regulation,
the law is enforced upon him as an individual. The city police do not
apprehend the passengers in the car, the driver's family, or his neighbors. He alone has violated the law and must suffer the consequences
if found guilty.

If a farmer in Adams County, Iowa, violates the state law against
carrying concealed weapons, the law is enforced upon him as an individual. The sheriff does not bring charges against the township in
which he lives or against the county Farm Bureau. Only the individual charged with the violation is apprehended, brought to trial, and
sentenced if found guilty.

If a worker in a munitions plant in Kansas City is charged with
violation of federal security regulations, the law is enforced upon him
as an individual. The federal enforcement officers do not bring charges
against the man's fellow workers, the company which employs him, the
city or the state in which the plant is located. Only the violator is
apprehended, and brought to trial to suffer the consequences if found
guilty.

If the governor of Florida violates the federal tax laws, the federal
government does not declare war on Florida or bomb Miami. The
governor of a state, like any other citizen, can be arrested, tried, and
punished if he breaks a law of the United States.

These examples clearly indicate the principle of enforcement upon
individuals. It is readily accepted at all levels of government. The
principle needs to be applied to the world.

Here is one fundamental difference between world law and "collective security." The latter acts only upon governments. If economic or
moral sanctions fail and attempts at negotiation are unsuccessful,
"collective security" has nothing to offer except war against the aggressor nation.

WHY INDIVIDUALS?   Enforcement of world law upon individuals will
require a sharp break with precedent. Historically, armaments races
and aggression have been considered national acts. Individuals, even

high government officials, have been considered free from personal responsibility as long as they carried out a national policy.

At the close of World War II, the famous Nuremberg trials in Germany and similar trials in Japan attempted to establish the principle of individual responsibility. These trials reflected the growing need to pin responsibility upon individuals who utilized their power as national leaders to precipitate war. But these trials came too late. The German and Japanese rulers were punished after the war was over. They should have been arrested, tried, and punished when they first began to rearm; but this was impossible because there were no world laws controlling armaments in the 1930's. The Nuremberg trials locked the barn door after the horse was stolen.

In addition, the Nuremberg trials created "ex post facto" law. The new principle, that national leaders could be tried by international courts for their crimes, was announced after the crimes had been committed. Many legal authorities question whether these trials were proper. Any attempt to make retroactive law is dangerous, both legally and morally. This is especially true when the victor in a war imposes a new legal principle upon the vanquished.

But the theory of individual responsibility is absolutely sound. It is accepted and practiced in the administration of law at all levels, up to and including nations. If, for instance, the officials of the City of San Francisco have violated a federal statute, the United States Government does not lay siege to the city in an attempt to enforce the law against the entire population. Rather, it obtains the appropriate warrant, taps the shoulder of the official accused of violation, and brings him to the bar of justice. Even though legal action may be taken against the municipal corporation, it is enforced also upon the individuals who are responsible for the violation.

This process is diametrically opposed to our unsuccessful attempts to prevent world war through "collective security." Nations have been considered the unit of responsibility in all previous attempts to eliminate war, reduce armaments, or take other steps aimed at achieving peace. Sanctions, when attempted, have been applied against nations. Military force, when used, has been directed against nations.

The trouble with this system is that an entire aggressor nation can be punished only by going to war against it. Yet the purpose of this "collective security" system is to prevent war. Enforcement against nations puts us in the ridiculous position of waging war to prevent war! The cure is as bad as the disease.

A "war to prevent war" is still a war. People still get killed. Usually, millions of innocent people are killed; the few guilty leaders often go unpunished. In trying to kill the rats, we burn down the barn.

Is it any wonder that "collective security" has never worked well, and has seldom even been attempted? Few nations are willing to "punish" an aggressor nation when the "punishment" includes the bombing, maiming, and slaughter of millions of civilians. Still fewer nations are willing to send their own troops into the battle and to take the risk that the aggressor will bomb their own cities. The sixteen nations which sent troops to defend South Korea against communist invasion deserve a great deal of praise. We had no world law in 1950, and this fumbling attempt to make "collective security" work was the best which could be done. But there must be a better way.

The alternative is to hold individual citizens, regardless of their rank or government office, responsible for violations of world laws controlling armaments and aggression. The adoption of this principle, accompanied by proper safeguards, provides a sound basis for enforcement. Failure to adopt this principle invites continued failure of a system which cannot cope with a future Hitler or Mussolini who undertakes to rearm his nation. Consider what would have happened in 1934 had there been such enforceable laws with respect to arms. As soon as inspectors discovered that Hitler was rearming Germany, contrary to the laws against manufacture or possession of weapons, he would have been arrested, tried, and punished. If we had had world law enforceable upon individuals, we could have stopped Hitler while he was still weak. We could have prevented World War II.

Furthermore, law enforcement upon individuals would make it easier for the U.N. to detect violations. Few citizens would support U.N. action against their entire nation. Many citizens would warn U.N. inspectors that a national official was stockpiling illegal arms. The desire for peace is a powerful force in this world. Many people would welcome the punishment of their government officials who were planning war, just as they would favor punishing grafters in their government.

The key to a workable system of law lies in this principle of enforcement upon individuals. Until it is accepted, all efforts at enforcement against major powers are doomed to failure.

FORCE AND LAW.   Establishment of a rule of law does not imply a utopian dependence upon the goodness of man. Quite the contrary. Police force is provided and used when necessary to cope with the criminal or the outlaw.

This is in fundamental contrast to the use of force under anarchy. Police force is in the hands of the institution of law which is responsible for peace and security. It is on the side of justice and the common good. When used, it is wielded to compel compliance with laws previously adopted and published.

Law is established because in every community—from the city to the world—there are "bad" as well as "good" citizens. Always some will not cooperate and will try to take advantage of neighbors. World law can deprive them of the implements of war and thereby limit their encroachment on others. World law can provide the force on the side of justice to restrain the "bad" national leader from using force.

Ordinary citizens have nothing to fear from such police power. They will not be building guided missiles in the basement or General Sherman tanks in the back yard. By limiting the sphere of world law to armament control and prevention of aggression, we make it almost impossible for private citizens to run afoul of U.N. laws. Only a small number of government officials, military officers, or munitions manufacturers would be capable of violating these laws.

The police force, on the side of law, is needed to protect the people against aggression or the manufacture and possession of the tools of war. Isn't this just the protection the world has so long desired?

ELEMENTS.   If the United Nations is to establish and maintain world law, it must be able to do the following:

1. By appropriate legislative processes, enact laws on control of armaments, disarmament, and aggression: matters directly related to the maintenance of a secure peace.

2. By adequate administrative methods, enforce these laws, apprehend violators, and maintain order.

3. By proper judicial procedures, assure equitable and just application of the world law, punish those who violate it, and provide a means for aiding peaceful settlement of differences and disputes between nations.

In other words, the U.N. must be able to enact, enforce, and interpret world law. These are minimum requirements for a secure peace, which will preserve freedom.

The changes required in the U.N. to accomplish these functions are discussed in Chapter 15.

DISARMAMENT CONTROL.   It is not unlikely that the beginning of world law will be forced by progress toward disarmament. It could even be forced by the "atoms for peace" program.

The current emphasis on disarmament will eventually compel us to realize that safe disarmament is possible only under world law.

Rather than revising the U.N. Charter at the beginning, the nations might agree on a definite plan for disarmament, including rules and regulations limiting armed forces and prohibiting major armaments. If they also created an enforcement agency to detect and apprehend violators, and a court to give accused violators a fair trial and punish them if found guilty, this would be a good start toward world law. Of course, such agencies would have to be set up with great care to make them as tyranny-proof as possible. In addition, the U.N. would soon have to be given some legislative power so that it could change the disarmament rules and regulations as needed to meet new conditions. As soon as possible, a thorough revision of the U.N. Charter would be essential.

ITEM FOUR—ESTABLISH A RULE OF LAW.   Recognize law as the keystone of order, peace and freedom. Make the United Nations responsible for establishing a rule of law adequate to control all armaments, prevent aggression, and aid peaceful settlement of disputes.

Chapter 14

DISARMAMENT

Industry is always ready to give up outmoded methods and procedures. It quickly accepts new scientific and engineering developments, particularly if they reduce costs without sacrificing quality or product. New methods and new approaches are the lifeblood of industry.

DISARMAMENT has long been linked to the idea of peace. A strong belief persists that peace can be secured if a way is found to reduce or eliminate the tools of war. Disarmament also offers reduced taxes and more beneficial uses of our resources.

Few contend that armaments are desirable, but most people consider them necessary for our security under present conditions. However, there is growing desire to find the conditions under which it will be safe to give them up. The task, however, is so extremely difficult and complex that many consider it impossible.

Disarmament has received renewed attention since the May, 1955, appointment of Harold E. Stassen as Special Assistant to the President on disarmament matters. Its current importance is indicated by the subcommittee on Disarmament of the Senate Foreign Relations Committee. This body, under the chairmanship of Senator Hubert Humphrey, is holding hearings and has a staff studying the subject.

President Eisenhower's proposals at Geneva in 1955 have been labeled as "gateways" to disarmament. These bold proposals deal with aerial inspection and exchange of military information. They were followed in August and October of 1955 by proposals which we submitted to the United Nations Subcommittee on Disarmament. More comprehensive proposals were presented to this committee in April, 1956.

The General Assembly's resolution in the fall of 1955 called upon the United Nations Disarmament Commission, and its subcommittee, to pursue diligently their studies and negotiations. This resolution urged study of the United States proposals, together with those made by other nations; it recommended the development of a comprehensive disarmament plan.

The growing specter of mass destruction makes disarmament an urgent necessity. But how do we achieve safe disarmament?

THE NEED FOR DISARMAMENT.   The usual case for disarmament is a simple one: Remove the implements of war, and nations will be unable to wage war. Take away the nuclear weapons, the supersonic bombers, the missiles, and the conventional weapons, and peace will result.

Unfortunately, such a stereotyped conception is too simple to stand close scrutiny. More than disarmament is required for peace. Scrapping of all modern weapons would temporarily make major war impossible. However, it would not permanently assure peace unless subsequent rearming were prevented. Moreover, it is at least theoretically possible for war to be waged without modern weapons. Wars have been fought with spears, stones, and clubs.

The case for disarmament, therefore, as a step toward a peaceful world must be supported in a different manner. A sound approach may be made by recognizing that the removal of arms from nations is only one need. It must be accompanied by other steps to secure every nation against aggression and to prevent potential aggressors from rearming. These steps require enforceable world law. Only thus will the void be filled which is created by abandonment of arms. Only thus will a substitute be furnished for the historic use of arms to protect national security, back up diplomacy, and settle national differences.

Once a rule of law makes disarmament safe, the need for national armaments will vanish. This expectancy frequently prompts the comment that disarmament will come as the result of world law, so why worry about it now? Such reasoning is as oversimplified as the idea that disarmament alone will bring peace.

Effective and complete disarmament and the establishment of world law are parts of a single package. Both are needed, and neither can be safely undertaken without the other. If we recognize these facts, the place of disarmament becomes clear.

BENEFITS OF DISARMAMENT.   Disarmament reduces the magnitude of the enforcement task associated with a rule of law. It is a fundamental precept that law enforcement requires an enforcing agency with power exceeding any likely combination which may be marshaled against it.

For example, the police force of an American city has sufficient strength to exceed the power of any group of criminals it is likely to encounter. States in our nation have long maintained a militia with sufficient power to exceed that which may be arrayed against it in any civilian uprising.

Power must be on the side of law, justice, and government. This was well stated by Blaise Pascal long ago when he wrote, "Justice without force is impotent; force without justice is tyrannical. . . . it is necessary therefore to put together justice and force and so insure that what is just shall be strong, and what is strong shall be just."

To obtain this power without disarmament the United Nations would require military strength superior to that now possessed by any likely combination of potential aggressors. This would require the United Nations either to maintain a huge military establishment or to rely upon contingents of national forces through collective security. Neither of these alternatives is attractive.

The first is undesirable because it adds to the total size and cost of world armaments. It also multiplies the problems of providing proper safeguards. No one wants to see the United Nations become an organization primarily concerned with its own military power.

This is exactly what would happen if it had to maintain military power equal to that now possessed by the Soviet Union or the United States.

The second alternative is undesirable because it places continued reliance upon "collective security." The inadequacies of this device were clearly demonstrated in the Korean War. It is never certain that a group of nations will act promptly; they seldom act at all. The call for collective action can be nullified by delay or opposition of one or more major nations.

It places an unfair burden on those few nations which may respond.

It is quite probable that Korea was the first and last attempt at major use of "collective security."

Disarmament under law limits the required size of the enforcement agency. If disarmament is complete and universal down to the level of militia required for internal security, the security forces of the United Nations can be comparatively small.

In addition, disarmament will make it easier for nations to rely upon world law to provide security. The mere possession of major armaments suggests dependence upon them in times of crisis and impedes reliance upon peaceful means. For these reasons, disarmament will aid in developing acceptance and confidence in the operation of world law.

Disarmament will also release great quantities of money and manpower for more beneficial uses. The potential savings are demonstrated by our budget, which currently includes nearly $40,000,000,-000 for military purposes. Add the expenditures of other nations, and the magnitude of the potential savings is tremendous. Not only at home, but throughout the world, national expenditures and taxes are closely keyed to military expenditures.

LEAGUE OF NATIONS.   Every past effort to disarm nations or to outlaw war has failed, including at least five attempts since the close of World War I.

The League of Nations was the first attempt. Its charter contained the following provisions in Article 8:

> The members of the League recognize that the maintenance of peace requires the reduction of national armaments to the lowest point consistent with national security and the enforcement, by common action, of international obligations.
>
> The Council, taking account of the geographical situation and circumstances of each state, shall formulate plans for such reduction for the consideration and action of the several governments.

Discussions aimed at implementing these provisions began with the first Assembly in 1920 and continued until 1934. At no time in this period did the League Council or the independent nations "formulate plans" which were submitted "for the consideration and action of the several governments." The League collapsed amid a growing armaments race.

WASHINGTON CONFERENCE.   The next effort was the Washington Conference which met on November 11, 1921, at the call of President Warren Harding. This conference resulted in a treaty for the limitation of naval strength with these ratios: United States, 5; Britain, 5; Japan, 3; France, 1.7; and Italy, 1.7. It included provisions for the destruction of certain ships and for a cessation of construction of capital ships by the three leading powers to achieve these ratios. It also limited additional fortifications by the United States, Britain, and Japan in the Pacific Ocean.

The treaty contained no provisions for enforcement other than an obligation for the contracting powers to consult in case a situation arose which, in the opinion of any one of them, should involve the application of the stipulations of the treaty. Thus, the treaty was without "teeth" and had no real provision for any kind of enforcement against a violator.

The results are well known. The United States respected her commitments, towed her ships out to sea and sank them, refrained from further construction, and honestly carried out the provisions of the treaty. So also did Britain, France, and Italy. But Japan, failing to heed her treaty obligations, expanded her naval force beyond the allowable ratio, and soon went ahead with expansion of fortifications in the Pacific. Even when these violations were recognized, the other nations did not use the only enforcement method—war—which was available.

KELLOGG-BRIAND PACT.   Another effort was the Kellogg-Briand Pact of 1929 in which all of the principal powers and most of the smaller nations of the world solemnly signed an agreement outlawing war. Two of the articles in this document follow:

1. The high contracting parties solemnly declare in the names of their respective peoples that they condemn recourse to war for the solution of international controversies and renounce it as an instrument of national policy in their relations with one another.

2. The high contracting parties agree that the settlement and solution of all disputes or contracts of whatever nature, of whatever origin they may be, which may arise between them, shall never be sought except by pacific means.

War would have been eliminated had all the signatories respected this pious declaration. But a review of the breaches of this treaty serves to list the actions which have precipitated war after war since 1929.

Japan signed this agreement, but in 1931 entered Manchuria, in 1938 invaded China, and in 1941 attacked Pearl Harbor and other points in the Pacific.

Italy signed this agreement, but in 1935 invaded Ethiopia.

Germany signed this agreement but, after successfully using the threat of military action to gain control of the Rhineland in 1936, Czechoslovakia in 1938, and Austria in 1938, invaded Poland in 1939 to start World War II.

The U.S.S.R. signed this agreement, but in 1940 occupied Lithuania, Latvia, and Estonia. Since World War II the Soviets have repeatedly used war and the threat of war to achieve their ends, usually maneuvering to have their satellites do the fighting, as in Korea and Indo-China.

The Kellogg-Briand Pact also lacked any effective means of enforcement. The sanctions, economic and otherwise, which the treaty called for, could be invoked only if the nations cooperated. Each time sanctions were proposed, sovereign nations reviewed the problem from their respective nationalistic positions and declined to take action. Even the call by Secretary of State Stimson of the United States to apply the sanctions after Japan moved into Manchuria in 1931 was met by a stony silence from the other signers.

UNITED NATIONS. The aggressions beginning in 1935 and culminating in World War II marked the end of disarmament efforts until the United Nations Charter was drafted in 1945. This document only weakly mentions disarmament, in the following language:

Preamble: . . . to ensure, by the acceptance of principles and the institution of methods, that armed force shall not be used, save in the common interest. . . .

Article 2, paragraph 3: All members shall settle their international disputes by peaceful means in such a manner that international peace and security, and justice, are not endangered.

Article 2, paragraph 4: All Members shall refrain in their international relations from the threat or use of force against the territorial integrity or political independence of any state, or in any other manner inconsistent with the Purposes of the United Nations.

Article 11, paragraph 1: The General Assembly may consider the general principles of cooperation in the maintenance of international peace and security, including the principles governing disarmament and the regulation of armaments, and may make recommendations with regard to such principles to the Members or to the Security Council or to both.

Without a clear mandate and effective procedures, the United Nations has been no more effective in achieving disarmament or eliminating war than the League of Nations. In fact, its pattern of frustration has been strikingly similar. Commissions have met but have not agreed on disarmament recommendations to be submitted to the Security Council and the General Assembly.

Efforts to set up a U.N. general staff, with designated contingents of national troops available as a collective security force, have been stymied by the Soviet Union. These failures have all been associated with disagreement on the means of enforcement and with the nations' refusal to surrender their prerogative to build and control military establishments. Therefore, until now the U.N. has failed to achieve workable disarmament.

UNILATERAL DISARMAMENT.   All of these efforts to achieve disarmament or end war involved agreed action by several nations. One additional experiment in disarmament was undertaken at the close of World War II.

This experiment was different from the others, for no international agreement was involved. We quickly dismantled the great United States military machine we had created to help win the war. It was a hectic demobilization to meet the pressing political and popular demand to "bring the boys home." We discharged millions of men, junked or abandoned billions of dollars' worth of equipment, and quickly converted industry to peaceful products. Rapidly our great military power was reduced to a skeleton.

We made this decision unilaterally, although it accompanied partial demobilization by some of our allies, the U.S.S.R. included. We did it, believing cooperation among the great powers would guarantee peace. The U.S.S.R. not only failed to follow our lead fully, but quickly took advantage of the weakness created by our demobilization to consolidate and expand its position in Europe and Asia. This disarmament experiment failed. It was not only unenforceable—it wasn't even a multilateral effort. But it is significant that a generous gesture of reducing military power by the strongest nation of the West kindled no desire in the U.S.S.R. to follow suit.

All of the five cases just outlined were complete failures. Such a dismal record of failure to achieve disarmament and eliminate war seems dispiriting. And so it is unless the underlying causes of the failure are recognized, understood, and avoided.

THE MISSING ELEMENT.   In all of these past trials at disarmament there has been adequate desire accompanied by sincere effort. Why then have they all failed? The reason is not hard to find. It lies in the fact that an effective method of enforcement was not provided.

In every instance, compliance depended upon the integrity of the participating nations. The contracting parties had no way to force any nation to carry out its commitment. They could discuss, request, negotiate, and plead, but if these efforts did not sway the violating power from its path the only recourse of the other nations was resort to war or threat of war. *Thus war, the very action which these disarmament programs sought to avoid, remained the only real means of enforcement!*

This situation, recognized at the time of negotiation, restrained nations from accepting complete disarmament. No nation could safely rely on a disarmament plan which was known to be unenforceable. Nations approached conferences with their tongues in their cheeks, desiring disarmament but firmly intending to depend on their own military strength for security.

Stated in a different way, these disarmament attempts failed because they became mere scraps of paper. They provided no effective way to prevent a contracting nation from violating the restrictions. Each nation reserved the complete right to do as it pleased. With no institution to police and enforce the agreements and to compel compliance, each of the attempts broke down whenever a single nation embarked on aggression. In the short span of fifteen years four major nations—Italy, Germany, Japan, and the U.S.S.R.—each under the domination of a militaristic dictatorship, took matters in their hands and used aggression to achieve their ends.

LAW AND DISARMAMENT.   Any realistic approach to disarmament must avoid the causes of past failures. Otherwise, it will lead once again to disillusionment. A bold new approach can be found only by coupling disarmament with world law.

If disarmament is undertaken simultaneously with the establishment of a rule of law, the responsibility for its enforcement can be shifted from the nations to the United Nations. The U.N. can become a supranational organization vested both with responsibility and with authority. No longer will the nations be dependent upon treaties, which are mere scraps of paper. No longer will the nations be dependent upon cooperation among themselves to enforce disarmament and prevent aggression.

Once world law is established and disarmament is achieved, the future control of armaments becomes a less complicated process. The development, manufacture, possession, and use of certain arms will be prohibited by law. The United Nations will be given the responsibility and the authority to assure compliance and to detect, restrain, and punish violators.

To repeat a statement of a previous chapter, it is unnecessary to debate whether world law precedes disarmament or disarmament precedes world law. Both are required, and neither can safely be undertaken without the other.

With this precept restated, let us look at some of the problems of achieving and maintaining disarmament under a system of world law.

THE DEGREE OF DISARMAMENT.   We have noted a vast difference in the meaning of the term "disarmament." It seems to mean different things to different people, ranging from the "outlawing" of certain weapons or even war itself, through various types of arms limitation to complete and universal disarmament.

Disarmament must be both complete and universal. To be complete it must call for the elimination of all national armaments down to the minimum level required for maintenance of internal order—the militia level. It must also include all types of military weapons—conventional, nuclear, and other. To be universal, disarmament must be applied to all nations.

Among the arguments supporting both complete and universal disarmament are these:

1. It is more readily enforced. If all armaments are prohibited, the detection of any indicates violation. On the other hand, if nations are permitted to maintain armaments at some arbitrary level, it becomes more difficult to assure compliance.

2. It lessens the magnitude of the inspection problem. For the

very reason that violations of complete disarmament are more readily detected, the difficulty of inspection by the United Nations is lessened. This will result in a smaller and less costly inspection operation. It will also lessen the danger of friction and resentment from the process of inspection.

3. It encourages peaceful settlements. The moment complete and universal disarmament is achieved, nations will be compelled to depend upon peaceful procedures to settle their differences. As long as they have appreciable national armaments, even if reduced and balanced, there is a continuing temptation to use them as an instrument of foreign policy.

4. It will produce maximum savings. Complete and universal disarmament will end the tremendous expenditures of men, money, and materials now going into armament programs. After a suitable transition, these resources will be available for peaceful uses.

5. And finally but most fundamentally, national armaments become unnecessary in a world of law. The responsibility for protecting national security will be lodged with a strengthened United Nations. The necessary armaments and military strength will be in its hands. The result will be similar to what happened a few generations ago in the "Wild West" towns where gunmen and outlaws created anarchy. Once a competent marshal or sheriff was employed, the responsibility for peace and security was placed in his hands. When the sheriff and his deputies had restored order, local residents had no further need for the six-shooters they had been carrying to protect themselves.

However, the key to our willingness to accept such complete and universal disarmament lies in enforcement. Unless the system of enforcement seems foolproof, nations will properly hesitate to accept complete and universal disarmament.

ENFORCEMENT.   Once universal disarmament is achieved, along with world law, the responsibility for maintenance of a secure peace will be transferred from the individual nations to the United Nations. One of its major functions will be the enforcement of the disarmament provisions which are adopted.

Enforcement requires the following:

1. U.N. inspection forces which will ensure that the various nations are obeying the disarmament agreements. The U.N. in-

spectors must also detect violations of the laws prohibiting manu-facture, possession, or use of major military weapons and the maintenance of military forces beyond the allowable militia level. The inspectors must be empowered to go anywhere and to inspect anything which looks suspicious.

The inspection forces should consist of civilians, highly trained and well paid. Inspectors would also serve as law enforcement officers. In this capacity they would lawfully apprehend violators and bring them to trial before the courts of the United Nations. These civilians become sort of an international F.B.I.

2. U.N. military forces adequate to maintain or restore order and patrol borders in case of threatened incidents or other aggres-sive actions. The strength of these military forces must be adequate to "put together justice and force and so insure that what is just shall be strong." Its strength must exceed the power which might be arrayed against it by any possible combination of aggressor nations.

Suggestions on the organization and operation of these U.N. forces are presented in the following chapters.

Problems involved in the safeguards which are necessary both for world law and for universal enforced disarmament are discussed in Chapter 16 together with special problems involved in the inspection and control of nuclear weapons.

STAGING.   Disarmament cannot be accomplished overnight even after agreement is reached to start the process. Physical problems involved in dismantling the huge military establishments of today will likely require several years, with the process being accomplished in several stages.

As disarmament is carried out, the United Nations must organize inspection and security forces. This will require time to recruit and train these organizations even after form and function are clearly defined. Obviously, these organizations must be built up to the desired strength before disarmament is completed, and certain stages of the buildup must parallel stages of disarmament.

Progress by stages will help reduce the fear and suspicion which are bound to surround the process of disarmament. Centuries of de-pendence on arms for security will not easily be broken even after the necessity is recognized.

During a gradual process of disarmament nations will retain portions of their military establishments. They will reduce from stage to stage only as all other nations do the same. Thus, relative balance of power is maintained from stage to stage. By this process the security of the United States is maintained at all times.

A number of suggested plans for executing disarmament by stages have been developed. Among them are those prepared by Clark and Sohn[1] and Charles Bolte.[2]

GATEWAYS TO DISARMAMENT. Any agreement on universal enforced disarmament, safeguarded by world law, is not likely to be brought about gradually or by a long series of steps. Such a major advance is likely to come only as the result of an earth-shaking decision to abandon war and anarchy in favor of law and order. Even if world law comes in two or three steps, the first step must be a great one if it is to be effective and safe.

Such a decision must be made by all the nations—or at least those which are military powers. Such a decision must be accompanied or promptly followed by the required revisions in the U.N. Charter. The "waging of peace" to achieve this crucial decision is dealt with in Part IV. Nevertheless, it is desirable here to touch upon some of the "gateways" which are often linked to disarmament in current discussions.

Many proposals have been made for plans which are less than universal enforced disarmament, but which are alleged to advance us toward this goal. These include: outlawing war, banning use of nuclear weapons, banning tests on nuclear weapons, reducing armaments or armed forces, establishing early warning systems, settling controversial issues, and others. Would any or all of these suggestions advance us toward universal enforced disarmament? It is on this basis that their merit should be judged, for no one of them alone is adequate to secure peace.

It is entirely possible, however, that certain of these suggestions can advance us toward disarmament. The various proposals for an "early warning" alarm system fall in this category. This approach, emphasized by President Eisenhower's proposals at Geneva in July, 1955,

[1] Grenville Clark and Louis Sohn, *Peace Through Disarmament and Charter Review*.

[2] Charles G. Bolte, *The Price of Peace* (Boston, The Beacon Press, 1956).

for aerial reconnaissance and exchange of military information, is aimed at lessening the chance and the fear of a surprise mass attack by nuclear weapons.

As outlined in United States memoranda of August 30 and October 10, 1955, to the U.N. Disarmament Subcommittee, the "early warning" system included ground inspection and other features as well as aerial reconnaissance. Other aspects have been included in proposals made to the Subcommittee in April, 1956.

Other proposals with the same aim have included inspection at ports of entry, examination of military budgets for expenditures, and similar devices. It is possible a combination of these suggestions can be accepted by the Soviet Union and the Western nations. If so, they should by all means be put into effect. By lessening the chance of surprise attack and the fear of it, an early-warning system may help create an atmosphere in which agreement to disarmament is more likely.

The establishment of a workable early-warning system will certainly involve some ground inspection. The acceptance of this principle would be a forward step toward the inspection powers which the United Nations must have to enforce genuine disarmament.

This plan would be of even greater value if the inspection operation involved the United Nations. This could be accomplished by delegating to the United Nations certain phases of the inspection process or by using joint national and U.N. inspectors.

Such action would begin the process of U.N. inspection and also develop wider support for the early-warning system on the part of the smaller nations.

OTHER INTERIM MEASURES.   There are other interim developments which could be helpful to the achievement of disarmament, although not of themselves disarmament. A number of these could be considered once the principle of inspection is accepted by the Soviet Union and by the major free nations. A few ideas follow:

1. A U.N. Information Center.[3] Such a center might be created in the secretariat to interpret and disseminate information on military establishments. Sources for such information might include public information and data (of which great amounts are available) and material voluntarily provided by nations. For instance, if a

[3] Gen. Carlos P. Romulo, Address at Miami, Florida, Feb., 1956.

reciprocal exchange of military information were agreed upon between the U.S.S.R. and the U.S.A., copies of such data and its verification by aerial and ground inspection might be turned over to the United Nations. This would begin the census which disarmament will require. It should also build favorable world opinion for the exchange of information between the United States and the Soviet Union.

2. Limited U.N. Security Forces. Establishment of U.N. security forces of a limited size to provide patrols in such areas as the borders between Israel and the Arab States would also be a forward step. In such situations, it would be far better to use U.N. men in U.N. uniforms than to employ national contingents. Such a program was once proposed by Mr. Trygve Lie, former Secretary-General. Such a force might be developed under the Secretariat as part of the "guard" forces, with the approval of the General Assembly and with no danger of veto. Such action would be a humble but useful step toward shifting the responsibility for peace and order to the United Nations. Of course, the larger U.N. military force suggested in Chapter 10 would be even more valuable.

3. Controlling Arms Development.[4] If the principle of inspection gains acceptance, effective controls could be placed on the development of the major weapons of tomorrow, the space satellite and the intermediate range and intercontinental ballistic missiles (IRBM and ICBM). It might be sensible to start disarmament by applying it to the weapons which are not yet developed. This would not upset any balance of power nor deprive any nation of weapons it now possesses.

Missiles and satellites appear to be ideally suited for such control. A review of the experience of Germany in World War II, and of missile development in this country since then, indicates that the process of perfecting a long-range missile is one of great magnitude and difficulty. Moreover, it requires repeated launching and flight tests. Such tests are detectable by a suitable inspection system with proper radar and other apparatus.

Suppose the United States and other Western nations propose to the Soviet Union that all parties agree not to test ICBMs unless the other one first violates the agreement. We should also propose

[4] Col. Richard Leghorn, "Letter to Editor," *Washington Post*, Feb. 14, 1956.

adequate inspection and observation by U.N. or national groups to inform all parties concerned of the occurrence of any tests.

This would be an effective control on the development of the weapon. Even though the U.S.S.R. and the U.S.A. continued experimentation and design within the laboratories and on the drawing boards, no ICBM could be perfected without repeated tests. If the Soviets violated the agreement we would be free to proceed with tests.

Early adoption of such a program might well avoid tomorrow's weapons which promise to add another dimension to man's destructive capability. More correctly, they promise to eliminate a dimension—time—by reducing the flight schedule between Moscow and New York to less than thirty minutes.

The adoption now of such a program would makes less probable a recurrence of the current situation with nuclear weapons—large stockpiles of warheads which are difficult to locate or detect. Future location and detection of ICBMs and their launching platforms may be very difficult. Now is the time to seek enforced controls before either side has long-range missiles.

Similarly, early control and regulation of development of space satellites may be desirable. Both the U.S.S.R. and the U.S.A. are working on such devices, and expect to launch them in 1957. While of great scientific interest, they are also expected to have major military significance.

They provide platforms for communication, observation, and perhaps for direction or launching of missiles.

Both the ICBM and the satellites are elements of delivery systems for thermonuclear weapons. Both advance the age of "push-button" war. These facts warrant the most serious study of means to place their development, manufacture, possession, and use under effective control at the earliest possible date.

4. Controls for "atoms for peace." Progress toward U.N. supervision of "atoms for peace" and creation of proper controls for fissionable materials can be helpful to the cause of disarmament. The advantages are twofold. First, the United Nations would gain experience in controls and inspections which will later be helpful for disarmament. Second, it reduces the probability of wide-scale distribution of nuclear weapons, which in the hands of a dictator of even a small nation could be a disturbing threat.

The need of inspection in connection with the "atoms for peace" program has been recognized by Admiral Strauss, Chairman of the Atomic Energy Commission. Commenting upon President Eisenhower's proposal of February, 1955, to sell nuclear materials, he implied that, of course, the United States would have to inspect the use of this material, to prevent its diversion to military uses.

But who is to inspect the use of uranium provided by the U.S.S.R.? The sensible control of "atoms for peace" under the United Nations can advance us toward disarmament.

CAUTION.   Caution must be observed with respect to all of the interim steps discussed above. It must be recognized that bans, limitations, and warning systems are not of themselves disarmament and do not solve our problem. Even now there are sufficient weapons in the world to launch a terrifying war.

In fact, adoption of some of the steps may raise a serious hazard: the assumption we have peace when we really do not. Every apparent relaxation of tensions brings suggestions that peace is here, that we can throw away our armaments, and that security is just around the corner. This hazard is particularly great in the United States; we tend to swing from one extreme to another.

To avoid this hazard there is dire need for an over-all disarmament goal or blueprint. Our objectives of universal disarmament, enforced by world law, must be spelled out, accepted, and supported by the public. Then we need not hesitate to accept any step which fits the over-all program and advances us toward our goal.

However, it needs once again to be emphasized that substitution of law and order for anarchy requires a major decision by the peoples of this earth. Without that decision, authority will not be delegated to the U.N. and disarmament cannot be enforced. We sorely need a blueprint of our objective so our footprints will move in the right direction.

UNITED STATES PROGRAM.   In recent disarmament discussions the United States has made many suggestions. Some of these deal with basic elements of disarmament. Others, such as the early-warning system, are aimed at reducing tensions and minimizing the danger and fear of surprise attack.

But in total they do not meet the crying need for an adequate, comprehensive program which meets the challenge of the weapons of tomorrow. We need an over-all plan for disarmament. It must consist of more than "first steps" or "gateways" or general statements.

The comprehensive plan must be stated in sufficient detail that it can serve as a basis for negotiation. Only in such form can it be understood, debated, and supported by public opinion.

The United States Government and its citizens need to develop a disarmament plan. We must determine our goals and objectives. Only when we have done this can we be sure that first steps will carry us toward the end objective.

If we are to grapple with the terrifying problems presented by ICBMs with thermonuclear warheads, only 25 minutes away from our shores, we must understand the problems. Moreover, we must have strong and dynamic leadership toward total universal and enforceable disarmament.

Adlai Stevenson underlined the urgency of disarmament in November, 1955, saying:

> The difficulties in the way of achieving an enforceable system of disarmament are immense. Maybe the problem is insoluble now as it has been in the past. But it seems to me that the urgency is such that we can settle for nothing less than a sustained and dogged search for effective disarmament with the best brains we can muster, and that we have no greater foreign policy objective.

ITEM FIVE—OBTAIN UNIVERSAL ENFORCEABLE DISARMAMENT. Clearly define our objective as universal enforceable disarmament. Recognize that enforceable disarmament and world law are intertwined, and that each needs the other.

Chapter 15

STRENGTHENED UNITED NATIONS

Reorganization is a common process in business. Organizations are constantly being changed to meet new situations and to perform new functions. Change is an indication of progress. Lack of change often indicates deterioration. Reorganization involves: determining required functions, adopting a suitable structure, and delegating authority with proper checks and balances.

WHAT CHANGES are necessary to enable the United Nations to do the important tasks of establishing world law and bringing about universal enforceable disarmament? These two functions are necessary for a secure peace. The United Nations as now constituted cannot perform them.

The general requirements for establishing a rule of law and for obtaining universal enforced disarmament have been outlined in the two previous chapters. Now we may concern ourselves with the specific powers, structure, and safeguards which should be provided in a revised and strengthened U.N.

Once again bold steps are required, which will break sharply with precedent. We can no longer hesitate. We must stop fumbling and mumbling that the problem is complicated. We must take a long, realistic viewpoint. We must use courage and foresight to develop a workable United Nations, capable of fulfilling its essential mission. General Romulo emphasized this when he declared:

In considering amendments, the yardstick should not be what seems possible in the context of the present international situation, but rather what is necessary to enable mankind to avoid atomic destruction. Accordingly, any and all proposals should merit careful consideration which would make it possible for the United Nations to cope with this imminent danger.

CORRECTIONS. The primary weakness in the present United Nations (discussed in previous chapters) is lack of authority to carry out the implied responsibility of maintaining international peace and security.

To correct this weakness the U.N. needs authority commensurate with its responsibility. This is a well known axiom in business and government. No organization can be expected to discharge a responsibility unless given adequate authority.

Four steps are needed to reorganize the United Nations to accomplish this delegation of authority:

1. Define the exact nature of the responsibility which the U.N. is to assume.

2. Give it the powers it must have to carry out these responsibilities.

3. Develop a structure which will permit the U.N. to exercise these powers and discharge its responsibilities.

4. Establish adequate safeguards, checks, and balances to assure that the strengthened United Nations, does not encroach upon the internal affairs of nations, nor upon the rights of individuals.

These steps require a thorough overhaul of the U.N. Charter. The procedure for amending and revising the Charter is outlined in Chapter 21.

RESPONSIBILITIES. Added responsibilities which the United Nations needs to perform have been pointed out in the chapters on "Rule of Law" and "Disarmament." They may be summarized as follows:

1. Limitation and control of national armaments and armed forces.

2. Prevention of aggression.

The United Nations also should continue certain existing responsibilities, such as:

3. Improvement of economic and social conditions by coopera-

tive action (as now done by the Economic and Social Council and the specialized agencies).

4. Supervision of the preparation of peoples for self-government. (This is now a function of the Trusteeship Council.)

5. Maintenance of means for peaceful settlement of disputes between nations (as now done by the International Court of Justice and various special U.N. commissions).

POWERS.   Additional powers must be delegated to the U.N. to allow successful discharge of the added responsibilities (1 and 2 above) pertaining to world law and disarmament. On the other hand, no additional powers are required for the current responsibilities (3, 4, and 5 above), except that U.N. courts should probably have compulsory jurisdiction over some types of disputes between nations.

The U.N. must have these six powers which it does not have now:

1. To prohibit by law the "right" of nations to use force or the threat of force in international affairs.

2. To make laws, binding on individuals and national governments, prohibiting the construction or possession of armaments and armed forces, except for the small forces required for internal police purposes. In this connection, the U.N. must also be empowered to administer an agreed schedule for universal disarmament.

3. To maintain adequate inspection forces (including law enforcement officers) to enforce the world laws controlling national armaments. These should be civilian forces, somewhat similar to the F.B.I.

4. To maintain United Nations military forces, strong enough to enforce world law prohibiting aggression and to support the United Nations inspection forces where necessary.

5. To bring to trial in world courts any individuals, including officials of national governments, who violate such world laws or obstruct their enforcement.

6. To raise dependable revenue under a carefully defined and limited, but direct, taxing power with a ceiling fixed by the Charter.

STRUCTURE OF U.N.   How must the structure of the United Nations be changed to enable it to exercise the six basic powers outlined above?

The following are the apparent minimum requirements:

1. Membership. All nations must be members of the strengthened U.N. It is vital that world law and disarmament apply to all nations.

2. Legislature. A suitable body of the U.N. must have the authority to enact world law in the limited sphere of armaments and aggression. Representation in this legislative body must be equitable. The present General Assembly can no doubt be revised to become a legislature.

3. Executive. The administrative functions of a revised U.N. must include those now handled by the Secretariat, plus those related to control of armaments and prevention of aggression: inspection, law enforcement, and supervision of U.N. security forces. The Executive might be created by entrusting to the Secretariat the administration of these new functions.

It is likely that some form of commission may be proposed to supervise disarmament and control nuclear weapons. Such a commission, reporting to the General Assembly, would by-pass the Security Council and its veto. The same result could be accomplished by revising the Security Council to eliminate the veto, alter the membership, and make it responsible to the General Assembly.

In any event the Executive must provide civilian control of all functions related to disarmament, arms control, law enforcement, and prevention of aggression.

4. Courts. A suitable U.N. court must have the authority to try violators of the laws relating to armaments and aggression, and to sentence those who are found guilty. The same court may try cases involving disputes between nations over the interpretation of treaties and contracts. In addition, the present International Court of Justice, with voluntary jurisdiction, may properly be continued to mediate other disputes.

Such a minimum structure is very similar to that found in every nation with a democratic form of government. With its traditional three separate branches—legislative, executive, and judicial—this structure makes sense to Americans. It is a familiar pattern which works successfully and protects individuals and minorities.

However, it must be emphasized again that the strengthened United Nations should have only the powers delegated to it in the limited field of control of armaments and prevention of aggression. It is not proposed that the U.N. otherwise interfere with national governments or undertake functions now handled by them. These matters are dealt with in greater detail after a look at the proposed structure.

MEMBERSHIP.   Membership in a strengthened United Nations must be universal. All nations must be members, without power of secession. This is the only way to apply to all the rules pertaining to armaments and aggression.

Why do we want the U.S.S.R., Red China, or other communist nations in the revised United Nations? For exactly the same reason that we want all citizens, "good" or "bad," to be subject to the laws of a city, a state, or a nation.

Presently, membership in the United Nations supposedly is based upon a nation's desire for peace. Since the U.N. is a voluntary organization of nations pledged to cooperate in assuring peace, such a requirement of good intention is understandable. But such conditions of selectivity vanish when the United Nations assumes the responsibility of enforcing rules in the field of armaments and aggression upon all nations, whether they be "good" or "bad."

We have every reason to expect that from time to time there will be nations governed by men whose aims are contrary to the good of mankind. We should not exclude them from the U.N. Rather, we want them in the world organization, subject to the U.N.'s controls and restrictions on armaments and aggression. We want them to be regulated by the established rule of law.

Exclusion of "bad" nations from the U.N. and from the rule of law makes no more sense than the exclusion of a criminal from the rule of domestic law. We regulate the criminal and put him in prison if necessary. We do not put him out of the community. We want him where our law-enforcing agency can reach him.

In the same way, universal membership brings all nations under the necessary laws regarding disarmament and aggression. Universal disarmament is impracticable without universal membership.

As long as U.N. membership remains an honor with no enforceable obligations, United States opposition to admitting Communist China to the U.N. has a sound basis. Red China clearly does not live up to the Charter's requirements for membership, and indeed is still at war with the U.N. in Korea.

However, we certainly could not disarm while Red China (or any other communist nation) remains free to build up its armaments. This

is why the communist nations must be members of the strengthened
U.N. Not because we like them or trust them. But Communist China
outside a strengthened U.N. would be like a gangster living across
the state line where our law couldn't reach him. U.N. laws could not
be enforced in any nation which remained outside the strengthened
U.N.

Moreover, withdrawal from the United Nations cannot be permitted and membership must be permanent. Of course, each nation would
decide for itself whether to accept or reject the revised U.N. Charter.
But once the nations have voluntarily joined the revised U.N., secession from it can no more be tolerated than it was when the Southern
states tried to leave the United States in 1861. The withdrawal of one
or more nations from the rule of law of the United Nations would
signal return to international anarchy. If unchallenged, a seceding
nation could upset the whole system of enforced disarmament. Such
a limitation on withdrawal may be hard for some nations to accept.
Nevertheless, it is the only practical basis upon which a strengthened
United Nations can function.

No nation will be physically forced to accept a revised U.N. in the
first place. The initial choice will be a voluntary one, compelled only
by the power of reason and common sense and the pressure of world
opinion. Once nations choose the protection of law and order they
are, in effect, signing a long-term contract. No one can compel them
to sign, but once they choose they cannot be allowed to break the
contract.

Universal membership, without right of secession, is the basic requirement for a strengthened U.N. It is the price that must be paid to
achieve peace and security, to substitute law for anarchy. Is there
any other way to assure enforceable disarmament and a rule of law?

LEGISLATURE.   The first step in establishing world law is the enactment of rules of conduct to control armaments, prevent aggression,
and allow peaceful settlement of controversies.

This requires a legislative body, presumably the General Assembly,
with revised representation. To it will be given the specific authority
to enact, by a suitable majority, legislation in the limited field of armaments and aggression.

The problem of representation is difficult. The present basis—one
nation, one vote—is inequitable and will become less and less acceptable to the larger nations. Unless a more suitable basis of repre-

sentation is part of the package, agreement on increased power for the U.N. is not likely. Several proposals for voting arrangements are discussed in the following chapter under the heading of "Representation."

The method of selection of representatives to the General Assembly must be left to the various nations. The ultimate and desirable objective most certainly is direct election by the people. But many nations are not willing to do this now, and the nuclear threat will not allow the reorganization of the U.N. to wait for democratic government in all nations.

We Americans champion the selection of public officers by direct election. We recall, however, that until fairly recently United States senators were selected by state governments, not popular election. Even now our delegates to the U.N. and other international bodies are appointed by the President. Allowing the nations to determine their own interim method of selecting delegates to a revised General Assembly avoids a sharp break with precedent and permits gradual progress toward popular election.

While a legislative body is necessary for a continuing rule of law, adaptable to changing conditions, it is probable that the initial rules concerning disarmament and aggression will be established by negotiation. They may be drafted by the Disarmament Commission and made a part of the Charter of the United Nations by the process of Charter amendment, under either Article 108 or 109. This approach is likely, as most nations will insist on examining detailed rules and regulations before they agree to the principles of world law and universal disarmament.

Even if this process is followed, it is still essential in the near future to give the General Assembly power to enact laws in the limited field of armaments and aggression. There are several reasons why a legislative body is needed:

1. To change the rules and regulations on armaments, as required by changing conditions. No group of men is wise enough to write perfect rules for all time. New weapons and new problems will often require changes in the armament-control laws. These changes should be made by a representative legislature, not by administrative edict.

2. To set up rules and policies for inspection and law enforcement.

3. To provide how the U.N.'s inspection and military forces are to be raised, paid, organized, and controlled.

4. To make appropriations and to raise the revenue required for the operation of the U.N.

5. To serve as a watchdog to ensure proper administration of the executive branch and its law-enforcement agencies.

In addition, the General Assembly should continue its present function of giving advisory opinions and recommendations on problems of the Economic and Social Council, the Trusteeship Council, and other cooperative U.N. programs. It should continue to provide a forum for discussion of world problems, even though it could not enact laws on subjects other than armaments and aggression.

EXECUTIVE.   The executive branch of a strengthened United Nations will have two functions:

1. The duties now performed by the Secretariat. These include the administration of the present activities of the U.N., its councils, commissions, and specialized agencies, together with studies, research, and special assignments.

2. The added duties related to control of armaments and prevention of aggression. These will include the administration of the inspection and military forces which are required to enforce world law and maintain a secure peace.

It would seem sensible and economical to combine these functions in an executive branch, just as they are combined in national governments. On the other hand, there may be reluctance to disturb the present Secretariat. Certainly there will be opposition to placing the control of inspection, police, and armed forces under a single individual, whether he is the Secretary-General or any other individual selected by the General Assembly.

It is probable, therefore, that a new executive body must be established with the responsibility of administering and enforcing the world laws established by a revised Charter or enacted by the U.N. legislature. It should be a civilian authority, small enough to act promptly, but with adequate controls to prevent misuse of its power.

Such an executive board can be created either by reorganization of the Security Council or by establishment of a new enforcement commission selected by the General Assembly.

In any event the executive body charged with enforcement should be selected by the General Assembly, report to it, and be subject to its review and authority. There must be no veto. Its members should be selected as individuals, not as representatives of nations. No more than one member should come from any given nation. Perhaps a majority should come from the small nations, which seem to have a greater appreciation of the need for a stronger U.N. Five to seven members would appear adequate for the executive board. It should operate by majority decision as does the Swiss executive board.

The new units needed for the executive branch, in addition to the Secretariat, are outlined below:

1. Inspection Service. The function of the inspection service would initially be to observe the various stages of disarmament and detect the failure of any nation to carry out its disarmament commitments. Thereafter, the inspection service would be responsible for detecting violations of the world law with respect to armaments and armed forces. Its functions would be those normally handled by a police officer; namely, the detection, apprehension, and arrest of alleged violators of world law.

The inspection service would consist of civilians of varied qualifications. The inspection process will be a complicated one (see Chapter 16). The inspection service must have the right to observe and inspect within every nation, to obtain information, and to investigate opportunities for violations. The granting of such authority to a world organization is another major but necessary departure from tradition.

2. Military Forces. The United Nations military forces would be established as a continuing deterrent to aggression. They would also support action of the inspectors, resist aggression should it occur, patrol borders, and restore order in case of armed conflict between nations.

Fairly powerful forces are necessary to serve as a continuing deterrent against aggression, or to resist aggression should it occur. Major aggression is unlikely in a disarmed world. If any nation tries to rearm secretly, the U.N. inspectors should be able to detect and stop the move before any substantial armaments have been built up. However, we should always prepare for the worst, and this means the U.N. needs substantial armed forces.

For this reason the U.N. needs military forces provided with the most modern equipment. These forces should possess supersonic bombers, long-range missiles, and nuclear warheads. Such weapons must be lodged with the law-enforcing agency where they will deter any sudden atomic "blitz" with hidden missiles. They are necessary to "put together justice and force and so insure that what is just shall be strong."

The size and equipment of this military force must be carefully selected. It must provide a military power stronger than that which can be mustered against it by nations which might attempt armed aggression.

A highly trained and mobile organization, its contingents should be placed at strategic points throughout the world. The size and the cost of maintaining such a security force will be small compared to the burden of the world's present military machine. Grenville Clark[1] has suggested that once disarmament is accomplished, such a force need not exceed 300,000 to 700,000 men.

COURTS.   A judicial branch is also required for the strengthened United Nations. Its function is the interpretation of world law, conduct of trials of individuals indicted for violations of the law, and the peaceful resolution of disputes between nations. Courts determine guilt and fix sentences within the limits prescribed by law. They back up the power to make and enforce law. They punish the guilty but protect the innocent through impartial court procedures.

There are four kinds of legal matters which need to be handled by U.N. courts:

    1. The interpretation of laws passed by the U.N. legislature and the review of these laws to determine their constitutionality. The court should have power to declare void any law which violates the United Nations Charter or goes beyond the powers delegated to the U.N. This is the function of a supreme court.

    2. The conduct of trials of persons charged with violating the law with respect to armaments or aggression. If the accused violator is found guilty, the court should impose appropriate sentence. This is the function of a criminal court.

    3. The conduct of trials to determine an equitable settlement of international disputes arising from treaties or contracts freely entered into between nations. The jurisdiction of the world court in such cases should be compulsory and binding. This is the function of a civil court.

[1] Grenville Clark, *A Plan for Peace* (New York, Harper & Brothers, 1950).

4. The conduct of hearings on other international disputes not the result of a contract or treaty. These cases often involve questions on which there is no clear "right" or "wrong." Such cases will require a special tribunal with powers of conciliation, arbitration, and recommendation. Such a tribunal will deal only with cases referred to it and hence should have voluntary jurisdiction.

A new court (or courts) of compulsory jurisdiction is required to deal with the first three functions, while the present International Court of Justice may be continued to deal with the fourth category.

REVENUE.   A strengthened United Nations must be capable of supporting its functions, including the enactment, enforcement, and interpretation of law. It must, therefore, have a dependable source of revenue. This means the U.N. must have a limited power to levy and collect taxes.

It is dangerous for the U.N. to remain dependent upon voluntary contributions from its members. These are subject to change on short notice, making it difficult to budget revenues and plan activities. Moreover, the withholding of funds by a single major nation can hamper the United Nations and interfere with the enforcement of the armament control laws.

The United Nations must, therefore, have direct and dependable sources of revenue sufficient for its limited functions.

The cost of maintaining an enforcement agency, including U.N. inspection, police, and armed forces, will of course depend upon the size of such forces. The cost of a 500,000-man force has been estimated at $5,000,000,000 per year. Add $1,000,000,000 for other U.N. functions, and a strengthened United Nations might need a budget of some $6,000,000,000 per year. This total budget is less than 20 per cent of the United States' present expenditures for its armed forces.

Numerous suggestions have been made as to sources of revenue, including:

1. Assignment of national quotas. The national governments would then collect the required amount of taxes for the account of the U.N. The type of tax could be specifically designated by the U.N., or each nation could be allowed to decide how to raise its U.N. taxes.

2. A tax upon international trade.

3. Royalties from mineral or other resources lying under international waters.

4. Royalties from resources in Antarctica (the continent around the South Pole). Since no nation has yet colonized Antarctica, it could properly be administered by the U.N. The U.N. could then license various companies or nations to develop its resources.

5. A tax on nuclear materials used for "atoms for peace" and licensed under the U.N.

Perhaps a better method than any of these suggestions can be found, or a combination of methods may be used. The important requirement is that revenue be dependable and be considered a tax, not a gift.

The task of collecting U.N. taxes will be made easier by the great reduction in national military budgets which a strengthened U.N. will bring. After enforced disarmament is established, every dollar paid to the revised U.N. will be balanced by a saving of five or ten or twenty dollars to the nation and its taxpayers.

For example, the United States now contributes about one-third of the U.N. budget. Our share of the estimated $6,000,000,000 U.N. budget would thus be $2,000,000,000 per year. But under a strengthened U.N., all or nearly all of our present $38,000,000,000 annual budget for current military costs would be eliminated. Thus a strengthened U.N. would mean a net saving to our government—and to the taxpayers, if we insist on proportionate tax reduction—of $36,000,000,000. This would be a net saving of $18 for every dollar we put into the revised U.N.!

But for the sake of argument, assume that our estimate of the U.N. budget is too conservative. Let us assume that a strengthened U.N. will cost three times as much as we have estimated—a total U.N. budget of $18,000,000,000. And to be even more pessimistic, let us assume that the United States will pay half, rather than one-third of all U.N. taxes. We would then be paying $9,000,000,000 per year for a secure peace. But we would still be able to reduce our national budget—and our taxes—by almost $38,000,000,000 (our current military expenditures). Any businessman would jump at the chance to save four dollars by investing one dollar. Here our saving is not only in dollars; our investment in a strengthened U.N. will also save our homes, our children, and our freedoms from the devastation of war.

However, taxes tend to go up instead of down, and we rightly fear that the power to tax may be used to destroy. Therefore, we should insist on one other change in the U.N. Charter: a ceiling on U.N. taxes. The Charter should clearly require that the total U.N. taxes collected from any nation and its citizens in any year cannot exceed a fixed percentage of that nation's gross national product (the value of all goods and services produced by that nation and its citizens) in that year. Perhaps annual national income, rather than gross national product, could be used as the base figure. In either case, the percentage should be low—perhaps 2 per cent or 3 per cent. A reasonable ceiling on its taxing power will not hamper the U.N. But it will assure that this taxing power cannot be seriously abused. We want this assurance.

SAFEGUARDS.   One of the most vital questions regarding the strengthening of the United Nations is that of safeguards. How do we provide proper precautions, checks, and balances? How can we make the U.N. as tyranny-proof as possible? This is a subject that must have exhaustive study and research by the framers of a revised Charter. What safeguards are needed?

For one thing, we wish to be sure that the strengthened United Nations will not interfere with domestic affairs beyond that minimum level required to enforce U.N. laws against development, manufacture, possession, and use of armaments. Therefore, we want safeguards which will prevent the United Nations from interfering in any way with any nation's economic system, form of government, culture, religion, or traditions.

Safeguards are also required to assure that the control of the United Nations cannot be usurped by a minority group of nations who might seek to use it as a tool of tyranny.

In addition, we need safeguards to protect the individual against abuse by the United Nations in the enforcement of law.

Those who have studied the subject have suggested many safeguards, including the following:

Federal Form. A strengthened United Nations should obtain its authority by utilizing the principle of federation. It would be a world organization but national governments would not be eliminated. They would continue as they are except that the responsibility for maintaining a secure peace would be transferred to the United Nations. This principle of federation has been successfully used in the United States, Switzerland, Australia, and other nations.

Limited Powers. The powers delegated to the United Nations should be "minimal" and strictly limited. No powers are proposed except those needed for the control of armaments and the prevention of aggression. These limited powers for the U.N. should be clearly defined in the Charter so that any attempt by the legislature or executive to enlarge them may be quickly nullified by the U.N. courts.

Delegated Powers. The strengthened United Nations should have only those powers delegated to it by the revised Charter. All other powers should be specifically reserved to the nations or their people. The U.N. Charter should contain neither a "general welfare" clause nor an "international commerce" clause. By omitting such clauses we can eliminate the principal sources for expansion of the U.N.'s powers by interpretation.

Proper Representation. The establishment of just and equitable representation is highly important. It must simultaneously assure both large and small nations, both rich and poor nations, that control of the organization cannot be seized by either group. The important question of representation is further discussed in Chapter 16.

Amendment Procedure. An amendment procedure should be provided to allow changes in the U.N. Charter in the event a heavily preponderant majority favors an amendment. The procedure, however, should be sufficiently difficult that Charter changes cannot be made without overwhelming support of the peoples of the world.

Diversification. Precautions should be taken to assign responsible positions in the executive and judicial bodies among peoples of the various nationalities. Careful attention to this can greatly minimize the possibility of arbitrary action favoring any specific nation. Problems of personnel selection and organization are discussed in Chapter 16.

Bill of Limitations. A revised U.N. Charter should provide a Bill of Limitations protecting individuals against arbitrary or unjust action by the United Nations; prohibiting interference by the United

Nations with rights and liberties guaranteed to persons by their own national and state institutions, and protecting the rights of any person who may be tried by U.N. Courts or accused of violating U.N. laws.

"WORLD GOVERNMENT"? The United Nations, strengthened as herein proposed, would take on the functions of government in a strictly limited field. It would enact, enforce, and interpret world law to the extent needed to control armaments and aggression. The United Nations would, therefore, become a world government, with limited powers.

There is no alternative. Government is required to establish world law, and world law is essential for a just and durable peace.

As *Time* magazine put it (April 12, 1954):

The H-bomb's existence requires the U.S. to put much more strongly the case for international control of atomic weapons. Such control might impair unlimited national sovereignty as the world now knows it. It might imply a measure of world government. But the U.S. need not flinch at this prospect. Its own political history encourages the chance of a constitutional solution of a force so big that it calls for supranational control.

Hence, we must have a form of world government. As it would use the principle of federation, in order to protect present national governments, and as its powers would be strictly limited, the strengthened U.N. would technically be classed as a "limited world federal government."

The proposed powers and the functions of a strengthened U.N. bear no resemblance to those of a national government such as the United States with its extensive powers and functions. The United Nations' sphere of authority would include only the enforcement of peace to prevent nations from using nuclear weapons to blast themselves off the face of the earth. This revised U.N. would have far fewer powers than the United States Government had even at its beginning in 1787.

Nevertheless, all proposals for the delegation of authority and power to a supranational organization—the United Nations—meet with violent and vociferous opposition from extremists of both right and left. Without distinction, opponents pin the label of "superstate" to any type of government on a world level. This designation is accompanied by charges that the adoption of the proposals would abolish the United States, destroy our Constitution, haul down the American flag, sell the United States down the river, put a Russian policeman on every corner, make us completely subordinate to the peoples of India and Red China, or other equally vivid and equally inaccurate contentions.

Such opposition often originates with sincere Americans who fear the encroachment of the United Nations on freedoms, liberties, and economy of the United States. Their love of country and respect for our Constitution supports their objections to any strengthening of the United Nations.

Unfortunately, such sincere opposition often engenders irresponsible outbursts from other individuals or groups having violent leanings toward an extreme variety of nationalism. Such irresponsible outbursts are usually made by highly emotional extremists. They tend to lump together all proposals for world government or a strengthened U.N. In fact, many of the attackers even go after the United Nations in its present form and propose: "Get the U.N. out of the United States and the United States out of the U.N."

The author is just as opposed to a world "superstate" as is anyone else. Nothing of the kind is proposed here. Rather, these discussions are concerned with finding a means of protecting our government, our freedoms, and our way of life from the hazards presented by nuclear weapons and communism, which are now at large in a world of anarchy.

It is very important to distinguish clearly between a "strengthened United Nations" to control armaments and prevent aggression and a "superstate" which would subordinate or replace our United States Government.

Unless we make this distinction there will be great confusion surrounding the simple question of delegating adequate power to the United Nations so it can maintain a secure peace with freedom.

ITEM SIX—STRENGTHEN THE UNITED NATIONS.   Revise the Charter of the United Nations. Give the U.N. the powers and structure required to administer and enforce a rule of law, to control armaments, and to prevent war. Erect the necessary safeguards, checks, and balances to protect the freedoms and rights of nations and individuals.

Chapter 16

PROBLEMS

"The difficult we do immediately, the impossible takes a little longer." This slogan ably expresses the American attitude toward problems in the scientific, engineering and industrial fields. Concentration of talent and effort overcomes seemingly insurmountable barriers.

DIFFICULT PROBLEMS can be viewed in one of two ways: as an excuse to block further effort or as a challenge to surmount the intervening hurdles.

Many problems and difficulties are involved in revising the United Nations to establish a rule of law which will make universal, enforceable disarmament possible. They are so substantial that faint hearts or tradition-bound minds can view them as valid reasons for accepting world anarchy and world war as inevitable.

Such a timid approach completely ignores the realities of our explosive age. These problems must be faced and solved. Our determination to win must be as great as it was during the trying war years of 1941 through 1945.

Secretary of State Dulles has called for such a bold and determined approach, saying:

The founders of our nation showed a political wisdom which has been rarely if ever matched. Surely, however, their efforts did not exhaust the political genius of the American people. They invented and bequeathed to us an ordered society of spiritual and intellectual freedom. Such a society ought to be able to produce the new ideas needed to meet changing conditions. This is for us to demonstrate. Now when new peril threatens, it behooves us to prove our worth. May we not, in our generation, emulate what our forefathers did in their generation, and find the way to develop international order to shield national life? That is the challenge of our time. Let us dedicate ourselves to meet it.

This chapter considers major problems in strengthening the United Nations, and examines the touchy subject of "sovereignty."

REPRESENTATION.   There is nothing fair about the present system of "one nation, one vote," in the General Assembly.

What equity is there in a single vote for the United States with 160,000,000 literate citizens and a highly developed economy? Nicaragua also has one vote for only 1,200,000 people with much lower standards of literacy and a primitive economy! France has already objected to one vote for its 50,000,000 citizens when the Arab nations around the Mediterranean Sea have seven votes for a comparable population. And we could certainly question the fairness of nine votes for the U.S.S.R. and its tightly controlled satellites while the United States has only one vote.

As the Assembly is given authority to enact laws regarding armaments and aggression which will be enforced upon all nations and peoples, the voting system must be made more equitable. Unless a change is made in the method of representation, the larger nations are not likely to accept a revised Charter.

So long as the U.N. has no real power or authority, the question of representation is not critical. There is little concern about fair representation when we have a veto in the Security Council and have freedom of action on every matter, collective security or otherwise. But once we give the U.N. the task of maintaining a secure peace, the voting system needs to be changed. It should be equitable and guard against tyranny. The U.N. must be able to give effect to the deep desires of the peoples of the world for peace and security.

One suggestion is representation on the basis of population, as in the House of Representatives of our Congress. This is simple and easy to administer, except for absence of accurate census data in many countries.

The weakness of such voting is that numbers control without regard to state of education and development. China, India, Indonesia, and Pakistan together would have about 40 per cent of the votes.

Representation based solely on population will not be acceptable to nations with high levels of education and economic development, including the United States. Probably the U.S.S.R. would oppose it, uncertain of her ability to control China permanently and to influence India, Indonesia, and Pakistan.

Therefore, some compromise must be found between the present system—one nation, one vote—and the democratic theory of representation proportional to population. The problem of developing an equitable basis of representation is similar to that which confronted the framers of our Constitution in 1787. They solved the problem by developing our familiar bicameral legislature.

Among the various suggestions for General Assembly representation are these:

1. Representation based upon population but with a ceiling of thirty votes per nation, which would give the U.S.A., U.S.S.R., China, and India thirty votes each. This proposal purports to give a safe balance of free-world votes against the communist bloc.[1]

2. Representation on a weighted basis, using factors indicative of economic development and education in addition to population. For example, each nation's number of delegates might be based one-third upon its population, one-third upon its gross national product (or upon taxes paid to the U.N.), and one-third upon its number of citizens who had completed a high-school education or its equivalent.

3. A bicameral legislative body with representation by population in one house and one vote for each nation—or combination of small nations—in the other.

4. A bicameral legislative body with representation by population in one house and representation based on economic and education factors in the other.

These and other methods require thorough study and extensive negotiation to develop an arrangement acceptable to the nations of the world. The adopted basis of representation will no doubt be a compromise. After a compromise is reached we have the right of review and rejection when we decide whether to ratify the revised U.N. Charter (see Chapter 21). This gives us protection against an unfair voting system. Before we accept any system we must assure ourselves that it provides adequate protection against tyranny and against control or obstruction by any group of nations with aggressive intent.

[1] Grenville Clark, *A Plan for Peace.*

INSPECTION.   An inspection system will be required to assure compliance with the disarmament schedule and to detect violations of the laws prohibiting development, manufacture, possession, and use of armaments. There are two phases of inspection. The first occurs during the period of disarmament. The second is the permanent phase, after disarmament has been achieved. There are certain differences in the conditions of the two phases which must be reflected in the inspection system.

During the initial period when national armaments are being reduced, the principal concern will be that all nations are meeting their commitments to disarm. The United States and its associates in NATO will want to make certain that the Soviet Union and her satellites are disarming. At the same time, the Communists will wish to make certain that the free world is carrying out its commitments. Inspection will therefore be concerned primarily with such items as the demobilization of military forces, the destruction of military equipment, the location and destruction or conversion of munitions, including nuclear stockpiles, and the conversion of munitions plants to peaceful uses.

The operation of an inspection system will commence only after agreement on a schedule for disarmament, which will probably be established by negotiation and later included in a revised U.N. Charter. Hence, inspection in the initial stages will be concerned with the execution of an agreed program. When such a program begins, a system of inspection aimed at "early warning" may already be operating. It may provide certain personnel, facilities, information, and experience which can be helpful to the U.N. inspection force.

The inspection program in the initial period will certainly require these minimums:

1. A schedule and program for disarmament which will have been previously agreed upon by the nations of the world.

2. Establishment of a permanent corps of United Nations inspectors.

3. Access for these inspectors to all facilities and establishments, and freedom of passage through all curtains, whether of "iron," "bamboo," or national prejudice. They must have the right to inspect any factory or base at any time, without advance notice.

4. Attachment to the U.N. inspection teams of observers from the great powers to give assurance their opponents are carrying out disarmament commitments.

5. A system of regular reports on the progress of disarmament to the United Nations and to the general public.

After disarmament has been accomplished and national armaments are reduced to the militia level, the process of inspection becomes somewhat different. Its aim will then be the detection of unauthorized buildup of military forces and weapons. It must be able to detect development, testing, production, or possession of prohibited weapons and munitions, and any other preparations for aggression. It will be concerned particularly with thermonuclear warheads, other weapons of mass destruction, and delivery systems such as long-range missiles.

The permanent inspection process will consist of more than teams of inspectors touring the nations, although these will be required. Such physical observation can be supplemented by many other sources of information, including:

1. Accounts of each nation's governmental expenditures.

2. Production and use of steel and other basic materials.

3. Production and processing of nuclear materials and operation of nuclear reactors.

4. Imports and exports of strategic materials.

5. Aerial reconnaissance.

But basic to the inspection process must be the right of U.N. inspectors to observe and inspect within every nation to obtain information and investigate opportunities for violation. Disarmament will not be safe unless we grant such authority.

The U.N. inspectors would probably be empowered both to inspect and to apprehend violators. If a violation is detected, the responsible individuals must be quickly arrested and brought to trial before U.N. courts. These individuals might be plant managers, military officers, or high officials of national governments. If a large-scale violation were detected, a large number of U.N. inspectors, or perhaps even the U.N. military forces, would be needed to take charge, disarm the violators, and prevent a further buildup of unauthorized weapons or armies.

If we want safe disarmament, we cannot separate inspection from enforcement, including the power to arrest, try, and punish individual violators. Neither inspection nor enforcement will be effective without the other.

SCIENTIFIC PROBLEMS.   Scientists and military experts are generally agreed that recent scientific developments make inspection more difficult for the reasons outlined below:

1. Detection of completed nuclear weapons is extremely difficult. There are no devices available which can easily detect the presence of hidden atomic or thermonuclear warheads. Inspectors would have no simple means of ferreting out such hidden weapons.

2. Atomic reactors used for power generation can also be used to produce materials for weapons. With widespread use of such reactors, many nations could produce nuclear warheads.

3. Sufficient quantities of nuclear materials to create atomic explosions could be smuggled into cities of a potential victim. These materials could be secretly assembled and hidden; the aggressor could then trigger them at any time.

4. Within five to ten years, intercontinental ballistic missiles will be developed which can be launched from underground facilities. These also will be difficult to detect.

Acceptance of these facts leads many to conclude that it is too late to disarm. They contend that a nation like the U.S.S.R. could accept a disarmament agreement, pretend to act in good faith but hide away enough power to destroy the rest of the world.

This school of thought further contends that because inspection is not certain, disarmament cannot be risked and we must continue indefinitely to depend upon armaments for security.

This reasoning holds back progress toward universal enforceable disarmament. Unfortunately, it has been accepted by many in positions of authority.

While we must admit the truth of the scientific facts stated above, we should challenge the validity of the conclusions drawn from them.

The fact that such conclusions can be drawn is a striking revelation of the misunderstanding surrounding the whole subject of disarmament, inspection, and enforcement under world law. Examination of the scientific facts in the context of universal enforceable disarmament leads to different conclusions.

HIDDEN WARHEADS.   It is true that detection of hidden nuclear war-heads and materials is difficult. It is also true that reactors constructed for peaceful purposes can produce nuclear materials for weapons, and that these weapons can be hidden.

Nevertheless, an alert and competent inspection force can do a great deal to reduce the quantities of hidden nuclear weapons. Let us examine some of the factors which assist them:

1. Disarmament agreements will call for the conversion or de-struction of existing nuclear weapons. The inspectors' problem will be concerned only with that portion of existing nuclear weapons which are not voluntarily revealed.

2. Reasonably accurate estimates can be made of the quantity of nuclear weapons and nuclear material for which any nation must account. The quantity of nuclear materials produced by given facil-ities can be computed. Competent engineers and scientists, with knowledge of the facilities used by a nation, can arrive at reasonable estimates. Their analysis can be verified by information made avail-able by other nations' present intelligence activities.

3. Once the process of disarmament is started, inspectors can de-termine the destination and disposition of all nuclear materials which are produced thereafter. Thus, further use of such materials for weapons can be detected and controlled.

4. Most nuclear weapons involve mechanism which must be main-tained to be kept in workable condition. If hidden and forgotten they will deteriorate and lose their usefulness. If serviced and main-tained their location becomes easier to detect.

5. When world law is established and nations no longer depend upon armaments for security, secrecy regarding weapons will be-come more difficult. U.N. inspectors will find it easier to obtain in-formation on the whereabouts of hidden weapons. Law enforce-ment on individuals will encourage reporting of suspected violations of world arms-control laws. With the overwhelming majority of the people of the world, including most Russians, wishing peace, alert inspectors will pick up gossip, rumor, and information which will help in the detection of hidden weapons.

6. It is not impossible that devices can be developed to aid detec-tion of hidden weapons. Certainly we should instruct our scientific experts to seek to develop satisfactory means of detection.

By the above means, the U.N. may find hidden nuclear weapons over a period of years and thus remove their potential threat.

But disarmament can be enforced even if we are never able to detect these hidden weapons. The hazard of hidden nuclear weapons has been greatly overrated. Even substantial quantities of them are not a threat, unless a would-be aggressor has the means to deliver them and the willingness to use them. The enforcement system provided by a strengthened United Nations can eliminate and control the means of delivery. But—of greater importance—it can make it unprofitable for a potential aggressor to consider use of nuclear weapons.

THE KEY IS ENFORCEMENT.   Enforcement, not inspection, is the real answer to the problem posed by hidden weapons. The enforcement system, as previously outlined, will include not only inspection forces but also military forces.

Let us see what a potential aggressor would face if he wished to attack another country, after the establishment of universal enforceable disarmament.

Perhaps he has secreted a number of ICBM launching platforms and has available a quantity of missiles with nuclear warheads. Perhaps he has hidden thermonuclear bombs or materials. However, he does not have conventional military forces—ships, planes, guns, and men. Large conventional forces cannot be hidden. Any attempt to build such forces would be detected by the inspection system and stopped by arrest and trial of the responsible individuals.

The United Nations military organization stands ready to resist aggression. Its strong units are scattered over the world (including perhaps a city of the would-be aggressor) and are equipped with modern weapons and equipment. It is prepared to move instantly. If aggression is launched, the U.N. forces will quickly move on the aggressor nation and arrest its rulers.

For an aggressor to succeed, he would first have to knock out the U.N. military forces. And he would have to do a complete job of it.

Unless he eliminated the ability of the U.N. military forces to resist and retaliate, the aggressor would have no chance to follow up his nuclear attack and consolidate his gains. Remember, he has only the limited conventional weapons allowed for internal security plus those he might have been able to secrete.

Only after he had knocked out the U.N. forces would he be able to build up the conventional forces needed to conquer the world. But, as previously stated, the U.N. military force must be of sufficient size and power to exceed the strength of any potential aggressor.

The chance of successful aggression is very remote once universal enforceable disarmament is achieved, and a strong U.N. military force is established.

MEANS OF DELIVERY.   The U.N. enforcement system also would prevent a potential aggressor from accumulating sufficient means of delivery for nuclear warheads.

The problem of controlling means of delivery is less difficult than preventing the hiding of nuclear warheads.

Universal enforceable disarmament would strip all nations of their military equipment for delivery of nuclear weapons. The inspection system which follows would detect any illegal attempts to develop or manufacture military planes, missiles, ships, submarines, or other means of delivery.

It would be a tremendous undertaking to manufacture sufficient planes or missiles for a major attack. The factories and bases required are so extensive as to be readily detected by the inspection system.

Some fear that underground ICBM launching platforms, constructed before disarmament, might be concealed. But a launching installation for an ICBM is of substantial size[2] and would be difficult to conceal. Let us examine some of the factors that would assist inspectors in finding them:

1. Many launching sites would be found and destroyed at the very beginning of disarmament. Their location may be voluntarily revealed or may already be known by the intelligence services of the other nations. Thus the task of the inspectors would be reduced.

2. Aerial reconnaissance would likely detect the presence of such an installation, which would be a major construction project. Aerial photography has amazing ability to reveal man-made changes to the earth, including attempted camouflage.

3. Secrecy regarding these installations would be difficult to maintain once world law is established. U.N. inspectors would find it easier to obtain information on previous construction projects

[2] Hanson W. Baldwin, "I.C.B.M.," *Collier's,* March 16, 1956.

which may have been launching installations, camouflaged as other structures.

4. Once the process of disarmament is begun, the U.N. inspection force could detect and stop any future construction of such installations.

Other potential means of delivery available to a would-be aggressor are commercial planes and ships which could be outfitted to deliver bombs or rockets with nuclear warheads.

Inspection of airports and seaports and of planes and ships can effectively limit the availability of these means of delivery. Remembering that a successful attack would require knocking out the entire military establishment of the U.N., the aggressor would accomplish little with only a few planes or a few ships. He would need a major fleet or armada to accomplish his aims. Preparation and mobilization on this scale would be easily detected.

Another means of delivery available to a would-be aggressor is smuggling. Undoubtedly it is possible to smuggle sufficient nuclear material for an explosion that would destroy a major city. The physical dimensions of the "critical mass" for atomic fission are sufficiently small to permit this.

Theoretically, any nation would possess the ability to smuggle and assemble nuclear bombs. But again, let's look at the problem from the viewpoint of the potential aggressor after the establishment of universal enforceable disarmament.

What would he gain by blowing up New York City, Washington, Pittsburgh, and Chicago with smuggled weapons if he could not follow up his attack? Without the conventional military forces to do this, he would first have to knock out the U.N. military establishment, not just a few cities of his proposed victim. Unless he could do this, the U.N. forces would crush him before he could begin to build his own conventional forces. He would have to smuggle and assemble hidden nuclear weapons in all major U.N. military bases, ships, and installations.

This would be impossible unless the U.N. forces were completely stupid. It is inconceivable that such widespread activity could be carried on without detection. Such an operation would require cooperation of many thousands of local traitors and a complete breakdown of security at U.N. military installations. Subversive groups of the size required could be infiltrated and exposed by U.N. agents, just as FBI agents successfully infiltrated the communist party in the United States.

Here again, enforcement deprives the would-be aggressor of any reasonable chance to use his secreted weapons successfully. He is not likely to use them if the only result will be his own defeat and punishment.

THE HAZARDS.   No one can deny that there are hazards involved in an inspection system. We must minimize these hazards and then accept them as lesser calculated risks than the present hazards of anarchy.

The fears of the experts are justified if we are talking about a disarmament plan which relies on inspection alone. We should truly be alarmed by any program which allows nations to keep substantial conventional armaments.

We should also firmly reject any system which does not give the United Nations the military establishment required to deter and prevent aggression. Equally disastrous would be any system which does not provide law enforcement on individuals.

Inspection by itself can neither prevent attack nor be certain of giving adequate early warning. The scientific facts listed above are manageable if, and only if, we add enforcement to inspection.

This requires U.N. military forces, world law enforceable upon individuals, and total universal disarmament down to internal police levels. All of these are proposed in Chapters 12 through 15.

Our scientific experts have accomplished one thing—they have proved the unworkability of any disarmament plan short of that proposed herein. Universal enforceable disarmament, under the safeguards of world law and administered by a strengthened United Nations, provides the only safe road to peace.

World law effectively enforced makes concealed weapons worthless and meaningless. No plan can be devised to prevent an aggressor from hiding some weapons, but the proposed plan would make it self-defeating for him to try to use them. If the aggressor can gain nothing from use of smuggled H-bombs or hidden missiles, the danger from them is reduced to the lowest possible level.

PERSONNEL PROBLEMS.   How should the personnel of a strengthened United Nations be selected and assigned? Most questions along this line are concerned with the inspection and military forces which would be required by the executive branch.

There are obvious problems involved in selecting and assigning these U.N. forces, coming as they must from many nations with many languages. But none of these problems is insurmountable. Actually, they will be easier to solve than such questions as representation in the legislature, because the solution is administrative rather than political.

All United Nations staff and armed forces should be made up of individuals rather than of national contingents. Of course, the individuals must come from various nations and will naturally have loyalty to them. Many checks and balances can be built into both the civilian and the military forces to reduce the chance of abuse of position by anyone favoring one nation:

1. Personnel should be recruited to meet strict qualifications. The recruiting must be done directly by the U.N. rather than by national governments. Definite limitations should be placed on the number to be accepted from any given nation. Such limitations can assure adequate mixture and balance of nationalities and geographic origins. Perhaps the majority of U.N. personnel should come from smaller nations.

2. Positions in every unit, department, or station should be carefully distributed among nationals of many countries.

3. Commanders and administrators in responsible positions, and even in subordinate ones, should be carefully assorted as to nationality. Never should an individual report to a fellow countryman. A Dane should report to a Frenchman who in turn reports to a Filipino, and so on. (Men of different nationalities can work well together in armies and police forces. The French Foreign Legion is an example. In the Korean War, large numbers of Koreans were assigned to U.S. Army units; Koreans and Americans lived, ate, slept, and fought side by side. This experiment was a success. The U.N. Secretariat and the international staff at NATO headquarters also show that men of many different nationalities can work as a unit.)

4. Courts, councils, boards, and commissions which make judicial or policy decisions and recommendations should always be made up of individuals from several nations.

5. Inspectors and military force units should be transferred from station to station at periodic intervals to diminish local preference or prejudice.

Such precautions as these can provide reasonable checks and balances. Over a period of time, however, the best safeguard should be the development of an esprit de corps with an international outlook. Significant progress along this line is already evident in parts of the U.N. Secretariat. Here, individuals from many nations are working together cooperatively with an increasing realization that the solution of the world's problems will benefit every nation.

Attractive rates of pay will hasten the development of a competent organization. This will not be difficult; modest compensation by United States standards will attract high-grade people from most parts of the world.

The language barrier is not a serious problem. The United Nations now uses five official languages: English, French, Chinese, Spanish, and Russian. U.N. armed forces would undoubtedly adopt a single language.

The armed forces of the United States have proved that a basic speaking knowledge of a foreign language can be taught in a few weeks of intensive training. Such training in a standard language would probably be part of the basic training for U.N. recruits.

WHAT IS AGGRESSION?   Another difficult problem is the defining of the term "aggression," which is to be resisted by a strengthened U.N. Its usual meaning is a military attack of the type launched by North Korea in June, 1950. There should be no difficulty in reaching agreement that such military action is clearly "aggression." Differences of opinion will arise, however, regarding the inclusion of other actions in the definition. A U.N. commission has been wrestling with this problem for several years.

What of an internal revolution aimed at overthrowing an existing national government? Is the U.N. to be concerned with such revolts or is it to take a hands-off position? Certainly it must prevent the spread of the armed conflict beyond the borders of the nation involved. The prohibitions on possession and manufacture of weapons would have two effects on such a revolution. It would limit it to the meager weapons of the militia within the country and it would deter the shipment of weapons into the country. Both of these controls would serve to limit the intensity of military action accompanying the revolution.

This leaves unanswered the question of U.N. intervention to restore peace and order. If the answer is yes, U.N. police forces would be required to intervene, invoke temporary military law, and restore order.

One suggestion is that the U.N. should intervene if, and only if, the national government requests U.N. intervention or if the national government is overthrown by force or by *coup d'etat*.

However, the U.N. must not be allowed to intervene merely to support the government in power. This result would be repugnant, especially if the people of a communist or fascist state were trying to overthrow their government. This problem could be resolved by requiring that when the U.N. intervenes, it must conduct a prompt election to resolve the issue which precipitated the revolt. This plan would let the people get rid of a tyrannical national government. However, it would prevent an organized minority (such as the Communists) from seizing and keeping control unless they could also win the U.N.-supervised free election.

This, or some alternative arrangement, must be defined. In any event, the U.N. must have the ability to prevent civil wars from spreading so as to threaten international peace. There must also be methods to prevent the illegal buildup of armaments during a civil war. This would jeopardize world security. Moreover, it is highly desirable that means be found to avoid wars within a nation while preserving the right of a dissatisfied people to change their government.

Another question of definition will center around activities, such as the Soviet's Cominform, aimed at subversion or overthrow of existing governments. It is highly desirable that such activities be eliminated. However, enforcement of such a prohibition would embark the U.N. on a difficult task of doubtful success.

Furthermore, the Communists might then demand U.N. action against American efforts such as Radio Free Europe, which give aid and comfort to the captive peoples of communist satellites. It would be better to leave national governments responsible for the control of communist subversion.

However, the strengthened U.N. would at least halt the expansion of communism by force and the threat of force. The nations of eastern Europe were enslaved while they were occupied by the Red Army. The Russian troops which surrounded Czechoslovakia in 1948 helped force that nation's surrender to communism. Communist victories in China and Indo-China were won by large armies supplied by other communist nations. By taking away all substantial armaments, a strengthened U.N. will prevent any more of these conquests. It will force communism to fight with ideas rather than guns; this is a battle which free men should welcome.

OTHER APPROACHES TO WORLD LAW.   The method of obtaining world law presented in the previous chapter is but one of several approaches listed in Chapter 8. There are sound reasons for eliminating the others.

The contention that the United Nations has a sufficiently flexible Charter to evolve into an institution capable of creating world law can be eliminated for two reasons:

1. The evolutionary process is too slow to meet the challenges of the Nuclear Age (see also Chapter 19). Furthermore, it is doubtful that a real delegation of authority can be accomplished by evolution. The necessary departure from tradition is too great.

2. Dependence upon evolution involves the hazard that the United Nations may develop in the wrong direction. If it can evolve toward a desirable pattern, it might also evolve in dangerous ways.

Change of the Charter by formal amendment reduces this hazard. It seems more honest and realistic to approach the issue head on, rather than to count upon evolution to bring new powers to the United Nations by the back door.

The proposals for regional federations may be eliminated as a basic vehicle for obtaining world law, even though we recognize the substantial benefits to be derived from such organizations—the United States is a living example. There are two reasons for this elimination.

1. Progress toward regional federations is slow and discouraging; consider the frustrated efforts to achieve a European Federation. It appears likely that progress can be more rapid toward strengthening the United Nations than toward the organization of a series of regional federations over the world.

Most regional federation proposals require nations to delegate far broader powers than would be required for a strengthened U.N. Because they call for more powers, these regional federations run into more opposition. In addition, some nations, such as Britain, feel they have world responsibilities and do not belong entirely to any one region.

2. Regional federations do not solve the problem of world peace. Conflicts of interest would arise between regional federations just as they now arise between nations. There might be six or eight regional federations; the United States, the U.S.S.R. and its satellites, a Federated Western Europe, China and adjacent communist countries, a noncommunist group in Asia, an Arab group, an African Federation, and a South American Federation. There would still be the need for a strengthened United Nations to deal with the problem of security and peace among such regional federations.

Nevertheless, regional federations should properly develop to help solve some of the local trade and economic problems.

The proposed Atlantic Union organization has many aspects of a regional federation, although its basis of membership is different. It should not be accepted as our path to world order for several reasons:[3]

1. It involves delegation of power to a supranational organization in many fields besides those of armaments control and prevention of aggression. It is extremely doubtful that the United States or other Western nations would delegate such broad powers in the fields of economics, trade, and currency.

2. Because it excludes the Soviet Union, this plan would delay bringing the Soviets under the rule of world law. Perhaps the Soviets are not willing to submit to world law and armaments control, but we should at least try to persuade them to do so.

3. It excludes all nations whose civilization and governments have not reached levels comparable to those of the United States and western Europe. Unfortunately, this exclusion creates a split primarily along racial and color lines. It would immediately be interpreted as a "white man's union" and as an insult to those not included.

On the other hand, a strong advantage of the Atlantic Union organization is its common defense system, more permanent and lasting than one maintained by treaties and alliances, such as NATO. In spite of the disadvantages of Atlantic Union, the Western nations may be forced to such an arrangement if they do not achieve a strengthened

[3] William Esslinger, *Politics and Science* (New York, Philosophical Library, 1955).

universal United Nations, enforceable disarmament, and world law within a reasonable time. If progress is not pushed aggressively, or if efforts fail because of Soviet intransigence, our alliances and treaties may crumble to the extent that adequate military deterrents are not maintained. This is already beginning to happen; NATO appears to be slowly falling apart.

However, the advantages of world law on a global basis seem so to overshadow those of Atlantic Union that the latter proposal should be considered only if the first cannot be achieved. Even then a free-world federation, open to all nations, would seem to be the better choice. It appears to offer some of the advantages of Atlantic Union with fewer disadvantages.

A free-world federation should not be adopted now as our road to world peace and security. It is an alternative to be pursued if communist rejection prevents the transformation of the United Nations into a world federation of limited powers. The time for its consideration will come only if a revised Charter for a strengthened United Nations is turned down by the Soviets. Then we should seriously consider a federation of the free world, leaving vacant chairs for the communist nations to occupy when they are willing. The crumbling of our alliances may well force us to federate the free world in order to survive the Soviet threat.

If the Soviets flatly say "no," the nations which have ratified the revised U.N. Charter could agree to be bound by it. They could set up the strengthened U.N. even while some nations remain outside. The revised Charter itself could provide for this procedure (see Chapter 21). Of course, the present U.N. (with the U.S.S.R. as a member) could be continued alongside the new organization until all major nations have ratified the revised Charter.

As long as the U.S.S.R. remains outside, the strengthened U.N. must have far larger armed forces than it would need when all nations entered. The transition from national to U.N. forces would necessarily be slow. The arms race would continue.

But at least this step would give us a head start in building a strengthened U.N., and would hold the free world together while waiting for Soviet ratification. A federation with its own armed forces and with power to make decisions would give the free world far more protection than it has today. A communist attack on any member nation would be resisted by the entire federation, just as an attack on

California would be resisted by the entire United States. This should prevent any more Korea-type wars and reduce the danger of World War III. The free world would also gain a moral advantage from actually taking a great step toward peace rather than merely talking about it.

Such a "federation of those willing" would be only a step toward our goal. It may be a vital step. If the Soviet answer is "no," the free world must become so strong that the Soviets will give up their hope of conquering it.

However, we must first seek to carry out the full Seven-Point Program, including universal enforceable disarmament. Its acceptance and execution would make a free-world federation unnecessary.

The other approach to world law which is eliminated is the "superstate" or world government of maximal powers. Such an institution is undesirable and dangerous. The United States would not, and should not, accept a superstate which would have broad social and economic powers. This approach, involving maximal powers and universal membership, could not possibly be accepted; the levels of education, economic development, and wealth throughout the world are too different. There is real danger that a government with such broad powers would destroy our way of life.

Moreover, love and pride of nation is so great throughout the world today that not only the United States but practically all other nations would oppose such delegation of maximum powers. Any such proposal is both completely undesirable and unattainable.

The great problem facing the world today is the elimination of war and the maintenance of a secure peace. We need this to survive. We need it to allow peoples everywhere to concentrate upon the building of a better world. This is a world-wide desire which must be implemented by the *minimum amount of world government*. To propose or consider more is to jeopardize the chances of obtaining the essential minimum.

AUTHORITY. What authority must the United Nations be given in order to discharge the responsibilities outlined above? It is around this question that much of the debate will revolve concerning a strengthened United Nations. If that organization is to establish and maintain world law, it must be the "supreme governing authority" in the limited field of operation which is delegated to it.

There is only one way in which it can receive this power and authority. The peoples of the world must give it to the United Nations. For, according to our beliefs, the supreme political power and authority rests with the people. They may delegate authority as they see fit to various institutions and governments.

This poses the great question which must be faced by the United States and all other powerful nations of the world. To date we have dodged it, and have sought to obtain peace and security through international cooperation and "collective security."

We have apologetically avoided the issue of delegation of power to the U.N. with the excuse that "the people are not ready for it." No real progress can be made toward securing peace until the nations of the world come to grips with this problem. No real leadership toward a secure peace can be provided by the United States until we resolve the question and recognize the utter necessity of giving the United Nations the minimum power it needs.

THE BUGABOO OF SOVEREIGNTY.   Consideration of the question of sovereignty frequently generates more heat than light; it is usually debated with more emotion than knowledge. Opponents of all proposals to strengthen the United Nations, when asked to explain their opposition, usually reply loudly that, "We must not give up our national sovereignty." It is therefore appropriate to ask some questions regarding sovereignty.

In the first place, what is sovereignty? It is defined as "supreme political power or authority." In a democracy the supreme political authority rests with the people, who in turn delegate powers to various governments but retain control of these governments. We hold this to be true because we believe men are created equal, and that their endowment of rights comes from their Creator. Our Declaration of Independence states, "That to secure these rights, Governments are instituted among Men, deriving their just powers from the consent of the governed."

The idea that a national government is "sovereign" is a highly un-American doctrine. It is directly contrary to the beliefs of our Founding Fathers, who maintained that sovereignty belonged to the people and that no government had sovereign rights of its own.

To talk of "national sovereignty" is to place the nation above the individual and give the nation a control over the individual which is repugnant to free men. As Americans, we believe that a national government has no sovereignty. It has powers and authority which have been given to it by the people and which may be taken away by the people.

In the United States we, the sovereign people, have delegated certain powers to local governments, to state governments, and to our national government. In each case we ask them to handle certain functions. Among the powers delegated to our national government is the authority to maintain peace and security.

But national governments can no longer successfully accomplish this function. Our government cannot prevent aggressors from forcing war upon us. It happened at Pearl Harbor; it happened again in Korea. Therefore, we propose to redelegate that power to the United Nations. We propose to transfer from national governments to the United Nations the limited power to maintain a secure peace. The delegation of other powers to local, state, and national governments will remain undisturbed. We clearly will not "give up" sovereignty or anything else to the U.N. Rather, we, the American people, will *get back* our sovereignty over war and armaments. Today we have lost that sovereignty, for our foreign-policy decisions are now largely dictated by the acts of aggressor nations.

Is there any doubt that on Sunday, December 7, 1941, when the Japanese struck Pearl Harbor, the power of decision with respect to war and peace was lodged not with us but with the Japanese? Similarly, on Sunday morning, June 25, 1950, when the North Korean armies crossed the 38th parallel into South Korea, the power of decision between peace and war lay with the aggressor, not with the United States. We now spend billions for armaments not because we want to, but because the Soviet threat forces us to arm.

In other words, the peace-keeping power which we delegated to our national government has got out of control. We have lost it, whether we call it "power" or "sovereignty." We cannot give up that which we do not possess. Rather, it is time for the people, from whom the power arises, to recapture and redelegate it to an institution—a stronger U.N.—which has a fair chance of maintaining peace. Thus we will regain control over war and peace, and will win back our lost sovereignty.

In so doing we actually give up nothing; the delegation of power to the U.N. will be beneficial, not detrimental, to the United States and its citizens. The only thing we will "give up" to a strengthened United Nations is the power to declare war and maintain armaments. Fundamentally, we do not want this power, for we have no aggressive intent. We will gladly exchange it for a secure peace, which will make it unnecessary for us to walk armed through the jungle of anarchy.

All of us live under city and state governments where we have "given up" the right to kill, steal, or destroy property. We do not consider this a loss, for we do not normally wish to kill, steal, or destroy property. What we have given up is a useless "right" that we have no intention of exercising. What we gain in return is protection against having other people shooting at us, taking our wallets, and burning our homes.

Exactly the same principle applies with respect to the authority and power we propose to give to the United Nations. We give up nothing of value; we get in return genuine protection of our lives and our freedoms. It is, therefore, a mistake to talk so much about the "loss" and so little about the "gain."

Approached from this point of view, "sovereignty" is something to be used, not given away. An understanding of these facts reduces the "bugaboo" of sovereignty.

Chapter 17

SPEAK FOR MAN

Something more than a policy is needed to achieve an objective. We must also have spokesmen who present the program with clarity and vigor, inform others of its objectives, and build the enthusiasm and inspiration to carry it through. In business, we consider this a basic element of dynamic salesmanship.

THE QUESTION of a spokesman for the great yearnings of the world's peoples was raised dramatically by Norman Cousins in his recent book *Who Speaks for Man?* No nation is as uniquely qualified as the United States to speak for man everywhere. Our history and traditions help us to express man's hopes and ambitions for a better world, and to demand that nations face the serious problems of the Nuclear Age and find the road to a sane and peaceful society. By accepting and performing this role of spokesman, we can render a significant service.

To do so requires only positive and repeated reaffirmation of the beliefs of our nation: those of our Declaration of Independence and our Constitution and those gained from 175 years of national experience.

We need only to advocate these eternal truths without hesitation or reservation, and to practice what we preach.

SOURCE OF RIGHTS. The most fundamental truth is that all rights man enjoys are God-given. No act or policy of nations should be allowed to hinder the development of these rights—neither communism, colonial imperialism, nor blind nationalism.

The rights with which man is endowed by his Creator are the foundation of individual sovereignty. The people may delegate some of their powers to various governments in order to safeguard their rights and to achieve peace.

All of this is much better said in these words from our Declaration of Independence:

We hold these truths to be self-evident, that all men are created equal, that they are endowed by their Creator with certain unalienable Rights, that among these are Life, Liberty and the pursuit of Happiness. That to secure these rights, Governments are instituted among Men, deriving their just powers from the consent of the governed.

INDEPENDENCE.   A second precept is that man is entitled to independence. The corollary of this statement is that colonialism has outlived its usefulness.

Progress toward independence should be as orderly as practicable. Adequate preparation should be provided for peoples who are not ready to govern themselves. But the process of preparation must not be hindered. Excuses of military expediency must not delay orderly progress toward self-determination and independence.

These fundamental principles need to be made clear to the Soviet Union and to Red China, which hold hundreds of millions of people subjugated with no opportunity for self-determination. But they need also to be said to France and any other colonial power which through procrastination, ineptness, or selfishness is delaying progress toward independence.

Colonialism is a most disturbing issue today. It is repeatedly injected into the United Nations, and affects positions taken by nations on many other issues. It is a wedge between the colonial powers and the neutral nations, hammered home by communist propaganda.

Our actions and attitudes on colonial problems have weakened our leadership of the free world. When we side with the British to prevent U.N. discussion of Cyprus, join with the French to block consideration of Morocco, and seem to favor Portugal in the Indian-Portuguese controversy over Goa, we are not making friends or influencing solutions to those problems. We appear to be acting contrary to our long-held beliefs in the right of self-determination. We give support to the communist claim we are "imperialists."

Many of these colonial issues are difficult and trying. Nevertheless, we need to exert a constructive influence toward their orderly solution. We must be the constant champions of independence. We cannot afford to let ourselves be labeled as procolonial even for security reasons. Even air bases may be less valuable than our world prestige.

There are many ways in which we can aid the cause of independence. We can offer to mediate, as we did successfully in Indonesia. We can call for U.N. discussion of troublesome colonial situations. We can urge that definite timetables be established for independence for each colony. Such steps, taken intelligently, can help bridge the apparent gap between the demands for military security and for self-determination and freedom of colonial people.

Is not this a proper role for such a nation as the United States? Why not resolutely advocate independence and match our words with action?

BETTER WAY OF LIFE.   There is also a crying need to express the universal human desire for a better life. But of equal importance is the news that a better way of life is now possible, using the tools of plenty made available by our great scientific and technical development. The time has come when increased production and transportation can make a decent living available to every man wherever he may live. Now is the time to surmount obstacles so that man everywhere may climb upward to a decent life. Of course, our speaking for man on this point must be supported by actual economic help (see Chapter 11).

Is any nation better qualified than the United States to speak up and to lead the way in overcoming poverty and misery?

WAR IS OBSOLETE.   Now is the time to declare that war is obsolete. It settles nothing. It is a constant threat to life and property, and the greatest hindrance today to the orderly development of civilization. Moreover, secrecy and military policies increasingly endanger freedom, even in peacetime. Preparation for war is essential in the present world; but it is also the most futile dissipation of time, energy, natural resources, and tax money known to man. Few of us can imagine the kind of life that could be created for humanity if all our resources were used for constructive rather than for destructive purposes.

But it is not enough to declare that war is obsolete. We must also proclaim that peace can and must be established and enforced. The methods of establishing a rule of law are known, tried, and proved. The price that must be paid for peace is cheap when we consider the tremendous benefits that will come from it. It is time for the leaders of all nations to overcome their inertia and develop a United Nations capable of enforcing peace and protecting peoples everywhere against the threat of war.

Here too the United States, having found the key to peace within this great nation, is peculiarly qualified to present to the world the challenge to end war. Why don't we speak up and show the way?

RESERVOIR OF GOOD WILL.   For over 175 years the United States enjoyed a unique reputation among the nations of the world. We have been known not only as the land of the free but as a land of great opportunity. We have been recognized as a leading champion of those rights for which man strives everywhere.

The belief that basic human rights are God-given is embedded in our traditions. Our form of government is an attempt to apply spiritual truths to the affairs of man. It clearly recognizes that sovereignty rests with the people, who may delegate certain powers to institutions of government to accomplish desired ends.

Our belief in independence has been known since 1776. We have practiced this belief in our treatment of the colonies which have come under our control, culminating with the granting of complete independence to the Philippines.

We have long been known as a nation which has not only advocated, but has also accomplished, great gains in material things leading to a better life. We have peace, prosperity, resources, and industry. We have obtained an enviable standard of living.

Throughout all of our history to the close of World War II we have been a nonmilitaristic nation, standing for peace and maintaining only nominal military establishments. In an age of imperialism we have largely avoided its temptations, kept to our own way, avoided entangling alliances, and sought to live at peace with the world. While trying to avoid war, we were also showing the world how diverse peoples in a great area can achieve peace. With our federal form of government, we have succeeded in maintaining peace over our vast expanse from the Atlantic to the Pacific. From this experience, we know that peace can be enforced.

By the end of World War II we had developed a great reservoir of good will. Peoples everywhere believed in the sincerity and unselfishness of the United States. We were regarded as leaders in man's revolution for independence, dignity, a better life, and peace.

DEPLETION.   But since the end of World War II, there has been a depletion of this reservoir of good will. This has been due primarily to misinterpretation of our motives and actions. And we have done much to encourage this misinterpretation by our ineptness and blundering in world affairs.

Containment of communism has been a necessary but negative program. It has lacked appeal and has distracted us from other positive steps. Frequently we have seemed too engrossed in military preparations, to the apparent neglect of the cause of independence and human dignity. We have equivocated on the colonial problem. We have often placed the demands of military security ahead of the cause of independence and freedom.

We have thought it necessary to side with our allies and have seemingly supported their colonial positions. We have misunderstood the needs and the aims of the neutral nations which have recently achieved independence.

We have not spoken out boldly to condemn war, nor have we promoted the measures necessary to achieve a secure peace.

Such inconsistency and uncertainty has raised doubts about our continued concern for freedom. These doubts have been encouraged and expanded by Soviet propaganda. We have been painted as "imperialists" and "warmongers."

Indeed, there has been a tragic evaporation of the reservoir of good will which we enjoyed only a few short years ago.

SPEAK OUT.   But in spite of this drain, the principles which have made the United States great still have real appeal to the world. Nothing we have done has tarnished their radiance. They are still accepted and quoted. For instance, the welcoming speech at the Bandung Conference in 1955 saw President Soekarno of Indonesia make reference to the ride of Paul Revere as one of the most significant events in the history of man.

Throughout this conference, representatives of the underdeveloped Asian and African nations paid repeated tribute to the principles of our Declaration of Independence and Constitution, which have made us the most successful and prosperous "revolutionists" in the world.

The time has come for us to resume our leadership. The time has come for us to speak out and raise a powerful voice for the interests of man everywhere, including ourselves. There are plenty of spokesmen for nations and national groups. But who speaks for man? We can do so if we will; we can do so because of our heritage and our traditions. By so doing, we can help lead the world to a secure peace in which freedom, independence, and dignity can prosper.

We can be the true champion of men everywhere if we have the vision to see the opportunity and the courage to lead the way.

We must do so if we are to regain the true respect of the world. Indeed, we must do so if we wish to keep our own valued freedom and traditions.

There is no greater need in the world today than the positive leadership of the United States toward a secure peace with freedom. Why then do we not speak out for man? Why do we not demand that which is necessary for man to secure peace, achieve independence, gain dignity, and improve his way of life?

ITEM SEVEN—SPEAK FOR MAN.   Champion the eternal principles of individual freedom and demand an end to the wanton and stupid destruction of war. Mobilize the opinion and support of the world to move forward together to a better life, greater freedom, and a secure peace.

Chapter 18

SEVEN-POINT PROGRAM

Inspection and quality control are standard industrial processes to assure that specifications and plans have been met. By observing, measuring, and testing, deficiencies can be detected and the desired standards obtained.

FROM THE many alternatives of Chapter 8, a seven-point program has been selected that could provide a powerful long-range national policy for the United States. The seven items comprising this program are restated below and are measured by the yardsticks suggested in Chapter 9.

THE SEVEN POINTS

Item 1. Maintain Military Strength. Continue our present program which has been identified as a "posture of strength." It involves maintenance of adequate military strength, in cooperation with our allies, to deter communist expansion and aggression. It is an interim step, necessary as long as nations are dependent upon their own military strength to maintain security in a world of anarchy. It cannot be abandoned until we have achieved a rule of law in the world and have provided other methods for preventing aggression.

Item 2. Lend a Helping Hand. Continue and expand our support of programs aimed at building a better world and creating a stronger world community. Broaden our efforts to include activities of private enterprise, nongovernmental organizations, our government, and the United Nations. Commit a portion of the

205

potential savings from disarmament to an expanded program of technical assistance and economic development.

Item 3.   Use the United Nations.   Decide that the responsibility for maintaining a secure peace must be delegated to the United Nations. Use and support the present United Nations to the maximum even as we seek changes to improve it.

Item 4.   Establish a Rule of Law.   Recognize law as the keystone of order, peace, and freedom. Make the United Nations responsible for establishing a rule of law adequate to control all armaments, prevent aggression, and aid peaceful settlement of disputes.

Item 5.   Obtain Universal Enforceable Disarmament.   Clearly define our objective as universal enforceable disarmament. Recognize that enforceable disarmament and world law are intertwined, and that each needs the other.

Item 6.   Strengthen the United Nations.   Revise the Charter of the United Nations. Give the United Nations the powers and the structure required to administer and enforce a rule of law to control armaments and to prevent war. Erect the necessary safeguards, checks, and balances to protect the freedoms and rights of nations and individuals.

Item 7.   Speak for Man.   Champion the eternal principles of individual freedom and demand an end to the wanton and stupid destruction of war. Mobilize the opinion and support of the world to move forward together to a better life, greater freedom, and a secure peace.

YARDSTICKS.   Having restated the policy, we may now see how it satisfies the yardsticks suggested in Chapter 9.

Preservation of Our Freedom.   The satisfactory execution of this seven-point program will not only preserve our liberties but will enlarge them. Freedom will thrive with lasting and secure peace. By removing the chaos, fear, and uncertainty that come with war, and by building a better world community, we will help the seeds of freedom to sprout and grow everywhere. The expansion of real freedom to more and more people will increase the security of our own liberty.

Maintenance of Our Security.   Item One of the program (Maintain Military Strength) proposes that our nation continue a policy of adequate military development and preparedness. Hence in the near future, no change is suggested with respect to security. But in the long run the achievement of a strong United Nations, capable of administering a rule of law, will allow universal enforceable disarmament and provide a means for the peaceful settlement of international conflicts. This will provide real security which is not possible now in a world of anarchy.

Containment of Communism.   The maintenance of our military strength will help us to continue the physical containment of communism. In addition, the two items in the program which promote a better world community (Lend a Helping Hand—Item Two) and champion freedom and progress (Speak for Man—Item Seven) will be of great assistance in containing the ideology of communism. Moreover, the achievement of world law, disarmament, and the elimination of war will reduce the chaos in which communism thrives. Under peaceful conditions the power of freedom will overwhelm the false ideology of communism.

Avoidance of World War.   The new and bold portion of the proposed program seeks to achieve this objective by an approach which has never been applied on the world level. War will be avoided only when law is substituted for anarchy and the responsibility for peace between nations is safely lodged in a stronger U.N. surrounded by proper safeguards.

By this process the weapons of this scientific age will be effectively controlled: thermonuclear warheads, atomic dust, supersonic bombers, rockets, intercontinental missiles, space satellites, and others yet unnamed.

This is the objective of much of the program: Use the United Nations (Item Three) but Strengthen the United Nations (Item Six) so that it will be able to Establish a Rule of Law (Item Four) and Obtain Universal Enforceable Disarmament (Item Five).

Development of a World Community.   This is the specific objective of Item Two of the program (Lend a Helping Hand). In addition, the goal will be speeded by the establishment of world law and universal disarmament, for these will free great resources, now channeled into armaments, for the constructive task of building a better world.

Increase of World Unity. This is the specific objective of Item Seven of the program (Speak for Man). However, all of the other parts of the program will contribute to increased world unity. Once again, the achievement of world law and universal enforceable disarmament will significantly accelerate world unity by removing the deep fears which now set nations against one another. Moreover, a better world community and world economy will promote greater understanding and unity. By proposing a positive alternative to communism, we will unite all free men around a great idea and weaken the divisive force of communism.

IS IT REALISTIC?   Another test which was suggested is that of realism. The proposed program, particularly regarding the United Nations, world law, and disarmament, is bold and imaginative. However, it contains only the minimum requisites for secure peace; namely, world law limited to enforceable disarmament and prevention of aggression. This is realistic, for it embodies only those minimum steps which must be taken to achieve the goal. Anything less would be unrealistic because it would not be adequate to secure peace. Anything more would be unrealistic because it would be too hard to accomplish.

The proposed program is realistic because it squares with our basic moral, spiritual, and political principles. It champions the ideas and ideals which have made our country strong, and it incorporates the political principles which have been so successful here in the United States.

The program is also realistic because it is in keeping with today's facts of international life. It permits and encourages the fulfillment of common human desires, but it proposes an international system which will protect the rights of all peoples to keep their diversities and their various national institutions. It opposes any attempt to force all peoples and nations into a common mold. It utilizes the tools of plenty to help man in his struggle for a better life. It recognizes the virtual collapse of colonialism, and the growing interdependence of nations. It seeks to end international anarchy and to stem the extreme tides of nationalism. It aims at utilizing scientific developments for good rather than for destruction. And above all, it urges the United States to accept its position of world leadership.

Furthermore, this program is realistic because it is geared to the divided and chaotic world of today at the same time it is aimed at the higher goal of secure peace with freedom. It sacrifices none of our present ability to contain communism. It greatly weakens communist propaganda. It steps up our aid and assistance to under-developed areas. Such a program can guide us on current problems and give greater consistency to our words and actions. Of even greater value is the world unity and morale which will result from sustained leadership and action by the United States toward such a forward-looking program.

And finally, it is realistic in that it does not impose any undue economic burden upon the United States. In fact, it offers the opportunity for a great reduction of our tax load when world law and disarmament are achieved.

ACHIEVEMENT.   Having outlined a minimum program to achieve our desired objective, we are ready to turn our attention to implementation and activation. The finest set of blueprints is of no value unless used as a guide for construction of the desired structure.

The execution of this program will not be easy. It will require sustained effort, patience, and sincere dedication. There is no easy road to peace with freedom!

Would it not be sheer folly to shun the difficult and follow a simple but inadequate program, however comfortable such a course might be? We may evade the problem and muddle on into war or slavery, but would not this be shortsighted? Throughout our history, have we ever hesitated to tackle difficult programs aimed at essential objectives?

To activate the Seven-Point Program with vigor, wisdom, and determination requires concentrated effort. Our determination to go forward, no matter what the obstacles, has made America great. This is no time for a retreat into whining, self-pitying defeatism. Now, if ever, the call to great leadership must be answered by America. *We must wage peace!*

PART IV

Waging Peace

"Let us have faith that right makes might, and in that faith let us to the end dare to do our duty as we understand it."
—ABRAHAM LINCOLN

"They shall beat their swords into plowshares and their spears into pruning hooks. Nation shall not lift up sword against nation, neither shall they learn war any more."
—Isaiah 2:4

"If we strive but fail and the world remains armed against itself, it at least need be divided no longer in its clear knowledge of who condemned humankind to his fate."
—DWIGHT D. EISENHOWER

"I am not an advocate for frequent changes in laws and constitutions. But laws and institutions must go hand in hand with the progress of the human mind. As that becomes more developed, more enlightened, as new discoveries are made, new truths are discovered and manners and opinions change. With the change of circumstances, institutions must advance also to keep pace with the times. We might as well require a man to wear still the coat which fitted him when a boy as civilized society to remain ever under the regime of their barbarous ancestors."
—THOMAS JEFFERSON

Chapter 19

WHY NOT EVOLVE?

> Good managers know the pitfalls of delay and the advantages
> of dealing promptly with important, though difficult, problems.
> Their proposals for major change are often met with negative
> reactions. A usual suggestion is that a little time will solve
> the problem and make drastic steps unnecessary. But positive
> action is usually required if the present path is one of hazard
> and danger.

A COMMON first reaction to proposals for world law and
enforceable disarmament is yes-but: "Yes, they are fine ideas and
would make a wonderful world, but they can't be realized in our
time." The next reaction is to leave the problem to history, confident
that within a few decades or generations civilization will reach the
goal by gradual evolution.

Having stated this point of view, the typical listener will wash his
hands of the problems, leave them to the experts, and return to pursuit
of more immediate activities. There is a widespread tendency to believe that gradual developments alone will solve the world's problems.
This is one of the greatest obstacles to aggressive action for world
peace. It lays the foundation for the dulling lethargy with which most
of us are infected. Why get excited? Why not let a secure peace come
by evolution?

I would not write this book if I believed we could reach our goal of
secure peace by gradual evolution. I do not believe we can. Rather I
think peace must be waged aggressively. This chapter, and those
which follow, suggest how we should wage peace using the Seven-
Point Program.

HAZARDS AND BENEFITS.   The urgency of creating an institution which will secure peace becomes apparent if we consider the risks involved in any delay. These hazards arise from two sources: nuclear weapons and the communist dictatorship.

As long as the potential release of nuclear weapons hangs over our heads, we live under a Sword of Damocles. The destruction of nuclear warfare can be released by intent or by accident, by desire or by inadvertence. Once released, it can cause almost instant slaughter and devastation. As long as the free world and the Communists are armed to their teeth with nuclear weapons, this threat hangs over us no matter how many steps are taken to create good will or to build warning and defense systems.

The second hazard comes from the aggressive program of the communist world, which continues to apply pressure at every point of weakness. The Communists stand ready, willing, and able to wedge into any voids or cracks arising from disunity among the allies and neutrals. Communism is like a great ocean pounding at a dike, ready to engulf the protected areas whenever a breach or leak occurs. It has shown alarming ability to capitalize on the confusion and lack of leadership which are inevitable in any alliance of nations.

In the business world it is always considered prudent to take the necessary steps to eliminate major risks and hazards. It is equally prudent for us to remove these twin hazards from the political world.

We may also consider the great benefits of a peaceful world. One, aiding every taxpayer in the United States, would be the reduction in federal taxes. Proposed spending for fiscal 1956 breaks down:

ITEM	BILLIONS OF DOLLARS*	PER CENT
Expenditures for Defense (includes armed forces, Atomic Energy Commission, and overseas aid)	41.46	66.5
Veterans Administration	3.83	6.1
Interest on Debt (almost entirely the results of our last three wars)	6.38	10.2
Total cost of present defense and previous wars	51.67	82.8
Other operations	10.74	17.2
Grand Total	62.41	100.0

* Fiscal 1956 request.[1]

[1] *Congressional Record,* House, Vol. 101, No. 7, p. 320.

A secure peace would eliminate most of the $41,000,000,000 defense budget, including Atomic Energy Commission and overseas aid. The offsetting expense of our share of a strengthened U.N.'s budget will be only a small part of our present military budget. (See analysis of this saving in Chapter 15.)

No appreciable reduction can be expected in federal expenditures unless and until armaments spending is drastically reduced, for 83 per cent of this year's budget pays for past wars and defense against future wars.

But there are other and more important incentives and benefits. A secure peace would release great resources of time, talent, and money for homes, schools, roads, and hospitals. It would reduce tension and help the underdeveloped nations and colonies to obtain their independence and accelerate their economic, educational, and social development. It would aid in reducing trade barriers and stimulate greater commerce and trade. This would benefit the whole world, including the United States.

And above all, by assuring peace, the Seven-Point Program would remove from our daily lives the restrictions caused by our great defense program: compulsory military service for our youth, interference of military security with our freedoms, and the demoralizing emphasis on war and destruction.

These incentives and benefits, if properly understood, provide adequate motivation to tackle aggressively the difficult problems. The great hazards are the stick, the real benefits the carrot which should move public opinion even though it be obstinate as a mule.

EVOLUTION NOT CERTAIN. Evolution offers no real likelihood of bringing a solution in time to cope with the ICBM. This is due to the fact that substantial departures must be made from traditional methods of conducting international affairs. A study of evolution shows that major changes seldom occur in nature until a catastrophe has compelled the survivors to change.

Undoubtedly the catastrophe of World War III would bring the world under one government and end the futile use of war. However, reliance upon this catastrophe to precipitate such evolution is not attractive. A world government resulting from World War III would almost certainly be a brutal dictatorship. In any event, few of us would live to see it; our chances of being cremated during the first few minutes of a nuclear war are excellent.

In order to establish world law and enforceable disarmament, major decisions have to be made. The United States and every other nation must make a world organization (the United Nations) the foundation of its foreign policy. We must delegate to it the responsibility for maintaining a secure peace, and the power to enforce disarmament by inspection and police action. Such decisions are diametrically opposed to the present situation, with every nation claiming the absolute right to do as it pleases. This is a sharp break with the traditions that have prevailed in international affairs for centuries.

There is nothing in history to indicate that such major decisions are likely to come gradually and easily. They are not likely to come in time to avoid a nuclear war unless the issues are forced by an aroused public opinion and by strong leadership. Evolution is too slow and too unsafe to do the job.

EVOLUTION IS DANGEROUS.   Dependence upon evolution introduces another hazard which should be avoided: adoption of piecemeal or halfway measures.

A strengthened United Nations cannot be constructed safely a piece at a time. Disarmament without adequate provisions for enforcement would leave the United States without protection. The development of a United Nations military force without a civilian agency to direct it, and without adequate safeguards, checks, and balances, would court tyranny. A conversion of the United Nations Assembly to a legislature would be worthless without the creation of an executive branch and courts to enforce the laws.

Evolution is likely to make such partial steps seem attractive. But half-measures are dangerous, and the process of learning this lesson might be fatal.

Evolution is also dangerous because inadequate progress toward secure peace will encourage the United Nations to assume greater power (see Chapter 21). It is much safer to maintain the principle that the U.N. is an organization of delegated powers. This requires giving it promptly the needed authority to perform its delegated task.

GOVERNMENTS MUST BE PRESSED.   There is a natural tendency for any organization to perpetuate itself, to defend its position from attacks, and to resist change. This is just as true of the institutions of national government as it is of local governmental, business, or private organizations.

Further, there is a strong tendency for the leaders of any organization to avoid any steps which lessen or diminish their power. Even in a democracy such as ours, we have little precedent for voluntary relinquishment of activities and authority, of power and prestige. The truth of this statement can be verified by a few days' tour of government offices in Washington, D.C., or by a study of the recent Hoover Report on reorganization of the government.

The author has observed these truths over a period of twenty years of personal contacts with our federal government. Such activities on behalf of clients have involved a number of different agencies and departments.

Governments, run by people, have almost human tendencies to resist change and retain authority. If this is the case in a democracy, how much stronger are the same tendencies in a government where the leaders are less responsive to public opinion and the ballot.

There is the further tendency of the officials in foreign offices and state departments to put great faith in the traditional methods of diplomacy and negotiation which have long been their stock in trade. Fresh approaches and new views seldom come from within and must ordinarily be compelled from without.

Normally diplomacy is a cautious face-saving device; a proposal is seldom made unless its acceptance is prearranged. It deals, therefore, either with broad aspirations, general and nonbinding, or with the day-to-day tasks of meeting crises, relieving tensions, and compromising differences. Such attitudes do not often generate the vision and the courage to propose and pursue the long-range programs we need now.

Top officials of our government, including our senators and representatives, haven't time to study adequately the complicated problems of securing peace. The pressure of daily duties and immediate issues makes it easy for them to delay in dealing with long-range problems. On many occasions congressmen have mentioned to me their great difficulty in finding time to read and think through any issue not immediately before them.

We have let the Presidency become so burdensome that our Chief Executive has inadequate time to develop and lead new programs. Even President Eisenhower, with his sincere desire for peace and his broad understanding of the obstacles which must be overcome, seems to depend on his staff and the State Department. Too often their proposals are concerned only with immediate crises rather than with an over-all program. This has nothing to do with partisan politics. For many years our government, Democratic or Republican, has been so preoccupied with the trees that it has seldom been able to see the forest.

For these reasons, the governments of the world, including our own, must be pressed by an enlightened and demanding public opinion to work aggressively for peace with freedom even though it means a break with traditional practices.

SPLIT PERSONALITY.   In the current crisis most national governments have bad cases of split personality. Committed as we are to a desperate arms race, our government is almost psychologically incapable of pressing at the same time for disarmament.

This is currently illustrated in the crash program for development of the ICBM. Fearful that we are behind the Soviets, our government properly throws its efforts behind a "crash" program to accelerate our development of the ICBM. But our leaders, convinced of the urgency of this activity, have little time for discussions of disarmament or elimination of war. This is not true of President Eisenhower, but many of his subordinates fail to give any serious thought to these problems. Any suggestion in this field is likely to be viewed as distractive and a waste of time.

And yet, if we are to make progress toward disarmament, we must also have a "crash" program aimed at enforced disarmament.

Support for this second "crash" program must be generated by an informed public opinion which will support those few officials sincerely interested in disarmament and which will urge and press the others. The situation is well illustrated in a statement by Donald McDonald:

Though there is an "office" for disarmament, headed by Harold Stassen, inside the White House, I do not think that we should expect that the government as such will make any spectacular progress toward disarmament, and with time running out that progress will have to be spectacular to be effective. Government is not an automatic machine; it is people and it seems to me that, given this fact, it is almost psychologically impossible for government to simultaneously launch and sustain two contradictory "crash" programs—a program for armament supremacy and a program for universal disarmament.

Mr. McDonald further said:

It is perhaps fitting that private citizens of the world, who share equally the stakes in this grim drama, should now find it their peculiar task to supply the motivation, the creative imagination and the moral urgency for solving this drama in favor of the human race.[2]

PEACE MUST BE WAGED.   Unless we are willing to accept the chance of nuclear war, we cannot depend upon evolution. We must wage peace with the same unity, drive, and determination with which we have waged world war twice in the last forty years. As citizens of this nation, we must become so alive to the problems that we create the public opinion which will support and compel our government to give top priority to the waging of peace.

If this nation can be aroused to make a determined effort, it holds a position of leadership from which it can exert immediate influence on world opinion. Such an enlightened and determined effort provides the only path to success. Peace will not evolve in our time. It must be actively sought after. Peace must be waged!

[2] Donald McDonald, "Ultimate Weapon in Ultimate Drama," *Catholic Messenger,* Jan. 26, 1956.

Chapter 20

STRATEGY

Salesmanship is vital to the successful business. Good salesmanship is based upon a carefully developed campaign to
overcome the objections of the prospect. Development of a
sales approach requires careful analysis of the prospect's
attitude.

HOW ARE WE to wage peace? If we cannot depend upon
evolution, what strategy should we adopt? It is not enough merely to
say that we shall carry forward the Seven-Point Program we have
outlined. We must also appraise the shifting world situation, anticipate
the moves of our opponents, and determine the emphasis to be given
various parts of our program.

THE OPPOSITION. We should develop our plans on the premise that
the Communists will continue to oppose and will not readily accept
a strengthened United Nations, world law, and universal enforceable
disarmament. We should assume that the Communists will accept
these requisites for peace only if they see that they will lose more
by opposing than by accepting.

It would be unrealistic to base our strategy on more favorable
assumptions, in the light of Soviet performance since the end of
World War II. Enforced disarmament under a strengthened U.N.
would destroy the Soviet plan for world conquest. It is wishful
thinking to expect the Communists to give up willingly their goal of
ruling the world. It is idle speculation to expect prompt change in
their attitude.

Rather, we should work on the assumption that the Communists will continue their present attitudes and objectives. We should expect them to seek greater expansion of their influence, their ideology, and their totalitarian empire. We should also expect them to seek increased security from the threat of external attack, just as every nation must in the world of anarchy. The arms race will almost certainly continue until enforceable disarmament is achieved.

The change in U.S.S.R. policy announced by Nikita Khrushchev in February, 1956, does not lessen the intensity of the communist drive for supremacy. It merely shifts major emphasis to the battle for the hearts and minds of the neutral peoples of Asia and Africa. The Communists claim to speak for the majority of the peoples of the world. If ever they actually control a majority of the world's people, they will have won their major goal. They will dominate the world.

Their change in policy is timely from their point of view. They have temporarily stalemated our nuclear threat and they may well be ahead of us on ICBM development. In any event, they can threaten western Europe with the IRBM before we can train the ICBM on Moscow.

The menace of modern war has grown so terrifying that the Soviets now believe they can win friends by emphasizing peace. Their talk of friendship and economic aid cannot be taken as sincere, but it is effective. We must meet and defeat the new Soviet policy on this front.

The Soviet rulers now seem to realize that a nuclear war would destroy them as well as us. However, we must not assume that the Soviets really believe "there is no alternative to peace." There are many intermediate positions between a decision against deliberate provocation of nuclear war on the one hand, and secure peace on the other. Total nuclear war may now be less likely, but there is no similar assurance with respect to "small wars." Such aggressions may be launched by the Communists with fair assurance that the United States will not retaliate with World War III. The current weakening of NATO and our other alliances makes another Korea more likely.

The shift in emphasis gives the Communists greater leeway to inject themselves, or their satellites, into local conflicts. It frees them to take advantage of political, social, and economic problems in the Middle East, Africa, and Asia.

Such are the attitudes and actions we should expect from the Communists if we are to develop a realistic strategy for the free world.

But at the same time we must not become so obsessed with such expectations that we blind ourselves to any real change in Soviet attitude. At some point, if our waging of peace is successful, there must be a turning point at which the Soviet rulers will realize that their own survival requires a secure peace.

We should base our strategy on the assumption of the most unfavorable conditions. But we must ever be alert to detect that crucial time when the struggle for peace can be won.

BASIC STRATEGY.   Our basic strategy must be to unify the free world and align it in support of giving the United Nations the responsibility and authority it needs. This free-world unity must be strong. It must create enough pressures and incentives to force the Soviets to join with the rest of the world in a strengthened U.N. The issue must be pressed by the entire free world.

In recent years we have emphasized containment of communism by military deterrents. This has been a necessary, but negative, program. While containment must be continued, the crying need is for positive, dynamic, and aggressive programs and policies.

We should implement the Seven-Point Program by using four strategic principles:

1. Seize the initiative and set the pace.
2. Mobilize world opinion.
3. Write the prescription for a secure peace.
4. Sell the benefits of a secure peace to the world.

SHIFT OF BATTLEGROUND.   Before discussing these four elements, it is well to consider the atmosphere in which they must be executed. The stage has shifted from Europe where the United States has until recently concentrated its containment policy. It was in Greece and Turkey that the threat was first recognized and the Truman Doctrine of containment first applied. The elements of our containment policy suited European conditions.

The Truman Doctrine, the Marshall Plan, and NATO have temporarily stabilized Europe and limited communist expansion. These programs were suited to European countries which were well advanced and industrialized. Moreover, they were adapted to a communist threat which was primarily external, once the war-damaged economies were partially restored. Our supreme deterrent, the threat of massive retaliation with nuclear weapons, fitted this threat.

Our propaganda emphasizing freedom, democracy, and private enterprise was also quite suitable to Europe, where such terms had meaning and value.

But now the emphasis is changing to a part of the world where our success in containing communism has not been good. Asia, Africa and, to some extent, South America have become the areas of contention. Conditions there are vastly different from every viewpoint. Most of these countries are backward and underdeveloped. They lack not only industry but even efficient agriculture. Food, not freedom, is the urgent demand of most of the population. Literacy levels are low. Government and business are usually in the hands of a few. Such terms as democracy and private enterprise are not understood. To many of these peoples, the words "freedom" and "independence" mean little beyond escape from the colonialism of the white man.

The methods which revitalized western Europe and turned aside the communist threat there will not work in the great Middle World— the area from Tokyo to Capetown.

Our great mistake is that we are tempted to apply the same programs that worked in Europe. To do so would be a tragedy because the conditions are completely different. If our leadership is successful it will be the result of a sustained effort to understand these peoples and fit our programs to their needs and problems.

INITIATIVE.   In any kind of controversy—military, political, athletic, or business—the side with the initiative has a distinct advantage. In a football game, a team is not likely to score and win while it is on the defensive. It must get possession of the ball, control it, and carry it forward.

The Western powers and the United States have been on the defensive too frequently since 1945. We have been countering "peace" proposals, meeting communist aggression, defending ourselves against communist accusations, and trying to offset communist propaganda. In only a few instances have we beaten the Communists to the draw and forced the issue.

One such instance was the Marshall Plan of 1947. Two others

were President Eisenhower's "atoms for peace" offer in December, 1953, and his bold proposal for exchange of military information accompanied by aerial inspection, made in Geneva in July, 1955.

On the whole, we are usually too late with too little, while the Communists keep the initiative. Four recent examples of embarrassment from lack of initiative are:

1. The admission of 16 new member nations to the United Nations in November, 1955. We were completely outmaneuvered. We stood firm on a policy of "abstention," and ended by antagonizing Japan and letting the U.S.S.R. take most of the credit for the admission of the new members.

2. The U.N. Disarmament Subcommittee discussions early in 1955. We were made to appear opposed to disarmament because we were unprepared to answer the communist call for an over-all plan.

3. Colonial issues. The Communists have cleverly and diabolically meddled in the economic and social problems of Asia and Africa. We have been made to appear to support the unpopular colonial policies of our allies.

4. The Middle East. The communist arms offer to Egypt caught us flat-footed. For many months we did nothing while the danger of an Israel-Arab war increased.

We cannot hide behind the alibi that a democracy moves slowly and takes time to reach decisions. If we want to win the battle for the survival of the free world and stop the spread of communist influence, we have to take the lead and hold it. We must know our objectives, and substitute positive action for negative reaction. We need a "crash" program. We require a speed-up of our actions and reactions. We must lead!

MOBILIZE WORLD OPINION.   Competition for world public opinion is a primary concern of our strategy. Unless our policies appeal to the world's peoples, we shall be unable to lead them. Ideas and opinions are the stuff of which world unity will be made.

The Soviet shift in tactics has convinced most nations that peace is now more likely. This makes it easier for both sides to influence world opinion by proposing new ideas.

The Soviet Union has already shown its alertness to this situation.

For example, in 1955 its disarmament spokesmen called for an over-all "plan of disarmament" as an answer to our proposals for aerial inspection. Having no comprehensive plan, we remained silent and were easily portrayed as opposed to disarmament. We can be sure the Communists will miss few opportunities of this type to proclaim themselves as champions of peace.

Colonial conflicts offer other examples. When these issues arise in the United Nations, the U.S.S.R. is almost always found on the side of those seeking independence. But the United States more often than not sides with the colonial powers, or seems to do so. The Communists are given the opportunity to present themselves as champions of freedom, while we are portrayed as "imperialists." The fact that the U.S.S.R. has a far worse form of colonialism does not prevent the Communists from winning friends. Colonial peoples are chiefly concerned with their own freedom, and are grateful for support from any source.

These are examples of how not to mobilize world opinion. They show us undecided, faltering, hesitant, and without a consistent idea of our objectives.

To win world opinion we must boldly and imaginatively champion great ideas. Independence, freedom, self-determination, and human dignity are great ideas. In its future meaning to man, world law is a great idea. It can be translated into freedom from fear and war, partial relief from taxation and bureaucracy, and opportunity for progress toward the great human needs and desires.

We should welcome the shift of emphasis to the battle of ideas. It is a field where we have much to offer and should be able to win. But to lead, we must be alert, imaginative, and persistent. Moreover, we must understand our aims and goals. If we meet these requirements, use ideas boldly and consistently, and support words with action, we can rally world opinion.

PRESCRIPTION FOR PEACE.   The ingredients for such a prescription— a strengthened United Nations, world law, and enforceable disarmament—have been discussed in previous chapters. However, it is not enough to have an over-all plan contemplating these steps. We also need to prescribe them to the world in terms which are unmistakable and understandable.

Such a prescription must be written. One device for doing this is a U.N. Charter Review Conference to draft a revised Charter, following the procedure discussed in Chapter 21. It is very important that these proposals be forcefully brought to the attention of all the world, including the Communists. We badly need this clear-cut prescription to define our ideas and coordinate our activities.

Furthermore, the written document—a proposed revision of the U.N. Charter—would stand as an alternative to the arms race and to world anarchy. It would state the conditions under which we can safely disarm. It would be an open invitation to all men everywhere to substitute law and order for chaos and death.

SELL THE BENEFITS. Businessmen know that incentives can be strong motivating forces. This is so whether they are applied to people or to nations. Therefore we need to sell the benefits as part of our strategy. We need to point out how everyone will gain from a secure peace. We need to include among these benefits the fact that a strengthened U.N. will make it easier to solve many of the current issues.

An understanding of these incentives can be a powerful help in obtaining world unity and mobilizing free-world opinion. It can also help push the Communists toward acceptance of the prescription for a secure peace.

An essential part of our strategy, therefore, must be an effective presentation of these incentives. Among the benefits of enforced disarmament are:

1. Security from outside interference and attack.

2. Freedom for every nation to proceed with its own development.

3. Release of vast expenditures of men, money, and resources, now going into armament, for constructive purposes.

4. Greater freedom to exchange ideas, information, and culture.

5. Improved trade and economic conditions.

6. Elimination of encroachments on freedom which now result from demands of military security.

7. Substitution of hope and optimism for fear and suspicion.

In addition to these real benefits, the achievement of a secure peace holds out the opportunity to settle many of the current issues. Such a problem as the unification of Germany can never be settled so long as the free world and the Communists are sparring for advantage. If dictates of military security dominate the thinking of the Communists and the free world, neither will permit a unified Germany which is not on its side. Hence, the inevitable stalemate can be broken only when the threat of war is eliminated.

Settlement of East-West controversies is unlikely except in conjunction with settlement of the greater problem of a secure peace. As we deal with current issues (Chapter 22) we must remember that many of them can be settled only when world law is achieved.

The door must be held open to achieve these benefits and to settle some of the controversies between East and West at the same time as the issue of a secure peace is resolved.

URGENCY.   A basic requirement of our strategy is an adequate sense of urgency. Certainly we need look no further than the recent news of that "absolute" weapon, the ICBM, to find a reason for urgency.

The impact of the ICBM on the public mind must not be allowed to wear off. It must not be permitted to become "just another weapon" in the public's mind. This has already happened with the A-bomb and is beginning to occur with the H-bomb. Such loss of concern results in apathy and dulls the desire to eliminate war.

It is the clear responsibility of thinking Americans to combat this tendency to dodge the unpleasant threats of today's weapons. It is the even clearer responsibility of our President and his administration to place the facts before our people and to give adequate urgency to our quest for peace. This is not being done now.

Unless this is done, the current shift in Soviet tactics may successfully generate complacency and reduce our sense of urgency. While we seek greater understanding, we cannot safely relax until the threat of a nuclear holocaust is eliminated.

This hazard of relaxation must be guarded against by constant emphasis on the dangers which face us until the world is securely disarmed.

Our survival requires an understanding of the entire program to achieve a secure peace. It requires a continuing sense of urgency which gives first priority to waging peace.

In speaking of the blindness and lack of action in the 1930's which allowed World War II to happen, Lester Pearson, Foreign Minister of Canada, says:

It was not so much that people did not know that a willingness to accept risks is sometimes necessary to the victories of peace as well as war, but that, necessary or not, they were unwilling to assume the responsibilities and sacrifices that action would involve.[1]

ON THE HOME FRONT.   In order to implement the strategy outlined above, we Americans all need to do our "homework."

We must understand what our objectives are and determine the general outlines of an over-all program and policy. This requires an informed public, with adequate information about international problems, disarmament, the U.N., nuclear warfare, and similar subjects. The American people need not be spoon fed. They have a far greater capacity to understand and use facts than they are credited with by most politicians. They are entitled to full information on the specifics that are required to obtain a secure peace.

We also need to educate ourselves on the principles of law and government. We can profit by re-examining the controversies of the 1780's over the need of a federal form of government to maintain a secure peace among our thirteen colonies.[2] We can then more easily appreciate the need of a rule of law in the world.

Not only is more information required; the American public, including its leaders, must also face the facts of international life, debate the issues, and unite on a program which will give us peace with freedom. We must prepare ourselves for a long operation, for there is no evidence that the task can be accomplished in a short time. And finally, we must resolve to provide more coordinated and effective leadership for the cause of a secure peace.

Only as we make these preparations on the home front will we be ready to move ahead to wage peace.

[1] Lester Pearson, *Democracy in World Politics* (Princeton, New Jersey, Princeton University Press, 1955).
[2] Carl Van Doren, *The Great Rehearsal*.

Chapter 21

TACTICS I—CHARTER REVISION

> After the function and purpose of a new plant are determined, engineers prepare plans or "blueprints." These not only show the over-all dimensions and shape of the building, but also the details of construction.

THERE IS a unique opportunity to use the device of U.N. Charter revision to move toward secure peace. By pressing forward toward review and revision of the United Nations Charter, it is possible to strengthen the United Nations, move toward disarmament and world law, and provide greater unity in the free world. Let us see how this may be done.

CHARTER REVIEW CONFERENCE. Suppose the delegates who met at San Francisco in 1945 to draft the United Nations Charter could repeat their performance today with the knowledge of the events since then. What kind of Charter would they propose? Would they give the organization enough authority and power to enforce disarmament and prevent aggression? Would they provide adequate means for control of nuclear weapons? Would they retain the paralyzing veto? Would they base their enforcement machinery on the assumption of big-power unity?

The probable answer to all of these questions is evident. The resulting organization would be stronger, more adequate, and better suited to the Nuclear Age. This probability is evident from the following statement by Secretary of State John Foster Dulles:

229

One inadequacy sprang from ignorance. When we were in San Francisco in the spring of 1945, none of us knew of the atomic bomb which was to fall on Hiroshima on August 6, 1945. The Charter is thus a pre-atomic age Charter. In this sense it was obsolete before it actually came into force. As one who was at San Francisco, I can say with confidence that if the delegates there had known that the mysterious and immeasurable power of the atom would be available as a means of mass destruction, the provisions of the Charter dealing with disarmament and the regulation of armaments would have been far more emphatic and realistic.

The drafters of the Charter wisely included procedures for amendment. Moreover, special provisions were included to encourage the calling of a Review Conference by the Tenth General Assembly in 1955. The tenth Assembly took advantage of this provision, initiating studies leading to a Review Conference. A committee of the whole is to report to the Assembly in 1957 with recommendations on time, place, and procedure for this conference.

If supported by a majority of the nations, this report should also lead to a Review Conference called under Article 109 of the U.N. Charter within the next few years. At that Conference, amendments can be proposed to correct the weaknesses of the U.N. and give it the authority and the means to enforce peace.

When such a revised Charter is submitted to the nations for ratification, a significant advance will have been made. The basis will have been formulated for a rule of law, enforceable disarmament, and peaceful settlement of disputes between nations. The proposed revision will stand as a challenge to all nations, including the Soviet Union, to line up on the side of peace and decency.

Such an invitation can be issued without the obstruction of the veto. This procedure provides a real opportunity to advocate forcefully a strengthened U.N.

AMENDMENT PROCEDURE.   The two methods by which the Charter of the United Nations may be amended are stated in Chapter 18. The first of these methods, contained in Article 108, states as follows:

Amendments to the present Charter shall come into force for all Members of the United Nations when they have been adopted by a vote of two-thirds of the members of the General Assembly and ratified in accordance with their respective constitutional processes by two-thirds of the Members of the United Nations, including all the permanent members of the Security Council.

The General Assembly may adopt amendments and submit them to the members of the United Nations for ratification. The action of the General Assembly in proposing amendments cannot be vetoed.

The other method of amendment, outlined in Article 109, is as follows:

1. A General Conference of the Members of the United Nations for the purpose of reviewing the present Charter may be held at a date and place to be fixed by a two-thirds vote of the members of the General Assembly and by a vote of seven members of the Security Council. Each member of the United Nations shall have one vote in the conference.

2. Any alteration of the present Charter recommended by a two-thirds vote of the conference shall take effect when ratified in accordance with their respective constitutional processes by two-thirds of the Members of the United Nations including all the permanent members of the Security Council.

3. If such a conference has not been held before the tenth annual session of the General Assembly following the coming into force of the present Charter, the proposal to call such a conference shall be placed on the agenda of that session of the General Assembly, and the conference shall be held if so decided by a majority vote of the members of the General Assembly and by a vote of any seven members of the Security Council.

Again it is significant that no veto is applicable to the calling of the Review Conference, nor to its recommending revisions of the Charter and submitting them to the members for ratification. Fear of a Soviet veto is no reason to delay proposing amendments to the United Nations Charter, by way either of Article 108 or of 109.

To become effective, amendments or alterations of the Charter must be ratified by two-thirds of the members of the United Nations, including all of the permanent members of the Security Council. At this stage, then, there must be ratification by the Soviet Union, the United States, Britain, France, and China and enough more U.N. members to add up to a two-thirds majority.

Ratification is to be accomplished by the normal constitutional processes of the respective members. Any of the Big Five can, of course, delay action by refusing to ratify. However, no nation, the U.S.S.R. included, can veto the amendments. Failure of any permanent member of the Security Council to ratify will not obstruct the process until two-thirds of the nations, including the other four permanent members of the Security Council, have ratified.

Of course, the Charter Review Conference would not necessarily be bound by the Charter provision requiring unanimous Big Five ratification. The Conference could include in a revised U.N. Charter a provision that it shall take effect when ratified by a smaller number of nations—perhaps a two-thirds majority, including any three of the Big Five. This would bypass the Big Five roadblock, but of course the revised Charter would bind only those nations which had ratified it. Our own nation set a precedent for this step. In 1787 the Articles of Confederation required unanimous thirteen-state approval of any amendment. But our Founding Fathers ignored this restriction. They drafted a new Constitution and provided that it would take effect when ratified by any nine of the thirteen states.

TIMETABLE.   The process of Charter review, revision, and ratification will span several years.

Favorable action of the 1957 General Assembly can lead to a Review Conference in 1958 or 1959. When the conference meets, it is likely that a year or more may be consumed in its deliberations. Perhaps after initial meetings it will establish commissions to study various aspects of Charter revision and reassemble at a later date to consider reports of these commissions. It is unlikely that such a Review Conference will complete its action before 1960, at which time the ratification process will start.

Ratification will be slow. If the proposals are substantial ones which give the U.N. real authority, a period of two years or more may elapse before the required two-thirds of the nations have ratified. Ratification by the United States may likely require a constitutional amendment. Only then will attention focus upon the permanent members of the Security Council. Only at that time will ratification by the Soviet Union or by the United States become a key factor. Such a situation is unlikely to occur before 1962. Hence, the elapsed time from the initial action of the General Assembly convening a Review Conference to the period of key decision by the permanent members of the Security Council is likely to be five or more years.

The above timetable is based upon the procedure under Article 109, using a Review Conference. If action is taken under Article 108, the General Assembly may adopt an amendment at any session; it then goes immediately to the nations for ratification.

This Article 108 process might well be followed for changes which are comparatively noncontroversial. It is quite possible it will be employed to alter the size and membership of the Security Council, the Trusteeship Council, and the Economic and Social Council and adjust them to the increased membership of the United Nations.

But an adequate revision of the U.N. probably requires a Charter Review Conference under Article 109.

INDUCEMENTS.   During this period of years powerful forces will be working to create a climate favorable for ratification. These forces include:

1. The growing realization of the increased destructiveness of modern weapons—the weapons of 1961 or 1962, not those of today. This means the ICBM, the space satellite, and more powerful thermonuclear warheads.

2. The overwhelming certainty that all participants in a nuclear war, faced with unstoppable "absolute" weapons, will lose.

3. The mounting pressure of the moral force of world opinion upon those nations which have not ratified and are impeding progress toward peace and security.

4. The growing desirability of adequate controls for "atoms for peace" to prevent diversion to military uses; also, the need for international control of space satellites.

5. The continuing cost of the arms race, and the slowing of progress toward a higher standard of living because of diversion of productive capacity to armaments.

6. The improving relations among nations which may result if the other parts of the Seven-Point Program are put into effect in time to bring economic, social, and political progress.

It is impossible to predict with certainty the attitude of the Soviet Union, or any other nation, toward the revised Charter until the nature of the revision is determined and the conditions when ratification is considered are known.

Faced with a true alternative to war and a continuing arms race, with mounting military strength of the free world, and with a revised Charter which will permit the U.N. to enforce disarmament but will not interfere with national institutions, the Soviets may well conclude that ratification is desirable.

Failure to move now for Charter revision because of fear of Soviet rejection would indeed be timid and hesitant. This defeatist policy would give the Soviets an absolute veto now over our plans for peace. The Soviets may say "no"; but if so, let us make them say it and bear the burden of blocking a secure peace.

THE SITUATION DURING RATIFICATION.   During the ratification period the present U.N. Charter would continue in force and all of the current activities of the U.N. would go forward. No present benefits which can come from the U.N. would be eliminated or diminished.

Furthermore, all projects and programs by which the nations seek to develop a better world community, including the specialized agencies of the U.N., would continue. Work would continue on other health, economic, social, educational, and religious programs now being conducted by governments or private organizations.

During this period the nations of the world would obviously continue individually and collectively to take those steps which they deem necessary for their security. They would maintain such armaments, regional organizations, and collective security methods as they consider advisable.

Thus, the nations of the world would lose none of their present rights and freedom of action while the ratification process is under way.

THE BENEFITS.   An analysis of the benefits of an early Charter Review Conference in 1958 or 1959 indicates that we have everything to gain and nothing to lose by going ahead. Some of the obvious benefits of a Review Conference are:

1. It would provide an opportunity for full-scale discussion and accelerated study of the accomplishments and weaknesses of the United Nations, and of the changes which are necessary to make it effective. Representatives of all nations would participate, not just the great powers who are now debating disarmament.

2. It could draft a "blueprint" for a strengthened United Nations. This revised U.N. Charter would describe in detail the powers and structure which the U.N. needs to control armaments and pre-

vent aggression. This would allow a definite comparison of the present U.N. with the proposed strengthened U.N.

3. The revised U.N. Charter would focus public discussion upon specifics rather than upon generalities. A definite "blueprint" should help the nations decide whether to delegate real authority to the U.N. in the sphere of armaments control and prevention of aggression.

4. The proposal of such a revised Charter would help to dispel the neutral nations' fears with respect to the aims of the United States. Our support of the revised Charter would show our willingness to disarm under adequate safeguards.

5. Greater unity should develop among the nations of the free world as they work together to draft a blueprint for secure peace and seek its ratification in their homelands.

6. For the first time, all peace-loving men would have a "Great Proposal" around which they could rally. The revised Charter would give the world a positive, specific answer to the twin threats of nuclear war and communist aggression. Those who seek peace are now riding many different horses in many different directions. A revised Charter would focus most efforts for peace on a single goal: to persuade all nations to ratify the revised Charter.

WHY NOT GO AHEAD?   Many strong supporters of the U.N. are fearful of Charter review now. This is so in spite of our government's support for a Review Conference in the 1955 General Assembly.

Those who have opposed early Charter review generally base their arguments upon fear that a Review Conference might weaken the United Nations or upon the premise that no progress can be made in a tense and divided world. Many of them also contend that the gradual or evolutionary approach is more satisfactory. Pertinent answers may be made to their arguments.

Some who fear a Review Conference claim that weakening amendments to the Charter might be adopted, or that the Review Conference would lead to discord which would harm the U.N. The danger of crippling amendments seems slight. The great majority of those who seek a Review Conference want to make the U.N. stronger, not weaker. The pessimists on this point completely underestimate the support for the U.N. in this country and throughout the world. They are unduly influenced by the noisy isolationists in the United States, who actually represent only a small part of our population. If discord could kill the U.N., it would already be dead. It is hard to imagine how debates in a Review Conference could be more bitter than many which have already taken place in the General Assembly and Security Council.

No one can guarantee that a Review Conference will not weaken the U.N. But this is a very small risk, and a calculated risk which we must take. The risk of doing nothing is far greater.

To await an era of cooperation and sweetness before proceeding with Charter review seems utterly unrealistic. The free world must press its peace offensive, fully expecting Soviet opposition and delay. Failure to do so gives the Communists control of the situation and allows them to set the pace.

Dependence on gradualism or evolution seems unsupportable for all of the reasons discussed in Chapter 19. There is the further objection to gradualism that it invites the United Nations itself to assume additional power and authority without the process of Charter amendment and ratification. Unquestionably, if Charter revision is long delayed, the General Assembly will seek to enlarge its powers to cope with world problems. Is there any doubt that citizens of the United States want the United Nations to have only those powers which have been expressly delegated to it rather than those which it wishes to assume? Any nation with our fundamental belief in a written constitution wishes the U.N. to follow constitutional procedures. Evolutionary growth of the U.N.'s powers could be a real threat to our freedom.

It is most difficult to accept the arguments which are raised against Charter review. The advantages are so substantial and the opportunities so great that we should adopt review immediately as one of our basic tactics. The free world needs this weapon to gain the offensive in waging peace. It can raise a standard around which peace-loving nations of the world can rally. It can give the free world far greater unity and determination to find a safe path to peace.

Remember that no nation would be bound by the revised Charter until and unless that nation ratifies it. Supporting a Review Conference will not commit the United States to ratify the revised Charter; we are not required to sign any blank checks. If the revised Charter is defective or dangerous, we can reject it. If, as we hope, it is a desirable document, we can ratify it.

The United Nations, like the League of Nations before it, will collapse unless it is given some real authority. While most Americans want us to stay in the U.N., they have little confidence in it because of its obvious lack of power. The American people sense what history demonstrates: the U.N. cannot survive unless it is greatly strengthened.

Advising a sick man to postpone an essential operation may be fatal. The United Nations is sick—desperately sick. Its worst enemies are its friends who timidly oppose a Review Conference—surgery which is already overdue. Its real friends are those who seek to strengthen the United Nations before it is too late.

Chapter 22

TACTICS II—ISSUES

Sometimes a project is built in several sections. Often one part is completed and put in service before completion of the entire project. The use of a comprehensive plan assures that the early phases of construction fit the over-all program.

OUR PROGRAM for waging peace should be directed toward transforming the United Nations into an organization capable of maintaining a secure peace. At the same time, we must maintain our posture of strength and play our part in developing a better world community.

But a gap is left which must be filled if our strategy and tactics are to be successful; namely, the troublesome issues which arise from day to day.

We dare not be so dazzled by our ultimate objective that we overlook the current issues. But neither dare we become so obsessed with current issues that we fail to see their relationship to our long-range program.

The Seven-Point Program can help with these current issues. It will not offer immediate solutions to all of them. For some there is no practical immediate answer. The Seven-Point Program will give some long-range answers. On some issues it will provide a sounder immediate position for the United States.

WHAT ISSUES?   The issues with which we are concerned here are those which keep Secretary of State John Foster Dulles hopping about the world. He has traveled more extensively than any former Secretary of State to attend conferences and negotiations aimed at solving the issues of the day. These issues arise from a chaotic world convulsed by war, torn by conflict, and stirred by the efforts of peoples determined to achieve dignity, independence, security, and a better life.

Some issues are directly concerned with war or its aftermath; for example, the controversies over Formosa, Matsu and Quemoy and the uneasy conditions along the Israel-Egypt boundary. There are also problems of nations split by war: Germany, Korea, and Viet Nam.

Others grow directly out of national efforts to obtain security from aggression: the operation of NATO and the problem of assuring its continued strength, and other defense pacts such as SEATO and individual agreements with Pakistan, Yugoslavia, Spain, and others.

There are problems concerned with independence and self-determination. Recent examples include the tense condition in Cyprus, the Suez Canal controversy, and the uneasy situation in Morocco and other African colonies. There is increasing evidence of the universal desire to end colonialism.

To this imposing list may be added those problems created by the efforts of the underdeveloped nations to strengthen their economies and raise their living standards. These are compounded by the competition of the Communists and the free world for the favor and support of the neutral nations.

Finally, there are the frustrating issues relating to nations which have communist governments: the attempt to admit Red China to the United Nations, recognition of other communist governments, and self-determination for the peoples of eastern European countries subjugated by the Soviet Union.

There is no shortage of issues. As fast as one is resolved, another arises. One fire is hardly extinguished in time to answer the alarm for the next blaze.

OUR DIFFICULTY.   Our handling of such important issues from day to day leaves much to be desired. This is true in spite of real progress in containing communism in Europe, in establishing military deterrents against World War III, and in creating a number of defense pacts and treaties.

No one can rightfully contend, however, that the situation is under control. It often seems that our State Department acts principally as a fire department, rushing from point to point to put out conflagrations. We are not doing enough planned prevention to lessen the number of four-alarm fires. Secretary Dulles often seems to be a fire chief instead of a policy maker.

There is no conceivable way of making easy the solution of these issues. The problems are complex and difficult, and we are usually faced by the harassment and opposition of the Communists. But our troubles are aggravated by five conditions:

1. Lack of an over-all plan and policy to guide action in specific instances.

2. Failure to appreciate the impossibility of solving some current issues except in conjunction with solution of the issues of war and peace.

3. Inability to anticipate coming problems and to apply preventive rather than remedial measures.

4. Political selfishness which pursues "politics as usual" in the face of world crisis.

5. Hesitancy to treat our waging of peace as a truly bipartisan project. Bipartisanship seems to end with military opposition to communism.

We just don't know where we are trying to go or how to get there. President Eisenhower no doubt has a general plan for achieving international peace and security. But details are lacking and he is frequently opposed by one wing of the Republican party. Actions and statements of members of his administration often indicate lack of agreement on any over-all program.

When the Democrats were in office, they had no comprehensive foreign policy; and they offer no such policy today. Even on the important issue of foreign aid, there is sharp disagreement among the leaders of the Democratic party.

We do have bipartisan support for a posture of strength and containment of communism. But even here there are sharp disagreements regarding the adequacy of our military establishment and the sufficiency of our containment policy in Asia.

As a result, we jump from crisis to crisis, usually late and often inadequate. We appear to change our minds without reason, to waver and to delay. The result is frequently diplomatic defeat. We cannot afford the luxury of politics and diplomacy "as usual" in the Nuclear

Age. The consequences are too great if we fail to avert nuclear war or to stem the onward march of communism.

REASONED APPROACH.   Some of these conditions causing our troubles could be removed by the adoption and implementation of an over-all foreign policy. The Seven-Point Program presented in Part III is the outline of such a program. To accept it, or a comparable one, will be to provide a guide for use in day-to-day issues.

Our crying need is for an understandable and workable program which can gain true bipartisan support. We do not need a Republican or a Democratic foreign policy; we need a truly United States foreign policy. Politically we may criticize the manner in which it is administered, but fundamental objectives which are good for the United States should be agreed upon.

If we know our destination, we will not vacillate and fluctuate on current issues. We can size up every problem by its relationship to our over-all objectives.

This will assist us in meeting intelligently our day-to-day problems. It will help us to take positions and to make decisions which advance us toward our objective. But it will also be of great value in those difficult problems which probably cannot be solved until our main objective of secure peace is achieved.

To support this statement, let us look at some pending or anticipated issues and see the benefit of a comprehensive foreign policy such as the Seven-Point Program.

U.N. MEMBERSHIP.   All current applicants have been admitted to the United Nations, except Communist China, Outer Mongolia, Japan, and the two halves of Korea and Viet Nam. (China is already a member of the U.N., but Red China claims the U.N. seat now held by Nationalist China.)

In the tenth (1955) Assembly the question of seating Red China was again deferred without extensive debate. In extensive maneuvering Outer Mongolia was balanced against Japan and their applications were vetoed, while sixteen other nations were accepted. No serious consideration was given to the two halves of Korea and Viet Nam.

It may be anticipated that in the next General Assembly there will be strong pressure to admit Red China as the price for admitting Japan. This will place the United States in an embarrassing position, for we have backed Japan while we have strongly opposed Red China.

It is even likely that the United States will not again muster sufficient support to keep the question of Red China off the agenda. Support for Nationalist China was weakened by the membership controversy in the tenth Assembly.

Most of the nations of the world believe Red China should be admitted. This is true of several of our allies and many neutral nations, including not only India but Pakistan, Burma, and other Asian nations. They contend that Red China will offer less threat in the U.N. than out of it.

We have logically opposed admission of Red China as not being "peace-loving." Actually, Red China is still at war with the United Nations. But our position was weakened when we did not oppose the admission of Albania, Bulgaria, Hungary, and Rumania—all Soviet satellites.

The current communist "peace" campaign will generate mounting pressure for admission of Red China. We are likely soon to be placed in a position where we must either permit admission of Red China or use the veto, which would hurt us badly not only with the neutral nations but with some of our allies.

Is there any alternative exit from this difficult situation?

If we approach the Red China situation from a long-range view, we see the necessity of its membership in a strengthened United Nations (see Chapter 15). Universal enforceable disarmament cannot be undertaken unless Red China is included. From this point of view, we might take a position opposing admission of Red China to the present U.N. but agreeing to admit Red China as part of a plan for a strengthened United Nations. This would not only strengthen our position with our allies but it would also give us initiative in pressing for Charter review.

If we coupled with this a requirement that the Nationalist Chinese government on Formosa must remain a member of the U.N., we would have a more sensible program regarding Red China.

This proposal would not conflict with our over-all opposition to the brutal Chinese Communist regime. Membership in a strengthened U.N. would require Red China to submit to world law and to turn over its armaments to the U.N. Sooner or later Red China will be admitted. We should prefer to admit Red China only to a U.N. strong enough to pull the teeth of the Red dragon.

BORDER DISPUTES.   The Israeli-Egyptian controversy is typical of the threats to peace which may be expected from time to time. Controversies over borders are as old as landownership.

Such cases should be handled by the United Nations. If we adopt the principle of United Nations responsibility for peace and security (Item 3 of the Seven-Point Program), we should first attempt to solve such situations through the U.N. We should call for U.N. action when such situations begin, not wait until they become serious.

Furthermore, if we adopt the objective of universal enforceable disarmament (Item 5 of the Seven-Point Program), it makes sense to refuse to give more arms to passionately aroused peoples.

The advantages of a small United Nations security force to maintain order in such cases were outlined in Chapter 10. Even comparatively small U.N. patrols would reduce the likelihood of outbreaks. Such patrols would represent the peoples of the world in their demand for peace. National armies would hesitate to attack U.N. forces because of the world-wide opposition which such an attack would create.

Such an approach would be very helpful in solving the threats to peace which arise from conflicts between smaller nations.

GERMANY.   Reams have been written on reunification of Germany. This frustrating and difficult problem is a subject on the agenda of nearly every East-West discussion. More than that, it is one which cannot be solved until a secure peace is achieved.

There is little doubt that both the U.S.S.R. and the free world would like to see Germany unified—provided it would be on their side. U.S.S.R. unification proposals call for a united Germany under Soviet influence or "neutral in favor of the U.S.S.R."

The West's proposals for unification usually call for a united Germany as a member of NATO, furnishing armed forces for the common defense of Europe.

These opposing positions are understandable and are to be expected as long as considerations of military security dominate the thinking of East and West.

Referral of this subject to the Big Four Foreign Ministers' Conference in October, 1955, was doomed before negotiations opened. Our demand that the U.S.S.R. agree to a united Germany as an indication of good faith will be ignored as long as Germany is an important military factor in Europe.

If we would recognize these facts we would save ourselves both effort and embarrassment. Quite likely only a disarmed Germany can be reunited and only a reunited Germany can be disarmed. If this be true, we should consider the German problem in the context of the over-all problem of peace and security.

Our position would be more sensible if we would realize that German unification must follow, not precede, world law and order. Such a position would add German unification to the list of benefits which may result from world law, and would thus increase support for strengthening the U.N.

LIBERATION.   From time to time American spokesmen call for liberation, usually meaning independence or self-determination for the peoples of the eastern European countries subjugated by the U.S.S.R.: Lithuania, Latvia, Estonia, Poland, Czechoslovakia, Hungary, Rumania, Bulgaria, Albania, and East Germany. On several occasions we have told the Soviet leaders that liberation of these nations would help prove the sincerity of their talk about peace.

We are on sound ground morally and ethically when we maintain that these peoples should have independence and self-determination. They are entitled to freedom from the communist form of colonialism just as other peoples are entitled to freedom from the more conventional kind of colonialism.

But we are completely unrealistic if we expect progress toward liberation until a secure peace is achieved. To state the principle of freedom is one thing; to expect early action from the Soviet Union is another. There are two ways by which these nations can be liberated in the foreseeable future:

1. By voluntary action of the Soviet Union, giving them self-determination, or

2. By forcible liberation undertaken by the Western nations.

It is wishful thinking to believe that the Soviet Union will release them from its control as long as war remains possible. The Soviet Union wants these nations for their manpower and industrial capability, and to provide a buffer area between NATO and the Russian homeland. There is no probability that they will release their tight control as long as these military demands continue.

Liberation by force means war. To force it now is to invite a rain of nuclear bombs or missiles on the United States and on the cities of western Europe. It would be completely irresponsible for the United States to take such action precipitating World War III, even in the name of liberation. There is little likelihood that Britain and the nations of western Europe would support us. They are in easy reach of Soviet bombers and missiles.

There is no likelihood of liberation until a secure peace is established. World law would eliminate the military factors which compel the East and the West to hold their present positions. The question of independence for these captive nations should be an item for East-West discussion simultaneously with negotiations to establish world law under a strengthened United Nations.

There is no guarantee that the Soviets would give their satellite peoples freedom to choose their own government even under this situation. They would rightly fear that this would mean the end of communist governments in these nations.

But at least there is a chance of this, while there is no possibility at all of liberation under the present situation. Hope of liberation is wishful thinking, except in the context of secure peace.

Much the same situation prevails with respect to liberation of China, North Korea, and North Viet Nam.

Hopes for liberation are keyed to the greater problem of eliminating the threat and fear of war. With the military compulsion removed, there will at least be long-range hope of achieving independence for these peoples.

DISARMAMENT.   A consistent approach to disarmament is one of the maximum benefits to be derived from the Seven-Point Program. We cannot exercise leadership toward disarmament until we know our objectives and have determined the conditions under which we will accept disarmament.

Now, we are constantly embarrassed in disarmament negotiations. Once we have a comprehensive plan which provides adequate safeguards, we shall find our position in these meetings much easier. We shall have something to guide us from day to day and month to month as we travel the long hard road to a just and durable peace. Now we are attempting to reach our destination without a road map.

The mounting tempo of scientific developments in the arms race creates greater need for decision on our disarmament objectives. Now is the time to be concerned with enforceable controls over ICBMs and "atoms for peace." Delay in formulating our specific goals only allows the situation to worsen and the problem of disarmament to become more complex.

NO PANACEA. There is no short answer that can be given to these varied and complicated issues. We shall not find a panacea, but an over-all plan will give us guidance on individual problems.

If we use such a plan, it will assist in the solution of those issues which can be resolved now. Each one can be considered in the light of our end objectives. This will give assurance that solutions will actually advance us toward our goal. It will help us avoid the crazy-quilt pattern that comes when there is no plan and when the easiest way out is adopted at each turn.

We may also use this plan to distinguish the problems which can be solved now from those which must wait for the achievement of secure peace. Such a classification will reduce the frustrations that come when we attempt the impossible.

Those issues which cannot be solved now should be related to the broader aspects of law and disarmament. We can thus tie them in to the basic questions that face the world. We should propose they be considered in negotiations between the East and the West as serious progress is made toward strengthening the United Nations.

Recognition that such problems cannot be solved by themselves will increase the force of our arguments for a supranational program to provide secure peace.

Chapter 23

THE $64,000 QUESTION

The element of calculated risk is always present in business enterprises. There is no positive way of assuring success before a venture is undertaken. Even after hazards are recognized and minimized, there remains an element of risk. Progress is made, however, only if the risk is accepted and the decision is made to proceed. But it is also wise to have alternative plans which can be used if the offer is rejected.

NO DISCUSSION of paths to peace lasts more than a few minutes before someone raises the question: "What about the Soviet Union? Will it agree to a strengthened U.N.?" In the parlance of the American television fan, this has become the $64,000 question. It is a proper question, for the Soviet Union has been the thorn in the flesh of efforts toward peace since World War II.

Anyone who could answer this question with certainty would indeed become an authority of world prominence. No such ambition or presumption influences the comments which follow. Rather, they are an attempt to outline some of the dominant factors which may affect the decision of the U.S.S.R.

QUESTION OF TIME.   Given enough time, the Soviet dictatorship will run its course, as have all others. Given enough time, the ideology of communism will collapse, as have all others which are contrary to human freedom and moral law.

But we are not here concerned with long-range evolution. We are interested in securing peace in the forseeable future—in time to avert the calamity of a nuclear war.

We dare not wait for the slow-moving reaction of an oppressed people to change their government. We cannot count upon a change in leadership to alter the path of the Soviet Union. Whether headed by Stalin, Malenkov, or Khrushchev, or "collective leadership," the Soviet Union is the same kind of government with the same attitudes and goals.

ANSWER UNKNOWN.   The surest comment on the question about the Soviet Union is that we do not definitely know what it will do. This is true in spite of our knowledge of communist ideology, of the history of the Soviet Union, and of its present opposition to efforts for a secure peace.

We do not know the extent to which the communist ideology will prevail if it conflicts with national interests or with the personal ambitions of Soviet leaders. We do not know the extent to which the U.S.S.R. will relax its aggressive aims if continuously confronted with a strong and alert free world. Neither do we know the degree to which it will modify its present opposition to disarmament, world law, and Charter revision if forced to accept or reject a definite blueprint for secure peace.

In developing a foreign policy for the United States, there are two alternative premises as to future Soviet conduct. One is that the Soviet Union will change its attitude and actions if confronted with world situations which make a change desirable, even though contrary to communist ideology and precedent. The other premise is that the Soviet Union is completely intransigent and that nothing can induce or compel a change of attitudes and actions within the forseeable future. We do not know which of these premises will prove correct.

We must develop a program which will provide pressures and incentives to compel or encourage the Soviet Union to accept world law. But this must be done in such a way that it gives us maximum security in case the second assumption proves correct and the Soviet Union remains completely uncooperative.

THE ALTERNATIVE.   If Soviet cooperation is not forthcoming within a reasonable period, the free world will need to re-examine its program. Then it must give serious consideration to proceeding with a free-world federation without the Communists (see Chapters 8 and 16). This alternative would enable the free world to maintain continued military deterrents, replace crumbling alliances and treaties with an effective federation, and build a more united posture of strength. This step should be taken only after a revised U.N. Charter has been flatly rejected by the U.S.S.R. It should be taken only if Soviet actions and attitudes indicate no reasonable chance of agreement on universal enforceable disarmament, world law, and a strengthened U.N.

Efforts directed toward achievement of the Seven-Point Program will help create free-world unity. If this fails to force Soviet acceptance of a strengthened U.N., it will make more likely a federation of the free world.

This opportunity provides us with an alternative if the Soviet rejects secure peace. Its availability provides one more pressure to compel Soviet acceptance of a strengthened U.N.

TRENDS.   There are powerful trends which may lead the Soviet Union to accept a rule of law. Although they have been mentioned in previous chapters, it is well to restate them here.

Perhaps the most impelling trend rises from the growing destructive and death-dealing capabilities of modern weapons. As Soviet scientists try to outstrip the free world's development of new means of terror, they constantly provide their governments with data on new weapons. As Soviet rulers recognize the havoc they can create by releasing such weapons against the free world, they must realize their vulnerability to similar attacks. As they develop the ICBM with nuclear warhead and analyze its devastating power, they must realize that war is obsolete. As they undertake the impossible task of developing an adequate defense mechanism against our ICBMs they should be able to see that safety can no longer come from arms.

The scientific fact that war is obsolete will inevitably become apparent. With it should come the urge to survive by eliminating war. The scientists of the world may well be the most effective messengers of peace as they report their fearful developments in death-dealing weapons.

There is another powerful trend, the desire of the Russian people for a better life. Regardless of their dedication to the ideology of communism, their desire for more butter and fewer guns is a constant pressure on Soviet leaders.

The trends are at work day by day regardless of the activities of the free world. Their tempo can be increased if we expertly dramatize the fact that war is obsolete and point out the vast differences of living standards between Russia and her Western neighbors.

But there are other pressures over which the free world has more control. The successful execution of the Seven-Point Program can bring strong pressure to bear on the Soviet Union.

PRESSURE.   Every element of the proposed Seven-Point Program will, if successfully executed, increase the pressures on the Communists to take the required steps for secure peace.

This program not only provides the requisites for a secure peace; it also provides steps to contain the Communists and to unite world opinion.

If we maintain a true posture of strength for both "major" and "minor" aggression, we discourage further physical expansion of the communist empire. If, as part of our posture of strength, we keep ahead of the U.S.S.R. in development of new weapons and maintain a stalemate of destructive capabilities, we neutralize the "blackmail" power of Soviet weapons.

If we intelligently lend a helping hand to the neutral nations of Africa and Asia and assist them in developing their economies, we can neutralize the Soviet economic threat.

If we make greater use of the United Nations, recognizing it as a keystone of foreign policy in the Nuclear Age, we shall help develop world unity.

If we work for the real alternative to world anarchy—a strengthened United Nations capable of enforcing universal disarmament under world law—we point the way to secure peace. We shall also take much of the wind out of the sails of communist "peace" propaganda.

And if we truly champion the cause of independence and freedom for all peoples, and support it by our actions as well as by our words, we shall bring the free world closer together and lessen the communist influence on neutral nations.

All of these objectives of the Seven-Point Program will foster a more united noncommunist world. All will intensify the pressure of world opinion on the Communists to join in establishing a secure peace.

DECISION.   Soviet acceptance of a strengthened United Nations is not likely until communist leaders conclude that it is to their self-interest.

Such a conclusion cannot be expected so long as their sphere of influence is expanding and they believe the free world fears them.

The Seven-Point Program of this book is aimed at limiting further expansion of the communist empire. These measures also seek to erase from Soviet minds any belief that the free world is afraid.

Once their expansion is contained, and the free world is united against their false ideology, the trends and forces discussed above may influence their decisions. The interests of the nation, its people and its leaders will begin to conflict with the communist ideology. At that stage, continued intransigence will only increase free-world opposition to the Communists. Moreover, it will interfere with Soviet economy, trade, and other activities. At some point the benefits of enforced disarmament and a peaceful world will become attractive.

When that occurs, the Communists will find it difficult to follow the dictates of their ideology. A workable plan for peace will be available to them. Abandonment of the communist goal of world domination may seem a cheap price to pay for national security. Leaders may be willing to trade an unattainable goal for their own positions and prestige.

Time magazine has expressed this opportunity, saying:

The hope of a legal solution to the H-bomb lies in efforts, over a varied field, to change the minds of the Kremlin's leaders. Conceivably, even they may be made to realize that aggression will not pay.

The Communists may well conclude, "If you can't whip them, join them," even though it ends their expansion. We need not fear that decision. In a world of peace, freedom will outstrip statism and communism.

No one knows when this decision may come. But no nation can forever defy the rest of the world. If we lead, eventually the Soviets must follow.

The Seven-Point Program is realistic. It applies strong pressures to bring the Soviets into a strengthened U.N. But if they refuse indefinitely, we are not helpless. We have the alternative of implementing a free-world federation without them. This would give the free world the great advantages of federation to reduce the danger of war and increase the pressure on the Soviets to join.

Will this policy guarantee success? Of course not. But we shall guarantee failure if we refuse to act because of Soviet opposition. The free world is divided, disorganized, and disunited; it is easy prey for communism. The Communists are setting the pace; we are on the defensive. If we let Soviet opposition block a strengthened U.N., we may give the world to communism by default.

Why should we let the Communists veto our foreign policy? By seizing the initiative, we can lead the free world to greater unity and force the decision on the Communists! Our chance of success will be proportional to the vigor and skill with which we wage peace.

Chapter 24

RAISE A STANDARD

No business venture succeeds unless it has enthusiastic support. The finest plans and programs fail unless there is a strong desire to achieve. There is no substitute for dedication and hard work.

THERE IS a question more vital to American citizens than "What about the U.S.S.R.?" It is "What about the U.S.A.?" Do we really want to wage peace? Is the price tag attached to peace and freedom too high? Can we maintain a united front through long years of hard climbing along rough roads? Can we substitute enlightened self-interest for shortsighted blundering?

These questions are of greater importance to us than those about the Soviet Union. This is so because we are the only ones who can answer them.

THE PRICE. Effective control of armaments and prevention of aggression must be a two-way street. The world organization which inspects the plants of a potential aggressor must be allowed to inspect our plants. If laws against development and use of arms are effectively enforced upon others, they will be enforced upon us.

We must make the same delegation of authority to the United Na- that we expect of others. We must give up the power to use war as an instrument of foreign policy if we want other nations to do so.

Are we willing to pay this price for a secure peace? Until we make this decision and implement it by our leadership, our friends throughout the world are likely to phrase their $64,000 question as "What about the U.S.A.?"

THE LONG PULL.   Never before has this nation been faced with the
necessity of choosing such long-range objectives in the field of foreign policy—goals which are not likely to be achieved promptly.

We are an impatient people who want immediate results. We have
a way of losing our enthusiasm if a project does not quickly produce
results. Our diplomats too are accustomed to dealing with immediate
crises. Our government has long-range aspirations expressed in general terms. But the active parts of our policies are concerned only with
the immediately attainable.

Now we need a sustained effort to achieve specific objectives over
a period of years. Can we accompany this effort with the steadiness
of purpose necessary to ride through turmoil, delay, and frustration?
Have we the determination to accept nothing less than world law and
enforceable disarmament? Can we raise this determination above
party politics?

Such is the long haul for which we must be prepared. Are we willing
and able to make this sustained effort?

ENLIGHTENED SELF-INTEREST.   To fulfill our role as leaders of the
world, we must think, speak, and act in its interest, as well as in the
interest of the United States. Can we rise above petty provincialism in
our attitudes and statements? Can we recognize that our own freedom
and survival depend upon freedom, peace, and prosperity in the rest
of the world?

Our background tends to keep us aloof; our nation was built by
people who came here to avoid the conflicts of Europe, and we were
protected for years by our isolated location. The majority of American citizens are not isolationists, but we do have difficulty in thinking
broadly and accurately about international problems.

Our great pride in our freedom, our economic and industrial development, our prosperity and our domestic peace make it easy for us
to adopt superior attitudes toward the rest of the world. Such attitudes
often lead to shortsighted policies based on emotion rather than on
good sense. No longer can we afford the luxury of looking down our
noses at other nations. For our own good we must lead in building
a better world.

By such leadership we can become real champions of independence,
dignity, freedom, democracy, and peace. By so doing, we not only help

the world, but also we help ourselves. Can we see where our true self-interest lies? Can we give the free world responsible leadership?

DECISION.   These questions will be answered by our acts of omission as well as commission. Before we answer them there must be some keen thinking and soul-searching by every American citizen who cherishes his right to influence public policy.

With an open mind every citizen needs to examine the requirements for a secure peace and think through the minimum essential. Is there any realistic alternative to peace? Can the weapons of tomorrow be controlled by anything less than a rule of law? Can world law be achieved in any better way than by strengthening the United Nations?

These are the questions which must be studied and debated, for unless one can honestly answer "yes" to them, the Seven-Point Program outlined in this document deserves—even demands—support. I have complete confidence that if we study and debate these matters with open minds, we shall be compelled to accept the need for world law and will work for a program which will accomplish it.

When we make this decision and implement it with our leadership, we shall have taken a great step forward. We shall have given the world a great idea—great enough to provide a true alternative to war and to the arms race. We shall have embarked not only on a plan for survival but also on the road to a just and durable peace.

Have we the vision to see that law must replace anarchy on the world level, just as our Founding Fathers recognized this need on the national level at the Constitutional Convention in Philadelphia in 1787? It is high time that we take the lead in bringing the rule of law into this troubled world. Have we the courage to make this goal a reality?

INDIVIDUAL DEDICATION.   Our communist opponents claim that we Americans are too complacent, selfish, soft, and lazy to wage peace effectively. The Communists are dangerous because they are so deeply dedicated to their false ideology and their goal of world domination. They match their depth of dedication with vigor of action.

Many non-Communists around the world have jumped on the communist bandwagon because the Communists seem to work harder for their goal than we do for our objectives. The Communists have convinced millions of people that the future belongs to communism.

Some Americans fear that this is true. For example, a recent editorial in *Life* magazine (March 5, 1956) stated:

> If religion were measured by the seriousness of its believers, Marxism would be one of the great world religions. It is now trying to appear less tyrannical, less violent and less irrational than it really is. But its real strength remains exactly what it was before: the undivided purpose of the believing Communist, to whom the important thing is "not just to interpret the world, but to change it."
>
> This purpose pervades all the Soviets do, from the training of engineers to the set of their foreign policy. Americans, by and large, do not seem to want to change the world, but to enjoy it. That equilibrium is not stable, and is not in our favor.

Is this indictment correct? Have we lost the courage and the dedication to freedom which made this nation great? Are we so busy making a living that we will not take time to make the world safe for peace and freedom?

I do not know the answers to these questions. Each American must answer them for himself.

One thing is clear: we shall fail unless enough of us clearly understand the need for world law, give it top priority in the use of our time, and keep working until it is achieved. In the past, our freedom has been saved several times by a handful of dedicated individuals. I have faith that enough dedicated Americans can be found to save our freedom now.

RAISE A STANDARD.   The battle for a secure peace will be long and difficult. But our task is so urgent that we cannot afford to quit, no matter what the odds against us may be.

Many years ago George Washington gave us some good advice. He was speaking to the Constitutional Convention at Philadelphia in 1787, when many of its members were discouraged and ready to give up. His words also speak to us: "Let us raise a standard to which the wise and the honest can repair. The event is in the hand of God."

History is looking for men and women who will do for the world what Washington and other great Americans did for this nation in 1787. The stakes are high. Will you accept the challenge?